Take Back Your Life!
Travel Full-Time in an RV

http://www.rvhometown.com

Take Back Your Life!
Travel Full-Time in an RV

by Stephanie Bernhagen

Bernham-Collins

Grateful acknowledgment is made for the use of the following material.

For survey data found on pages 207, 224 and 225 of *Over the Next Hill: An Ethnography of RVing Seniors in North America* by Dorothy Ayers Counts and David R. Counts, published by Broadview Press, Ontario, Canada, 1996.

An abridge version of the article *Whistle While I Work* by Janice Lasko, published originally in the February 1994 *Camperways*.

Excerpt from *On the Road Alone* by DeAnna Satre, copyright by DeAnna Satre. Reprinted by permission of DeAnna Satre. Originally printed in the July/August 1996 issue of *RVing Women.*

For data found in *Recreation Vehicle Weight & Tire Safety Handbook* published by A'Weigh We Go.

In order to protect privacy, some individual's names have been changed.

Cover Design and Photo by
Paul Jones

ISBN 0-9700263-0-7

Library of Congress Card Number: 00-102625

Printed in the United States of America
First Printing—October 2000
Second Printing—November 2000

This book is dedicated to those with the unrestrained courage to chase their dreams as a child chases a firefly.

Table of Contents

Appendixes

Resource Directory

Acknowledgments

On a typical day in a campground you will find a vehicle surrounded by men. A call for help or discussion went out the minute the hood went up.

On another morning word spreads quickly from motorhome to trailer, Jane's husband Joe is in the hospital. Soon, the neighbors, whose names she doesn't yet know, have arranged to accompany her to the hospital every day. When Jane learns her husband will be in the hospital for a while some of these neighbors move her home on wheels to the hospital parking lot.

It was this same kind of support from the full-timing and writing communities that has made *Take Back Your Life! Travel Full-time in an RV* possible. Without the support of the following people and many others you would not hold this book in your hand today.

Fifty six young full-timers share their stories and experiences in this book. Many others shared their stories, but there just was not space to include them all. I am grateful for all of the stories shared with me. They have enriched my life and will touch yours as well.

Over and over and over again this book was edited and proofread. Mostly by RVers, full-time and wannabees. Some with writing credentials and others with a desire for or love of the full-timing lifestyle.

Jim and Cindy Cook, experienced full-timers and writers, did a complete edit of the book. They nudged and encouraged me all the way. Without that encouragement and their attention to detail this book might never have been.

The day I found Donna Yeaw online is one of the golden moments in my life. From that first e-mail Donna and I built a friendship that blossomed. Donna is also a writer and RVer. When she heard about the book she quickly offered to do some editing for me. Donna didn't even know me, yet she was willing to make a huge commitment to help me out. She didn't stop there either. She used one of her web sites to get the word out about this book and more. She was also a wealth of information for publishing, web site construction and many of my other questions. Visit Donna's RV web site at *http://www.myprimeyears.com/rv*.

Paul, my husband, also edited the book. Besides the typos he caught, he was my chief technical expert. As an engineer and hands on person there isn't much he can't figure out. Paul also gave up many hours of play with me while I worked on the book and waited patiently for the small windows of time when he could use our computer.

Alice Zyetz, author of *You Shoulda Listened to Your Mother: 36 Timeless Success Tips for Working Women* was also a big help with the editing. Her communication and English knowledge came to my rescue several times.

Marilyn Abraham, author of *First We Quit Our Jobs: How One Work-Driven Couple Got on the Road to a New Life* and co-author of *The Happy Camper's Cookbook* shared her publishing career background in helping me develop the current layout of the book.

Other editors include: Theresa Collins, Don and Shirley Gassen, Jaimie Hall and Dianne Harlan.

Barb and Ron Hofmeister, authors of *Movin' On: Living and Traveling Full Time in a Recreational Vehicle* created another golden moment in my life. They too only knew me by e-mail. When I started firing self-publishing questions at Barb she met the challenge and led me tirelessly through the hoops. Both she and Ron read the partially typeset manuscript, giving me valuable feedback. Ron also supported me in some of my business hurdles. Visit them at *http://www.movinon.net*.

One would think a title would come easily. Not so! After lying awake many nights pondering titles I put the word out that I needed help naming this book. Suggestions rolled in by e-mail and snail-mail. One of those e-mails was from Debbie Keller, a full-timer wannabee. In the e-mail she shared how those she worked with felt about their lives and the changes they planned to make in their lives. Four words popped out of that e-mail at me, "take back their life."

The next step was to send five titles to Donna Yeaw, to post in a survey on one of her web sites. Nearly 40 percent of the votes were for the title stimulated by Debbie, *Take Back Your Life! Travel Full-time in an RV.*

When I became hung up with the cover design I called Paul Jones, a photographer and fellow full-time RVer. Paul was boondocked in the southwest desert at the time, running his computer on electricity provided by the sun. Less than 24 hours after my call Paul had selected two pictures from his files, laid them out as book covers and sent them off to me. One was the beautiful Alaska scenery on the cover. Once the selection was made he went to work to create the entire stunning cover.

Then there are those who kept me motivated with simple comments like: "How's the book coming?" "Young full-timer wannabees do need their own book." "I wish there had been a book like that for me to read." "We can't wait to read it." "I have a friend who needs the book."

With so many contributing to this book it is impossible to list everyone and their contributions. My gratitude goes out to all of the contributors: be it stories and experiences; editorial assistance; title input; cover design, encouragement or word of mouth about the book.

SKP Hugs to all of you!
Stephanie

Introduction

On January 4, 1994, with arms full, I walked out of an office building in Denver, Colorado. A few minutes later I climbed on a city bus. With a throbbing head, lump in my throat and fighting tears I wondered what lay ahead. After planning for four years we were leaving the traditional lifestyle behind to become nomads!

When I climbed off the bus at a Park-n-Ride I looked around and saw our pickup with U-Haul in tow. Paul was walking towards me with his arms out for a hug. Afterwards I stepped back and with a silly grin on my face said, "I'm Free!" With that we climbed in the truck, with our dog Tiffany, and our journey began.

As we made tracks west to pickup our new home on wheels my head continued to pound. What was around the next bend or over the next mountain for us? So much was uncertain, yet we were confident we were doing the right thing.

Today, six years later, I look back at the growth we have experienced, the many friends we have made and the wonderful places we have visited. Fewer people ask us when we plan to stop. And for those that do the answer is when we find something better to do. There is still plenty out here to experience! Besides, I don't know if we could stop. There is this bug called hitch-itch that creates a need to be in perpetual motion.

I was fortunate to have the opportunity to start living this rich lifestyle, known as full-timing, when I was only 36. It only seemed right to share that opportunity with others, which is why I wrote *Take Back Your Life! Travel Full-time in an RV.*

You are about to obtain a glimpse of this unique lifestyle only few are fortunate enough to experience. You will come to understand why those too young to retire chose this lifestyle. Woven between the stories and experiences shared by young full-timers is the knowledge necessary to get you started, should you want to become a part of the full-timing lifestyle. Even those traveling alone, with kids, with pets or with disabilities will find useful information. An extensive *Resource Directory* has been included to make individual research easier.

I have made every effort to provide a broad perspective by including input from 56 young full-timers. However, you must realize the full-timing lifestyle is as unique for each individual as it is in the traditional lifestyle. Also, Paul and I are fifth-wheel people, so my perspective tends to lean that way. Not to say it is right or wrong. The right way is what is right for you. Also, keep in mind that full-timing as a lifestyle is evolving rapidly into something much larger than it has been in the past. Therefore, some things that may be accurate in this book today may be ancient history tomorrow. If you want to make this lifestyle yours I encourage you to visit with as many full-timers as you can and read everything you can find on the lifestyle.

It is my hope that when you finish this book that you will be able to expand your life into an area that you have only dreamed of until now. It doesn't need to be the full-timing lifestyle. But if this book helps your dreams become reality I will have accomplished what I set out to do.

May your journey through life be ever evolving!

Stephanie

Disclaimer

This book is designed to provide information on the full-timing lifestyle. It is sold with the understanding that the publisher and author are not engaged in rendering legal, accounting or other professional services. If legal or other expert assistance is required, the services of a competent professional should be sought.

It is not the purpose of this book to reprint all the information that is otherwise available, but to complement, amplify and supplement other books and resources. You are urged to read all the available material, learn as much as possible about the full-timing lifestyle and to tailor the information to your individual needs. For more resources see the *Resource Directory* at the end of the book.

Every effort has been made to make this book as complete and as accurate as possible. However, there **may be mistakes** both typographical and in content. Therefore, this book should be used only as a general guide and not the ultimate source for making a major lifestyle change. Furthermore, this book only contains information on the full-timing lifestyle up to the printing date.

The purpose of this book is to educate and entertain. The author and Bernham-Collins shall have neither liability nor responsibility to any person or entity with respect to any loss or damage caused, or alleged to be caused, directly or indirectly by the information contained in this book.

If you do not wish to be bound by the above, you may return this book to the publisher for a full refund.

The Future is Now

1

Grab the Future

Something seemed to be missing in our lives. We had good jobs which provided more money than we cared to spend. We spent our free time building custom homes while toying with the idea of starting our own business. Having completed our second home, we pondered what to do next. We decided we were not ready to start a business. With that decision made, we thought we would have lots of free time to play. However, chores quickly got in the way. Before we knew it, Monday morning would arrive and work would call. With sudden clarity, we knew what was missing in our lives. Time to sit back and enjoy life.

It was a perfect Sunday afternoon when we faced a turning point in our lives. The sun was bright in the cloudless azure sky and the view of the Rocky Mountains off in the distance was superb. Paul and I had the ***Denver Post*** scattered between us in the living room. How much better could life get? Then Paul looked up and said, "Why don't we take a year off and see the United States?" I agreed this was a great idea, but how would we do it?

Over the following weeks and months we pondered our dream to tour the United States. We came up with a five-year plan. We needed to save enough money so we would not have to work. We constantly brain stormed our options. It took no time at all to figure out that living out of a car, suitcase and motel rooms was not our style, nor could we afford it.

We soon realized RVs (recreational vehicles) were a solution to our dilemma. We had our doubts, however, as we recalled RVs of days gone by. Camping? Who wants to live in dirty, dusty campgrounds full of ticks and mosquitoes and cook over a campfire? We had never camped and were not sure we were ready to start.

We began attending RV shows and visiting dealerships. We could not believe what we found! RVs had become condos on wheels. I would not have to spend my days cooking over a campfire. I could prepare meals in minutes in the microwave!

We began to devour books and magazines about the RV lifestyle. We visited with anyone and everyone who knew anything about camping. We soon became aware of a lifestyle known as "full-timing," where people travel and live full-time in their RVs. Full-timing is a lifestyle normally adopted by seniors who have the time and freedom to wander.

As our excitement grew we realized one year would not be enough to see the United States. Our dream expanded to two years and finally we decided we would not put a limit on our journey.

After four years of planning we were about to be footloose and fancy-free. Paul had an opportunity for a voluntary layoff. The market was right to sell our house. Finally, a review of our full-timing budget and our finances indicated we had saved enough money. ***It was time to hit the road.***

As we traveled we found few people close to our age living in RVs. Our community was one of seniors. We were completing our second year on the road when we discovered where all the young full-timers were hiding! To our surprise, there were hundreds of them!

We were fortunate to be able to retire when we were 36 and 38 years old. But, we were not unique when it came to the full-timing lifestyle. Hundreds of people who had not reached retirement age were living this way. With each year the numbers increased, quickly growing to thousands.

Traveling full-time. Taking time to smell the flowers; visit with a neighbor; watch the moonrise and listen to coyotes howl. Peace and tranquility. *Footloose and fancy-free.*

You too can have this lifestyle, even if your finances will not let you retire yet. Even if you have kids! *Take Back Your Life: Travel Full-time in an RV* will walk you through the steps to getting on the road as a full-timer. You will learn from many other young full-timers' experiences. Along the way you will evaluate your own situation, determining your own needs and the steps you must take to become a full-timer.

Let's start our journey by learning what caused other young people to *take back their lives* with the full-timing lifestyle.

Turning Point

Tom and Nicole, Real Estate developers, found themselves caught up in the hustle and bustle of life. They needed a way to spend time together while taking a break from the stress of their careers. Their solution was a six-month tour of the United States.

With six months off and the house closed up, Tom and Nicole set out in a van to travel from Florida to California and back. They discovered they enjoyed camping. Although they would have liked more of the conveniences of home, they found the van suited their needs perfectly for this trip.

One day Tom and Nicole were standing in line, waiting for Carlsbad Caverns to open. The conversation they struck up with the couple behind them would change their lives.

The couple was in their mid-sixties and had just retired. The wife told Tom and Nicole that she had never had the opportunity to travel and now her dream of being able to travel was coming true. A few minutes later the Caverns opened and they started down the steep grade into the cave.

About 50 feet into the cave the retired woman fell, breaking her hip. She had waited all those years to be able to enjoy herself and now her dream of traveling might never happen. "That was just like God sending us a message," Nicole said of the experience.

For *Al and DeAnna* it wasn't someone else who had the accident, it was them. They were out on Al's motorcycle one day when a city bus struck them. Recovery took two years, leaving Al with disabilities from head injuries and DeAnna on edge whenever she rides in or drives a vehicle.

Some good did come from the accident. When the accident happened, Al and DeAnna had only begun their relationship and they had not tested the waters of commitment and trust. The accident forced them to depend on each other, creating a strong and delightful bond. "While we were recovering we decided life was too short," DeAnna says. "The most valuable gift in life is time and we wanted to spend quality time together, enjoying new experiences. We may never have much money, but we have all these wonderful experiences and the quality of our relationship is priceless for us."

Betty loved her job as a human relations director until a new boss appeared. As tension in the office grew, Betty found herself ending each day in the tub, soaking her misery away.

Lin, Betty's husband, filled his days of retirement with chores around the house and his favorite hobbies: cooking and gardening. On weekends, Lin and Betty would escape to nature in their RV.

Betty came to the realization it was time to confront the stress in her life and do something about it. She could go to work for a different agency, but she was really toying with the idea of completely changing careers. Then the thought crossed her mind, "I could do something really different!" Since both Betty and Lin enjoyed their weekend camping trips they decided to sell everything and move into their motorhome.

Janice and Gabby were city folks who escaped to their mountain condo every weekend, a 500 mile round trip. One day Gabby suggested they say good-bye to the city, move to their mountain condo and see what it was like to live with less.

"That was not so hard," Janice said. "We love to ski so we took jobs that allowed us to ski. We just totally turned our lives around because we wanted to travel and ski. We only needed enough income to play, which is exactly what we did."

Life was good for Janice and Gabby, but one day they stumbled into an even better lifestyle. As they walked along a street they saw a motorhome. Curious, they went into the business next to it and asked, "Who owns the motorhome?" It was a small town so you could do that type of thing. When they learned who owned it they asked if they could see it. The owner replied, "Sure, but it's not for sale." Two weeks later Janice and Gabby owned the motorhome.

After a year and a half of camping excursions, Janice and Gabby were experiencing problems with the old motorhome. They decided the next time the motorhome acted up they would replace it with a fifth-wheel trailer and truck, then sell the condo. Only two hours later the motorhome broke down in the middle of the highway. They limped into a dealership and traded their motorhome and VW for a fifth-wheel trailer and truck. During the next week they put their condo on the market. It sold in three days and closed in two weeks! That was more than 10 years ago and they still love full-timing!

Susan and Jeff had traveled before. When they were first married they went to Europe where they learned many Europeans travel for long periods of time. Susan said, "It just blew our minds because, before this, we did not know of anyone who traveled for long periods of time." Susan and Jeff took off from their careers several times for extended trips and each time they successfully restarted their careers.

Then Samantha was born. Susan was in her early forties and wanted to focus life around her child, making the most of every moment she could grab with Samantha. Careers were demanding too much of their time. Both Jeff and Susan were ready for another extended vacation.

So, Jeff and Susan set off to do what they enjoyed most—travel—but this time three month old Samantha went along. Ten years later they are still traveling. Jeff and Susan homeschool Samantha and all three enjoy their time together.

Jessica and Sam were living near a nuclear power plant. Jessica's long commute to work kept her away from home for 13 hours a day. While on vacation Jessica and Sam stopped at Custer State Park in South Dakota where they met their first full-timer. He told them about the full-timing lifestyle and obtaining jobs on the road.

Jessica was not happy with her job and Sam was ready for a change, so they pulled their life together and sold their house to the first person who saw it. They now do seasonal work in the national park system and travel the rest of the year. Jessica views this change in her life as just another step in her personal growth. One lesson she has learned is, "By letting go and facing fears, it is amazing how things work out!"

Fred was a fire captain. "I was doing what I was good at," Fred said. "It was fairly easy and I was making good money, but I wasn't doing what I wanted to do." Seeing some of his fire department friends die before they turned 50 Fred realized, "It is my responsibility to enjoy life." He and Peggy quit their jobs, sold their house, moved into a trailer and got married.

When Fred and Peggy took responsibility for their lifestyle the energy in their life changed. Things quickly became possible and fell into place, which is a common experience among young full-timers.

Megan Edwards and her husband Mark hit the road when their house burned to the ground. Imagine poking through the ashes of your smoldering home and seeing opportunity. This is what Megan and Mark did. You can read about their journey in Megan's book *Roads from the Ashes: An Odyssey in Real Life on the Virtual Frontier.*

Do any of these stories sound familiar? Are you anxious, ready for a change? Maybe what full-timers call "hitch itch" has set in and it is time for you to move on. Let's find out how you can become a full-timer and take back your life.

2

SURPRISE!
You Can Afford Full-timing

Today's Budget

You probably think you must be rich or work your entire life to be able to afford the full-timing lifestyle. Not so! The majority of full-timers find their expenses are 40 to 50 percent less than that of their previous lifestyle.

Biker Chuck looks back and says, "I was just amazed that full-timing was possible. I think if I had realized how easy full-timing is and its financial aspects, that you can live relatively inexpensively, I probably would have left a lot sooner."

So how do you put together a full-timing budget? First you must understand your expenses in the traditional lifestyle. This understanding shows how affordable full-timing can be and helps with the financial transition between lifestyles.

The first step is determining what it costs to maintain your job. (Yes, there are costs to having a job.) Your expenses may include your commute to work; buying and maintaining clothing you may not otherwise need; daycare, if you have children; vacations you would not take if your job did not provide the stress you need a break from; coffee breaks with others in the office; lunch out when you otherwise would have prepared your lunch and so on.

Along with the cost of buying these material things or the services necessary to maintain a job, there is a cost for your time. For example, think about the many hours a year you spend commuting to work and how you could use those hours to do something you enjoy instead.

Let's examine a basic example of what maintaining a job can cost. Assume you make $12 per hour and work 40 hours per week. Your wages total $480 per week. Next estimate the amount of time and the expenses incurred as a direct result of your job.

	Time	Expense Incurred
Commute	10 hours per week	$25.00 per week
Clothes	1 hour per week	$15.00 per week
Lunch out	5 hours per week	$20.00 per week
Totals	16 hours per week	$60.00 per week

Note: *Time* is based on time spent commuting; time spent shopping for clothes and doing extra laundry; and time spent eating out when there are other things you would prefer to spend your lunch hour doing. *Expense Incurred* is based on the cost of driving and paying for parking or taking a bus; the cost of new work clothes and dry cleaning; and the cost of meals eaten out rather than a homemade sandwich for lunch.

Allowing for these expenses your effective weekly wage is:

Weekly Wage	$480
Weekly job related expenses	$ 60
Effective Weekly Wage	$420

or $10.50 per hour

Next we acknowledge your job requires 56 hours of your time (40 hours of work plus 16 hours communting, etc.) This drops your hourly wage to $7.50. Ouch!

$$\frac{\$420}{56\,\text{hours}} = \$7.50 / \text{hour}$$

Chances are your cost of maintaining a job are much greater than estimated here. To take this exercise a little further let us assume you can work at home doing the same job with the same wage. What is the impact of this? You no longer need to commute, dress up or have lunch out. This eliminates the expenses tied to maintaining your job as well as your personal time spent maintaining the job. This means your effective weekly wage has increased from $420 to $480 per week and you now have 16 additional hours per week to spend on yourself!

Of course, you have been getting by with $420 per week, so what about only working enough hours to make the $420 per week? At $12 an hour that would be only 35 hours, giving you five more hours of free time per week. I know, I know, the boss won't agree to it, but you can dream can't you?

Ah, let's dream a little more. What if you could cut your living expenses by 40 to 50 percent? Now you only need to work 21 to 18 hours per week. Okay, so cutting your cost of living by that amount means getting rid of certain material possessions, especially the house. How much money would you have working for you if you sold your house and other possessions? Could you cut your hours of work per week back even further? **Maybe even eliminate the need for a job!** Let your mind travel freely along this line of thought. What you come up with may surprise you.

As you can imagine, there is a great deal more to this thought process than there is time for in this book. Understanding your current expenses, using the above approach, will help you determine how much money you must have for the full-timing lifestyle. Either *Your Money or Your Life* by Joe Dominguez and Vicki Robin or *Two Incomes and Still Broke* by Linda Kelley will help you continue this thought process. Once you have completed the financial exercises in one of these books you will be able to develop a full-timer's budget with confidence.

Expenses That Go Away

When you become a full-timer some of the traditional expenses will go away. For example, you may want to sell your house. If the market is good and you have equity the house may be a good source of funding for your new lifestyle. Selling the house will definitely do away with mortgage payments, property taxes, maintenance expenses, insurance, and utility bills. It may do away with phone and cable TV charges, as well as the homeowners' dues required in some neighborhoods.

Admittedly some full-timers opt to hang on to their home for various reasons. Some have kids or parents living in the home; others just are not sure if they really want to live full-time on the road; and still others keep the house as investment property.

Think twice before turning your house over to one of your kids. We met one couple in Tennessee that had just started to full-time for the second time. The first time they let their son take over the mortgage on their house. About a year down the road they learned he was not making the payments so they started making the payments again. However, their budget could not cover this additional expense and within a few months they decided to go home and sell the house. A quick inspection of the house showed that their son had done a great deal of damage. Seven years later the expensive repairs were behind them, someone else owned the house and they hit the road again.

Traditional lifestyle families often own two or more vehicles. When full-timers hit the road they normally eliminate vehicle loans, insurance, maintenance, licensing fees and fuel for one or more vehicles.

And don't forget those job related expenses: the work clothing; commuting costs such as bus, van pool or parking; the cost of meals and breaks directly tied to your job and whatever other expenses you have uncovered in your current expenses. If you have kids and pay for child care you can deduct that from your budget.

Taxes are also a factor to consider. Uncle Sam will always get his portion, but in the new lifestyle it will probably be less, maybe even zero. And did you know you may be able to get rid of your state income taxes? Legally, of course. How to do this and many other things mentioned in this chapter will be discussed in detail later in the book.

New Budget Items

You will also need a tow vehicle if you have a trailer, or a vehicle to tow if you have a motorhome or bus conversion. Of course, if you have a small motorhome that is easy to park you may be able to get by without a towed vehicle. This is assuming you do not mind packing up your house and disconnecting the water, electric and sewer connections every time you want to go somewhere. Then you have to hope no one has taken your spot in the campground when you return.

The type of driving you do will be completely different from that in your current lifestyle. During the first year you are likely to still be in a vacation mode, rushing from one place to the next, feeling you have to return to your previous life tomorrow. Eventually it will dawn on you that you don't have to return and your pace will slow.

What you need to consider is how frequently and how far you believe you will be moving during a year. This is a question only you can answer and it is likely to change the longer you are on the road. Paul and I have been fairly consistent, covering about 19,000 miles a year, half of which is towing our fifth-wheel. Others we know will make two or three trips across the country in a year.

How much of your mileage will be with your RV and how much with just your sightseeing vehicle? This will impact fuel and vehicle maintenance costs. Many full-timers have told us they, like us, drive about half their miles without their RV. Others move their RV short distances and stay in one place longer. Most of their miles are without their RV.

Don't forget to factor in the role family plays in your travel plans. Also the type of camping you will be doing. Will you be staying in expensive campgrounds near the attractions you want to see or camping less expensively miles away? Do you prefer to stay at parks with lots of amenities or those that just provide you a place to park?

Estimate the miles you think you will travel in a year and show this expense in your full-timing budget. When money gets tight full-timers look for ways to cut expenses. Fuel is a major expense so many full-timers will slow their pace to reduce their fuel consumption. If you use campgrounds you may want to stay long enough to get weekly or monthly camping rates, which are typically less than daily rates.

Once you sell your house you will not be able to tie your RV insurance to your homeowner's insurance. Therefore, your RV insurance will be more expensive. Your vehicle and RV registration costs can also vary significantly, depending on your state of residency.

Okay, so you no longer have a house to maintain, but now you have an RV to maintain. The cost of this will vary depending on the type of RV you buy, the age, quality of construction and your own ability to make repairs. If you are uncomfortable estimating maintenance costs, talk to others who already own the same brand and model of RV you plan to buy. People living this lifestyle love to share their experiences and talking to them can save you a lot of money. Make sure they are sharing actual maintenance expenses and not the cost of adding options such as solar panels or ceramic heaters. Don't forget to factor in the cost of maintaining your tow or towed vehicle as well. You should be able to estimate this from your current budget.

When you move out of the house the annoyance and convenience of a phone goes away. Now what? Many full-timers use a message service. However, this is changing as cellular phone costs come down. You can even get nationwide service with no roaming charges now.

There is also the question of how you will get your mail. Some people have family members forward their mail, others use a mailing service.

While you no longer have a mortgage on the house you do have camping fees. These can vary from absolutely nothing, to a nightly charge of $30 or more, to a one time expense of several thousand dollars to buy into a membership camping system with annual dues.

As you might guess, TV reception across the country varies from crystal clear to absolutely no reception. Many full-timers have opted for satellite TV service. If you can't live without your TV for a few days you will want to add the cost of satellite TV to your budget.

If you plan to travel with your kids you will need to factor in the cost of homeschooling supplies, unless you plan to stay in one community during the school year.

When the full-time job goes away so does the health insurance coverage, unless you are one of the lucky few to receive an early pension that includes health insurance. The biggest dilemma for many young full-timers is whether the budget can bear the expense of health insurance or if they can bear the risk of not having health insurance.

The above expenses are those full-timers typically find to be different from their traditional lifestyle expenses. These expenses will be discussed in more detail in the following chapters. You may find other expenses depending on your individual needs. You may also decide to increase or decrease your standard of living when you become a full-timer.

For example, most of us choose to give up many of our material possessions when we become full-timers. Where would we keep them? Maybe we don't have a jet ski to maintain or insure; this effectively lowers our standard of living, but not our quality of life. Others will find a way to own all those toys, possibly more than they did in the traditional lifestyle, thereby increasing their standard of living. After all, now they have time to play with their toys. If you plan to take your toys, keep your eyes open, there are many creative ways to take them along!

How Much Money Do I Need?

Once you know what your budget will be you can determine how much money you will need to save to be a full-timer and not work. Let's say you have determined you can live on $16,000 per year and you can make six percent annually on your investments. The amount of money you must have invested at six percent would be:

$$\frac{\$16,000}{.06} = \$266,667$$

If you can earn more on your investments you will need less money. Say you can make 10 percent on your money. Your investment would need to be:

$$\frac{\$16,000}{.10} = \$160,000$$

The most practical choice would be to raise sufficient funds before hitting the road. However, if you do not have sufficient funds to invest, there are other choices.

If you feel your time is running out or you just can't wait, consider working on the road. Many young full-timers do work on the road. We will look at working on the road in more detail later in the book.

If you have sufficient funds in one or more retirement plans, or if you are lucky enough to have a good pension when you are older, there is another option. You can determine how much money you will need between now and the time your retirement funds kick in. Once you have raised this amount of money you can hit the road. If you plan and invest well, your money will not run out before your retirement funds kick in.

Still another option would be to take the equity from the sale of your home and other possessions and live as long as you can on it. This is risky from a financial standpoint. Additionally, if you are a non-working full-timer you may find it very difficult to return to a structured working lifestyle when the funds run out.

Let's say you decide the risk is worth taking. What happens if you come up with $50,000, which you invest and it earns 10 percent. Your cost of living is $16,000 per year. Let's assume you will use the interest on your money first, then you will tap into the capital.

We will use a simple, but not exact, way to determine the interest here. Take what you have at the beginning of the year and what you have at the end of the year after the entire $16,000 has been removed. Add these numbers and multiply them by the interest rate. Divide this number by two to obtain the average interest. For year one the calculation would be:

$$\frac{(\$50,000 + \$34,000)(.10)}{2} = \$4,200$$

Now, how long will the money last?

Year	Capital In Bank	Interest	Capital Reduction (living expense-interest)
1	$50,000	$4,200	$16,000-$4,200=$11,800
2	$38,200	$3,020	$16,000-$3,020=$12,980
3	$25,220	$1,722	$16,000-$1,722=$14,278
4	$10,942		

To determine what remains in the bank for the next year subtract the capital reduction from the capital in the bank. Therefore $50,000 minus $11,800 gives you $38,200 for year two. With the capital you have left in year four you will need another income by the ninth month.

This may not be the most financially sound way to get on the road, but it is an option and the choice is yours.

ACTUAL BUDGETS

Budgets are a personal thing and there are as many different budget options as there are people. Some feel they must have health insurance before becoming a full-timer. Others will risk not having health insurance in exchange for the joy of being on the road. Some will give up eating out if it puts them on the road while others feel trying local restaurants is part of being on the road. Only you can make these decisions.

Rather than sharing individual budgets we will look at survey responses Dorothy Ayers Counts and David R. Counts received when they were writing their book *Over the Next Hill: An Ethnography of RVing Seniors in North America.* The following are questions the Counts' asked and the responses they received on surveys done in 1990 and 1993-1994. You will find this information on pages 207, 224 and 225 of *Over the Next Hill.* Included is their question on age of the respondents since age can affect a person's budget.

In my experience, the RVing lifestyle (276 responses)

1.	is an expensive way of life	(14)	(5.1%)
2.	costs about the same as a sedentary way of life	(94)	(34.0%)
3.	is an inexpensive way of life	(168)	(60.9%)

What do you spend during a normal month (either a specific figure or a range)? (244 responses, percentages calculated out of 230 responses specifying amounts.)

1.	<$300 month	(9)	(3.90%)
2.	$300-499 month	(3)	(1.30%)
3.	$500-699 month	(19)	(8.26%)
4.	$700-999 month	(31)	(13.50%)
5.	$1000-1199 month	(30)	(13.00%)
6.	$1200-1499 month	(28)	(12.00%)
7.	$1500-1999 month	(50)	(21.70%)
8.	$2000-2499 month	(27)	(11.70%)
9.	$2500-2999 month	(22)	(9.60%)
10.	$3000+ month	(11)	(4.80%)

Note: 60.2% spend between $700 and $1999 per month.

How old are you? (294 responses)

1.	under 40	(1)	(.36%)
2.	41-55	(37)	(12.58%)
3.	56-65	(146)	(49.60%)
4.	66-75	(93)	(31.60%)
5.	over 75	(17)	(5.78%)

Note: 62.6% of the respondents are 65 or younger.

Responses to the second question indicate 74 percent of full-timers live on less than $2,000 per month. We are part of that group and do not feel like we must skimp. We travel 19,000 miles a year, see many sights and attractions, visit amusement parks, stay in full hook-up campgrounds half to three quarters of the year, maintain our truck and RV and can even afford health insurance. Our budget does not allow for replacing our truck or trailer, nor does it allow for expensive toys like computers, boats, ham radios, etc. These expenses would push us over a $2,000 a month budget.

Throughout this book you will find resources that will allow you to determine your budget using the cost for specific services that will work best for you. While it will entail some work for you to put your budget together, the time spent will give you more confidence with your personal budget and your ability to become a full-timer.

You will find a worksheet in *Appendix A* that will help compare your budget today with your proposed full-timing budget. Remember you can expect to see some categories go away, such as mortgage and work related expenses and some new categories appear, such as mail forwarding and camping fees. The budget for some categories may remain the same, such as groceries and eating out. While the budget may go up or down in other categories, depending on how you change your activities when you change lifestyles.

Eventually RVs wear out and need to be replaced. Some people like to replace their RV every couple of years, although a good one could easily last 10 to 20 years. Don't forget to include this expense in your budget considerations. Keep in mind, unlike houses, RVs lose value over time.

If you have not been tracking your expenses you may find it will take a few months of tracking every receipt to get a handle on what today's expenses are. It will also take time to develop your full-timing budget. About the time you think you have it all figured out another piece of information will appear. This is just part of the lifestyle since one of the favorite pastimes is sharing information.

As you work to develop your full-timer's budget remember you are making a big lifestyle change. Seldom do lifestyle changes happen overnight or without planning. The more time you spend putting your budget together the more likely you are to be successful in the full-timing lifestyle.

3

Reality vs. Dream:
Full-timing as a Lifestyle

So what is this full-timing lifestyle and what makes it so great? Have you ever experienced a vacation you did not want to end? Well, full-timing is about as close as you can come to a full-time vacation. Full-timing has nothing to do with vacations though, it means living full-time in a house on wheels and moving when the mood strikes you.

"Camping!" you say. "Who in their right mind wants to camp for life!" Well, if you have never camped, as we never had, maybe it is time to look at the latest motorhomes and trailers. Today they offer everything condos and houses offer, with the exception of square footage. By the way, when talking to full-timers they will tell you they **do not camp**. They are simply living life in the same home while changing yards.

What Do You Do With Your Time?

A typical question asked of full-timers is, "What do you do with all your time?" Just the other day someone asked me this question. I could not give a clear and concise answer. This is because we do many of the same things on the road that others do at home. So what do you do with your free time?

As for chores, some will take longer while others will take less time. Laundry is a chore that will take longer. RV washers and dryers are small and only do half as much as household washers and dryers. This means it will take you twice as long to do the laundry. RV washers and dryers take up valuable space, add weight and require a full hook-up site. You may find it easier to go to the Laundromat. You will not be able to do other things at home while you are doing laundry, but you can get it all done in a couple of hours.

Grocery shopping is another chore that takes longer, as every store has a different layout. Some full-timers enjoy this chore because they can check out regional foods and unfamiliar products while they shop.

When it comes to passing time, most people can quickly make a list of things they would like to do if they had the time. Once you have made your list, determine if these are things you can do while you travel. If they are, good. If not, you will have to consider which is more important, the things on your list or full-timing.

When you become a full-timer the change in your lifestyle can be as dramatic as when a person retires, even for those full-timers who must work. Chili Chuck says, "I have met so many people who don't know what to do when they retire. It is as if they lived in a vacuum. They went to work and they came home. Don't you have something you want to do? Only for you?"

Maybe you have heard retirees say, "I don't have any free time." The same is true for full-timers. Most of us do not stay put long, a few days, a week or two, then "hitch itch" returns and we know it is time to move on. With so much to see and do there is no free time! Many of us will tell you, "I wake up with nothing to do and go to bed with it only half done."

There is little structure and a great deal of whim in the full-timing lifestyle. Sightseeing will be the agenda some days. Other days' chores, such as washing the outside of the RV, vacuuming (which now takes only 10 minutes), or changing the oil in the vehicle, will keep you busy. There is often time to relax with a good book, or to go for a hike or bike ride. If you need structure, however, don't look for the full-timing lifestyle to provide it. Learning to live without structure can be a challenging adjustment.

In a campground you are likely to find yourself on a walk, stopping along the way to visit or look at different RVs. This is a great way to make new friends and find answers to questions like: can you afford to buy a satellite dish or should you install an exhaust brake. One of the best parts of the full-timing lifestyle is meeting new people. You will also make friends when doing the laundry or participating in planned activities.

Some people cannot afford the cost of campgrounds or just do not like being packed like sardines into a campground. They enjoy hearing only the sounds of nature at night and during the day prefer not to listen to the neighbor's TV with the hottest new talk show blaring. These people choose to boondock or camp without water, sewer and electric hook-ups. Cheryl's description of boondocking is "*TOTAL FREEDOM* from full hook-up parks to enjoy the 3 S's—Silence, Solitude and Spectacular views, while avoiding the three R's—Reservations, Rules and Regulations."

In the winter, boondockers find themselves parked in the desert. Summer takes them to mountains, lakes and streams, either by themselves or with a few friends. These locations have no water, electricity or sewer hook-ups. A true boondocker has an RV with large holding tanks, solar panels, a generator and maybe even a wind generator. They are true environmentalists.

When we started out we had no interest in boondocking. We felt it was too primitive and we liked the modern conveniences hook-ups offer. Two years later we learned the tricks to making boondocking fit our needs and we now boondock half the time. So never say "never" to boondocking. With the right knowledge and equipment you would probably enjoy it!

Determining Travel Plans

Another question we frequently hear from those considering full-timing is, "How do you determine your travel plans?" In our case we decide what states we plan to visit, obtain a state visitor guide and talk with others about what there is to see. Paul puts our itinerary together, studying the visitor guides, selecting sights to see and evaluating where they are in relation to our membership campgrounds and available boondocking sites. When the sights are more than a half hour from our membership campground or a boondocking site we decide if the attraction is worth the cost of a public campground nearby.

Family time is also a factor that gets worked into our travel plans. A bonus to being a full-timer is being where you feel you need to be. If there is a family crisis, such as an illness or death, you can provide the necessary support, while staying in your own home.

One of our goals was to tour the United States. With 47 states checked off, we now plan less and return to places we have enjoyed before.

Some people are even better at being prepared for an area than we are. Nicole makes notes every time she reads about something of interest to her. It may be a couple of years, if ever, before she gets there, but her archives of information result in great experiences! Others keep an envelope for each state and when they see an article of interest they put it in the appropriate envelope.

Chili Chuck is a historian, so his travel plans take him across the country by way of various historic trails. He and his wife Ginny have done the Oregon Trail, Little House on the Prairie and the Spanish Missions from north to south, just to name a few. "I have 30 trips outlined," Chili Chuck says. "Now I just need to live 30 years so I can do them all."

Those who work on the road can either decide where they want to travel and find work along the way or they can decide what job they want and go where it takes them.

Then there are the full-timers who have no plans, or at least no more than being south in the winter and north in the summer. If they wake up one day and feel the urge to move they move. They may or may not have a destination in mind. That is about as close to total freedom as you can get!

We belong to a group called "Boomers," who you will learn more about later. When Boomers talk about their schedules they talk about their schedules being carved in *Jell-O*®. This is their way of saying their schedules are flexible and likely to change on the spur of the moment. Recently we left Oregon for the San Francisco area, but it was raining there and we were looking for sunshine, so we turned toward Palm Springs instead. That is *Jell-O*® planning. You never know where you will end up!

By now you should be getting a feel for young full-timers. Their traits include a love of fun, people and travel; independence and willingness to take a risk; a pioneer spirit; a willingness to share knowledge and experiences and little interest in material possessions. They are also adventurous, spontaneous, resourceful and accepting of others.

Is Full-timing Right For You?

This brief glimpse at full-timing has probably given you an idea of whether this lifestyle is right for you. To further evaluate the lifestyle for yourself, go knock on a full-timer's door in a campground and tell them of your interest in full-timing. Chances are you will spend the next couple of hours hearing more than you can absorb!

How do you know a full-timer from a weekend camper as you walk through a campground? One good way is to look for the Escapees RV Club decal—a circle with a red wagon hauling a blue and white house. The Escapees RV Club provides a support network for full-timers. Look for license plates from Florida, Texas or Oregon, as many full-timers are residents of these states. Also look for an energized Escapees decal with the red wagon and white house leaping out of a yellow star burst. People with this decal belong to Boomers, a subgroup of Escapees for young full-timers.

If you are serious about the idea of full-timing you may want to look into one of two educational programs to help you prepare. Escapees have a five day Escapade at a western location in the spring and a eastern location in the fall. Escapades offer many seminars to help those considering the full-timing lifestyle as well as those already on the road. It is also a great place to visit with hundreds of people already in the full-timers lifestyle.

This lifestyle has become so popular that in 1996 the University of Idaho started offering a five day Life on Wheels program. It was such a success that the summer 1997 Life on Wheels program was full by December 1996. The program has been extended and now offers extension courses across the country.

It is not necessary to have an RV to attend either Escapade or Life on Wheels. You will find the addresses and phone numbers for these programs in the **Resource Directory** at the back of this book.

Be honest with yourself when evaluating whether full-timing is the right lifestyle for you. It is not right for everyone. In fact, it is not even right for most people. For example, consider how you feel about change. Successful full-timers enjoy the many wonders of the lifestyle because they expect and thrive on change.

If the lifestyle is right for you, but not for your significant other, it probably will not work. Do not lose hope yet, however! Sometimes significant others just need a more in-depth introduction to the lifestyle.

4

Moving into the Dream

"I knew that once I left our house and things behind that I would become a different person in the eyes of the world. You go through your life building status and when you leave all those status things behind you are looked at differently. It was interesting to leave that behind. It is kind of like here I am, naked before the world again. It's like getting a second chance at life and it is another step in finding who you are." This is how Nicole viewed the transition into the full-timing lifestyle.

How do you start this second chance at life smoothly, with the least amount of stress and the maximum amount of joy? We will look at some of the mental and emotional obstacles that may occur and how you can deal with them. This is not a complete discussion of what you might expect, however. Take a moment to think about the obstacles or fears you may have to confront. Then visit with full-timers about these obstacles and ask how they dealt with them.

Confront The Obstacles

It is important to allow enough time to mentally prepare for a lifestyle change. While some people require little mental adjustment, others may require years. If it takes a while to adjust to the idea of a new lifestyle, don't worry. Your values have grown up with you over many years. You cannot expect them to change overnight. And even when you are ready to make the transition, remember those close to you may not be able to accept your new lifestyle so readily. You may need a great deal of patience and understanding for those close to you, as they struggle with what you are about to do.

As you deal with your emotions you will also be dealing with those of your friends and family. With luck they will support your decision to become a full-timer. While many will be envious, only a few will admit they would never have the courage to do what you are doing. Some may tell you that you are throwing everything away, or that what you want to do isn't possible. Others may tell you the lifestyle isn't safe, or make other discouraging remarks.

Guilt is an emotion society has taught us and some people are masters at using it. A college student might say to his parents, "But you can't sell the house. Where will I go during breaks?" Or parents might say, "We need you here to help with things." It is hard to remember that it takes two to create guilt—one to give and one to accept.

Other emotions may come into play. One young couple told how both their parents thought they were being so irresponsible that they took them out of their wills. Who do you think won in this situation?

Just like you, your family has fears. Do you know what their fears are and the role these fears play in their reaction to your lifestyle change? Understanding this may help the transition.

Your life is a gift and it is your responsibility to figure out how to make the most of it. In most cases, adult children and parents can stand on their own two feet. When they need assistance, the skills of specialists will exceed your ability to care for them. If guilt or other emotions cause you to change your plans, chances are you will grow to resent the intrusion in your life. As a result the relationship with this person is likely to deteriorate.

This isn't to say you should not be with your family when they need you. The lifestyle makes it easier to be with family in a crisis. Your lifestyle is mobile and you can take it wherever you feel you should be.

Dealing with these issues is not easy. However, the decision of what you do with your life is yours, and only yours. A copy of this book and others may help those close to you through your transition.

Doubt

Many people will never consider the full-timing lifestyle. Some would just never enjoy it. Others are not risk takers, have self-doubt or simply fear what the lifestyle may bring.

Your intrigue has brought you this far, but how will you confront the doubts surrounding a major lifestyle change? Doubts, such as where the money will come from, the loss of a career and what will happen if full-timing isn't for you?

Jessica said, "My belief is that if you really want to do something, you will find a way. If you find a way, go for it because it is not a life or death situation. I know that if we decide we don't want to be on the road we could always go somewhere, get jobs, an apartment and do whatever we have to do. I wouldn't feel like we had been failures. It would just be a new choice or new decision based on the circumstances."

"It is amazing how when we are afraid to make a change that we can find so many things that help us see how it is not possible," Fred says. On the other hand, "when that thing snaps in our mind and we say 'This is possible,' it is amazing how many things take on a positive force. We can do this. It is amazing, the different energy that we draw to ourselves."

Fred's wife, Peggy expressed it this way, "Once we had the idea in our hearts everything around us started to work out in a manner that hurried up our plans, and allowed them to happen sooner, encouraging us to do it sooner. Not in a fearful way, just like everything was cooperating to help us move this up."

As Jessica, Fred and Peggy share, much of our doubt is overcome with how we look at the lifestyle we choose.

We are not the only ones to have doubts. Our friends and family may have even more doubts about our choice in lifestyle than we do. It is important not to let their doubts drag you down.

Jessica's daughter-in-law and husband were apprehensive. They said, "Well, what if you are making a mistake?"

Jessica responded, "Well, there is no mistake. This is a decision we are making now. We can always make a new decision if we want to."

It is easy to get wrapped up in the "what ifs" and completely miss out on a wonderful opportunity. Are you willing to take risks to live life fully and follow your dreams? Or will you let life dwindle away and only have your lost dreams to look back on?

Make a list of your doubts. Then go back and look at each one. Ask yourself, "What is the worst thing that could happen?" Write these answers down. Finally write down your "reality" regarding the worst case. Jessica's family raised a doubt that she might write down like this:

Doubt

Are we making a mistake?

Worst Case

Full-timing isn't for us.

Reality

Our skills make us very employable and finding housing will be no problem.

Hmmm, that doesn't seem like enough to lose sleep over. Continue to add to your list as doubts come up. Also review your list periodically to reassure yourself that you are heading down the right path. Doubt should help you avoid obstacles—not destroy dreams

Self Esteem

Some people will struggle with self esteem. I did and it took me six months to realize what was happening! The following quiz will help you determine if you may face a struggle with self esteem.

Self Esteem Quiz

1) Do you play a more important role in
   a) your home life.
   b) your work life.
   c) your community.

2) Can someone else step in and take over your job?
   a) yes
   b) no

3) Where do you get your pats on the back?
   a) family and friends
   b) on the job
   c) community

4) Can you walk away from a half completed project?
   a) yes
   b) no

If you answered "b" to one or more questions you may struggle with self esteem when you change lifestyles. If you answered "b" to all the questions you can almost count on a struggle with self esteem.

Responses of "c" may also indicate a struggle with self esteem until you are able to establish yourself in your new community. You may want to consider becoming involved in your new community before hitting the road to minimize your struggle. We will focus on community for full-timers later in the book.

Overcoming a struggle with self esteem will take time. It is a matter of adjusting to your new lifestyle and finding your own niche. For me, sharing my knowledge on full-timing and other interests has helped.

Making The Break

What about the emotions you face when you finally take off? "Emotionally it was like a jail break," Peggy said. "There was a lot of grief from leaving all that stuff behind and there was a lot of excitement at the new stuff we were doing. There was a lot of dread about what if we are doing the entire wrong thing? The worst dread was, what if they caught up with us and made us go back?"

"I was making a radical break," Biker Chuck said. "There were some emotions at first I guess. I was leaving for Cape Cod and I drove 70 mph for the first day. Then I thought, now wait a minute, this is a whole new thing, I'm not rushing anymore. It took maybe a day to gear down and recognize it, but after a couple of days it felt natural."

Then comes the realization that you are now living in a very small home with your partner 24 hours a day. As Bethany's husband liked to tell people, "Can you imagine living in a 32 foot by 8 foot island with her?" Bethany went on to say, "Every once in a while you are allowed off the island, or someone else comes on, but basically you're on a deserted island together." As you can imagine, this will be very trying on a relationship, so if you don't get along now, you should definitely reconsider.

Disposing Of Your "Stuff"

Disposing of "stuff" is an overwhelming task for many. While it is a great load off your shoulders to get rid of your "stuff," most people have a few things they are not ready to let go of. But what do you do with it when there isn't space for it in your home on wheels?

Obviously you could rent a storage unit, but this gets expensive and is one more bill to worry about. Also, if you decide to give these things up down the road, it is very difficult to have a garage sale from a storage unit. Maybe you will be storing family antiques, or other items that need to be in a controlled environment, not too damp, not too dry. Something more to worry about.

Full-timers have settled this dilemma in a couple of ways. Some will give things they care about, and cannot yet let go of, to their children. This way they can enjoy them when they visit their kids. Of course brothers and sisters, parents and even close friends could help here as well.

Others loan their stuff to family members or friends, with the understanding that they get it back when they want it. In the mean time, those close to you are enjoying and caring for your things. This is what DeAnna and Al did. "But with time we got less attached to it, so it became theirs," DeAnna said.

Now, what about the things that you are ready to let go of? There are garage sales, auctions and charities that can help. You might even be able to sell some things with your house. Creativity can make this experience fun and give you an opportunity to make others happy as well. It isn't time to get hung up on what this "stuff" is worth. If you get hung up on the value of your stuff you probably are not quite ready to hit the road.

Peggy invited people from her office to come to their yard sale before the public. "They actually bought up a lot of the nicer things at decent prices." Then when the public came, Peggy said,

"I was talking people down [in price]. It was ridiculous!" But the experience left her with a good feeling.

Another person accepted lower prices as their garage sale came to an end—providing the buyer took something they were having a hard time getting rid of. Jessica and her husband gave some of their stuff to a friend who had just come out of a divorce with only a bed and a lawn chair to her name.

Lin and Betty threw a going away party for themselves and invited all their neighbors and close friends. Betty said, "We had all these little odds and ends of funny liquors, you know, you've got a recipe and it calls for two tablespoons of cherry liquor, or something ridiculous." Lin continued, "I set them out on a table and we told folks as they came in, 'When you leave you will take a bottle with you.' 'Oh no, we can't do that,' they said. 'Yes, you will do that or you can't come in!'"

When it came time to get rid of our own stuff Paul came up with an idea that worked well. We took pictures of everything we wanted to get rid of and made up a price list. Paul then took the pictures and list to work, explaining that some of the stuff would not be available for a couple of months. That did not seem to bother anyone. People lined up at Paul's desk to put their names on things. Often four or five people would sign up for the same item, hoping those who had signed ahead of them would not want the item.

As the departure date approached I told my coworkers that I was leaving and brought in the price list and pictures to work. My car was one of the items still on the list and we had yet to set a price. One person came to me and said, "I want your car. How much do you want for it?"

"I don't know," I said. I went on to tell him the problems the car had and commented that he wouldn't be able to get the seat back far enough to accommodate his six foot six inch frame.

"I'm not concerned. Just let me know how much you want for the car," he said.

No cost for running ads, no stress from dickering over the price with strangers and the buyers moved most of the stuff out of the house. It took three of the largest U-Haul trucks for us to move in and we moved out in one pick-up load. What a way to go!

The Transition Continues

As you continue through this book, take time to make a transition plan. Start with a list of tasks and obstacles you foresee. The following chapters look at additional steps to include in your plan. Also estimate how long you believe each step will take. When the list seems fairly complete determine their order and set target dates for completion of each step. Use of such a plan will make the mental adjustment of shedding your old life for a new one occur naturally and at a comfortable pace.

One of the most exciting steps you will take is selecting your home on wheels. This will take more work than selecting a traditional home and will require you to put more thought into your needs. Selecting a traditional home is second nature since your needs developed around the homes you grew up in.

The next five chapters cover selection of a home on wheels. Even if you already have an RV that you plan to call home, take time to read these chapters. You may find some things to reconsider.

As you tackle each step in your plan, look for ways to make it fun. Your creativity is all it takes to turn a chore into something fun. When your plan seems overwhelming, step back from it and choose a smaller step or portion of a step to work on. Trust yourself and your intuition. Overcome your fears by getting to their roots and turning them into positive thoughts. Give yourself the gift of time, don't kill yourself getting there. And finally, remember you can always go and do something different if full-timing isn't your thing.

Preparing to Hit the Road

5

Selecting A Wheel Estate

We have seen full-timers living in some interesting RVs. One senior couple and their greyhound lived in a camper van, a single lady and her dog lived in a trailer small enough to pull behind a motorcycle, and then there was the couple with two kids, ages twelve and four, who lived in a folding camping trailer. These people were willing to sacrifice comfort in exchange for this lifestyle. However, most full-timers do not go to this extreme.

If you have never camped or seen the inside of a motorhome or trailer, you will be surprised. The only thing missing from these homes on wheels is square footage. Check them out by spending a day visiting RV dealers or go to an RV show, but don't buy anything yet! Once you have a feel for what motorhomes and trailers have to offer, sit down and consider if an RV will meet your needs.

Throughout the rest of the book the terms recreational vehicle and RV will often be replaced with the term "wheel estate." It is time everyone recognizes the difference between camping, as an activity, and full-timing, as a lifestyle. This starts with our homes on wheels, which need more storage capacity, durability and payload than an RV used for camping. The term "wheel estate" helps to establish this difference.

Additionally, the term "wheel estate" establishes legitimacy and reality to full-timing as a lifestyle.

Selecting a good wheel estate will be more challenging than selecting traditional housing. You will need to consider things like durability, will your home on wheels last a couple of years or 20 years? Storage, not normally a problem in traditional housing, becomes a priority in the full-timing lifestyle. Even how frequently you plan to move and whether you can drive or pull your home on wheels must be considered.

Paul and I are fifth-wheel people and you are likely to see that bias in the next few chapters. Others you visit with will also have a basis. The best wheel estate is the one that is right for you and only you can make that determination.

You will want to carefully research RVs before buying. Read as many articles on RVs as you can. Also visit with full-timers to find out why and how they selected their wheel estate. This will help you match your needs to what each RV has to offer. The more research and thought you put into your selection, the more likely you are to get the right RV for you.

It is not always possible to foresee the right choice in wheel estates, as Jessica shares. "We went back and forth between a fifth-wheel trailer and a motorhome. We ended up deciding a motorhome would be better. As it turns out, for the lifestyle we have lived so far, we probably would have been better off with a fifth-wheel trailer because we end up being parked somewhere for six months while we are working. Even when we do travel we haven't done as much traveling as we thought we would, so I think a fifth-wheel trailer might have been more spacious and we would have only had one vehicle to maintain."

While a fifth-wheel trailer may have given Jessica and Sam more space, their motorhome does a good job of meeting their needs. They remodeled it to include a large office area, while maintaining their living space. If you cannot find the right RV, or purchase an RV only to learn it does not meet your needs, don't hit the panic button. Consider the options remodeling may offer instead.

The next five chapters cover how to select an RV. When you understand and follow the process laid out in these chapters you will be more knowledgeable than 99 percent of RV buyers. You will also be more knowledgeable than most salespeople.

Do you need to be this knowledgeable? No, but without the knowledge provided here and from other resources your chance of buying an RV that does not meet your needs increase. Worse yet you may buy an unsafe RV or a "lemon!"

Shopping for the perfect wheel estate is the beginning of your dream come true. It is fun and exciting! So what is a little extra time spent on this step if it will save you money and headaches down the road?

The first step is to determine what type of wheel estate will best meet your needs. We will look at motorhomes, travel trailers and fifth-wheel trailers in this chapter. Bus conversions will be covered in a separate chapter.

Motorhome

Motorhomes offer the most security. You can pull into rest stops and other places for the night without ever leaving your home. If a problem arises you simply drive off.

As you travel down the road your partner can fix a meal, go to the bathroom or catch the things you forgot to tie down. If you want to do some sightseeing, without the wheel estate, and you aren't ready to head to a campground, no problem. Simply pull into a shopping center and disconnect your towed vehicle. No one knows you are not shopping inside.

The floor plan in motorhomes are the least flexible of all wheel estates. Generally the driving compartment becomes part of the living space. This places the kitchen in the center of the motorhome with the bathroom and bedroom to the rear of the unit.

Many motorhomes have a convection oven and no gas oven. This increases the kitchen storage, but can you forego the gas oven? While you may not believe it today, you are likely to find yourself camping without electricity at some point in the future.

A motorhome offers the most options in the type of vehicle you take for transportation. If you like comfort while sightseeing you can take a car. If you need additional storage, you can take a van or a pick-up with a topper. We have seen motorhomes pulling two story trailers that carry all the toys, making it possible to take along a car, boat, jet skis, ATVs and motorcycles. We have also seen motorhomes towing enclosed trailers that carry a car, motorcycles or business supplies. Keep in mind that motorhomes do have limits on the weight they can safely tow. Also, be aware some vehicles are not designed to be towed.

The drive train in a motorhome will increase maintenance. It also means that when the drive train has a problem your entire home is in the shop. When you tow a vehicle behind a motorhome you have two drive trains to maintain. This increases your costs. Will you be able to find reliable mechanics? Or can you do the maintenance yourself?

If you are shopping for a large motorhome, keep in mind that some states require drivers of large motorhomes to have a CDL Class B driver's license. Check the requirements in your state of residency before buying a large motorhome.

Betty had concerns about driving a motorhome. Here is how she overcame her fear.

We went out to look at some motorhomes and I kept thinking, those are too big. But we looked at a few, just looked at the exteriors, then one day we actually went to a dealership and got inside. We were looking around and the salesman came up to us. I guess we were looking at a 34 foot and I kept saying, "This is too big, we'll never be able to manage it. This is more than we need, let's look at one of these little ones." Which wasn't very practical.

The salesman said, "Well why don't you take it for a test drive and see how it drives." He backed it out of the lot, which was crowded, and said, "Here."

So I sat in the driver's seat and he said, "Just drive it."

I said, "I don't want to drive this."

He said, "It drives just like a car. Just drive it."

You know, it did drive just like a car. I mean, it really was not hard to drive.

So do not be concerned about driving a motorhome until you have taken one for a test drive.

Travel Trailer

Travel trailers are less expensive than motorhomes since they do not have an engine. They are also less expensive than fifth-wheel trailers which have a more complex structural system. For the same reason travel trailers weigh less than fifth-wheel trailers.

A wide variety of tow vehicles are available due to the lighter weight and the trailer being hitched behind the tow vehicle. The low profile makes travel trailers more aerodynamic. This increases fuel mileage and reduces the chore of scrubbing bugs off the front of the trailer. It also makes it possible to go under low trees and bridges.

Travel trailers generally have less storage than other types of RVs. A few offer basement storage, which improves the storage situation but also increases the height of a trailer. People who have motorcycles will frequently choose a travel trailer. This way they can tow with a pick-up that will also carry their motorcycle. Those who work craft and trade shows may tow with a van, pick-up topper combination, or a commercial truck. This provides an easy way to carry products and supplies along. Those who like to travel to Mexico and Alaska in a small RV can install a pick-up camper for those trips and tow a travel trailer the rest of the year.

The floor plan of a travel trailer is extremely flexible. Some even have an enclosed patio or garage on the back to haul motorcycles, ATVs or other toys. Travel trailers are the most likely of all wheel estates to offer a second sleeping area for children or parents that may travel with you.

The light weight and hitch location makes travel trailers less stable when a semi truck passes or when driving in high winds or on rough roads. There are special hitches and stabilizing bars to improve stability. Travel trailers are also the most difficult to hitch-up; however, special equipment makes it possible for one person to accomplish this task.

Fifth-Wheel Trailer

Fifth-wheels are considered the most livable of wheel estates. This is because they tend to have the most storage and usable living space for the length of the unit.

Generally bedrooms and bathrooms are located in the upper portion of a fifth-wheel trailer. Occasionally you will see living areas in this location or infrequently a kitchen. Normally the kitchen will be located in the center or rear of the trailer and the living room will occupy the remaining portion of the lower section.

Unlike other RVs, fifth-wheel trailers are built on two or three levels. Therefore a fifth-wheel trailer may not be a good choice for those who have difficulty with steps.

The tow vehicle will be a pick-up, medium duty truck or even a semi truck, since a fifth-wheel trailer must hitch to the bed of a truck. Occasionally we see modified vans towing fifth-wheels.

Fifth-wheel trailers are more stable for towing in high winds or on rough roads than travel trailers. This is because fifth-wheel trailers hitch in the bed of a tow truck. The weight of a fifth-wheel trailer also adds stability.

One person can easily hitch up a fifth-wheel trailer. Installation of a dual-pivot action hitch allows for easy hitching and unhitching in unlevel sites. Without this type of hitch you may find yourself leveling the truck before you can unhitch or hitch-up.

Trailer Living Space and Tow Length

When comparing fifth-wheels and travel trailers keep in mind a 33 foot travel trailer provides only 30 feet of usable living space. The hitch accounts for the other three feet in length. The living space in a fifth-wheel is the same as the overall length of the trailer. This is because the fifth-wheel hitch is below the upper living space and does not extend much beyond the trailer itself.

When hitched, a fifth-wheel trailer overlaps the tow vehicle by three or four feet, while a travel trailer is completely behind the tow vehicle. This means the combined length of a tow vehicle and fifth-wheel trailer is six to seven feet shorter than a travel trailer with the same living space. Due to the additional length and the location of the hitch, travel trailers require more space to turn and maneuver than fifth-wheel trailers.

Selection Based On Tow or Towed Vehicle

The type of vehicle you choose to get around in, once you park your RV, may play a role in selecting your wheel estate. If you prefer to sightsee in a car, you will probably be looking at motorhomes. Few cars are rated to tow a travel trailer and it takes a truck, a good sized truck, to tow a fifth-wheel trailer. Occasionally couples will take a second more comfortable vehicle along for sightseeing and use their tow truck only to tow the trailer.

If you will be towing a vehicle behind a motorhome, you need to determine if it can be towed with all four wheels on the ground or if a tow dolly or trailer is required. **Do not** rely on the vehicle salesperson for this information. Too many people have bought a vehicle because the salesperson told them they could tow it, only to learn later that they could not tow it. Check the owner's manual to see if you will be able to tow the vehicle. You will also want to determine what steps must be taken to tow the vehicle. Can you live with those steps or are they too much of a hassle?

In a later chapter we will look at weight ratings for the tow or towed vehicle and the RV. The results of this analysis will help you decide between types of RVs and tow versus towed vehicle.

If you are considering traveling in a motorhome without taking a towed vehicle along you may want to reconsider. Here is what Bethany has to say about traveling without a towed vehicle.

Our transportation is two mountain bikes. So if we happened to be camped for a week and we're eight or nine miles out of town and need a loaf of bread or a quart of milk, we ride our bike. Once we have set the bus up we don't move it.

I would like to have a towed vehicle. I don't like being dependent on other people, like having to ask if someone is going into town that I could possibly catch a ride with. I prefer to be a little bit more independent.

I think if we had a towed vehicle we would stay in one place longer and see more of the area. We don't go into cities because the campgrounds are quite a way out of

> *town in most places. Twice we rented a car, but you can't do that all the time.*

Sue's experience is similar.

> *We used to travel almost every day or two in order to go and see the sights. Since we had to take the coach, we might as well boondock someplace different. Now with the car we can see a little more of the town before we move on.*
>
> *It just got really tiring to pick up everything and move to see things all the time. I get a great feeling of freedom from having the car. Just the fact that I can go someplace by myself, which I could not do before.*

Once you select the type of RV you believe will best meet your needs, it is time to evaluate the equipment your wheel estate should have.

6

Equipment for the Wheel Estate

The second step to selecting a wheel estate is deciding what equipment and features you need. Never assume that manufacturers know what full-timers need in a wheel estate. Few manufacturers have lived full-time in an RV. Many have never even owned an RV!

Also, few salespeople have spent time in an RV. You may want to ask the salesperson:

★ How often do you go camping?
★ What is the longest period you have spent in an RV?
★ What type of RV do you own?

This will give you an idea of how knowledgeable they are about the lifestyle. Regardless of their experience, do not let them talk you out of anything you feel you need. Only you know what is important to you.

Let's take a look at some of the features you may want to consider for your wheel estate. As you read this chapter, make a list of the items you *must* have in your wheel estate. Also list the items you would *like* to have, but may be willing to sacrifice. Making this list before you shop will save you from buying an RV that may not meet your needs. This list will grow as you begin to look at RVs and decide what will or will not work for you.

Wheel Estate Construction and Living Space

Floor Plans

The floor plan of an RV may determine the type of RV you would like. As previously mentioned, the floor plans in motorhomes are very limited. Front to back you have living space, kitchen, bathroom and bedroom.

In fifth-wheels bedrooms are normally located in the upper level of the trailer. The living room and kitchen will normally be on the lower level. Occasionally you will find upper living rooms or kitchens. In that case the bedroom is at the rear of the trailer.

Travel trailers have the most flexibility and therefore the most options in floor plans.

In most wheel estates, access to the bedroom is either through the bathroom or a hall alongside the bathroom. A few manufacturers will locate the bathroom in another location.

Where do you enter the RV? Does this work for you? What floor plan works best for you?

Kitchen

Is there sufficient counter space? Storage space? Are the electric outlets where you will need them? Does the wheel estate have a gas oven? If not, can you live without it? Remember you may not have power to run a convection oven. Is there room to store your bread maker, large mixer or pots and pans? Is the sink large enough for doing dishes easily? Where will a waste basket go? Is there a pantry? Does it have fixed shelves or do the shelves pull out for easy access? Are the shelves deep enough for your plates and other kitchen equipment? Where will the silverware go?

Do you want a dinette, which will give additional storage, or a traditional kitchen table and chairs, which provide more flexibility? Do any of the chairs fold for storage elsewhere? If your table is in a slide room and you turn it sideways, placing it on the floor next to the slide room, do you gain space for other things? One couple made space for their electric keyboard this way.

Be sure the refrigerator can operate on both gas and electricity. Custom and modified RVs may have refrigerators that operate only on electricity. With the combination unit you can keep the food cold during a power outage or while boondocking.

Electronic refrigerators have a high failure rate. In fact, if you ask RVers about equipment failures you are more likely to hear about refrigerator failures than any other equipment failure. If you can select your own refrigerator, check with the refrigerator manufacturers to see if they offer a manual refrigerator. In our current trailer we have a Norcold model 1082 refrigerator. It is a household refrigerator and comes with an outer wrapper. However, when the outer wrapper is removed it is the same size as an RV refrigerator. While we have to manually flip between the gas and electric modes, we will not have to deal with electronic failures that can cost more than $400 to fix. This refrigerator also pulls no power when boondocked.

You will hear stories about dishes breaking in rear kitchens. We have had two trailers with a rear kitchen. We had little breakage in the first trailer. In the second trailer we broke dishes we had carried for four years in the first trailer.

We have a unique situation, as our second trailer was a custom duplication of our first trailer. So what caused the breakage in the second trailer? One possible cause was a change from a shock, leaf spring and equalizer axle system to a rubberized axle system. Another possible cause is the second trailer has a stiffer structural construction, which does not allow the structure to give as much when we hit bumps. The axle manufacturer was unable to offer any solutions.

What finally helped was to let a few pounds of air out of the tires. However, safety, performance and life of the tires must be considered before doing this. See the Chubby Wheel Estate chapter for more on this.

It is impossible to tell from one trailer or motorhome to the next how it will ride. One salesperson actually told us that an RV goes through a perpetual earthquake! You may want to go for a test drive down a rough road to see how it rides. The salesperson may think you are crazy, but so what. We are talking about your future home, not his. Keep in mind that many states have laws against riding in a trailer, so you may not legally be able to do this.

We took our first trailer down a washboard road and took turns riding in it to see how everything rode. It was noisy and everything shook, but nothing broke. Don't expect it to be a quiet air ride.

To minimize breakage in a trailer's rear kitchen you can limit or eliminate glassware. You can also place padding between glass or ceramic plates and bowls. We use Corelle® dishes which did not break for over five years. Then one day going down the road six pieces of Corelle® tumbled out of the cabinet to the floor. Of those six pieces only one, a bowl, broke. Early in our travels a Corelle® cup fell out of a cabinet and removed a large piece of enamel from the sink. We continue to use that cup six years later.

It is hard to determine in advance if a particular RV will have a problem. Visit with owners of the same brand and size RV you are considering to see what their experience has been.

Living Room

Try the furniture. Is it comfortable? Consider two recliners instead of a couch. Not only are they more comfortable, they also make it possible to put a bookcase or additional storage behind them. Do you need a hide-a-bed or can guests sleep on an air mattress? Remember you will sit on the couch every day while your guests will only visit for a few days. If you do not like the furniture, delete it when you buy your wheel estate.

A trend in the RV market is to have entertainment centers. Where is the entertainment center? Manufacturers give little thought to comfort when locating an entertainment center. Their goal is to finding an easy and inexpensive way to incorporate it into the floor plan. Some manufacturers will even install the entertainment center in the kitchen! So sit on the furniture and determine if the entertainment center is in a good location for you. Will it be comfortable to watch TV for long periods of time? Is there space for the size TV you want? Are the electrical outlets where you will need them?

Slide Rooms

Slide rooms offer great expansion opportunities. They are rooms that slide out when you park the RV and slide in when you are ready to go down the road.

Evaluate what will be behind the slide room when the room is in. If you stop for lunch on the road will you be able to get to your silverware, pantry or microwave without putting the slide room out? What if you spend the night in a location where you cannot put your slide room out—will you be able to watch TV? Slide rooms do fail—can you survive with a slide room in for several days until it is repaired? Thermostats and heat ducts behind slide rooms can also be a problem when the slide room is in.

Does a slide eliminate basement storage or make it harder to access? Slides with a bed in them will greatly reduce or eliminate under the bed storage.

Does the slide have power to it for lights and other equipment? Does a power cord run from the slide to the main room to get power to the slide? Besides being unattractive, should you forget to unplug this cord before you bring the slide in you could cause some damage.

What is in the slide? In some slides you will find kitchens with refrigerators or stoves. This means there are water, drain and gas lines going in and out with the slide. Will these cause maintenance problems? You be the judge and don't let the manufacturer or dealer sway your judgment. They have little to lose since they are not likely to have to deal with the long term problems you might have.

Is the ceiling of the slide high enough that you do not bump your head when you stand up? Try the slide furnishings and see if they are comfortable. If the slide has a raised floor are people likely to trip on it? Can you use the furnishings the way you would expect to use them? We saw one trailer where the raised floor of the slide made it impossible to slide a chair up to the desk in the slide.

Where are the controls to run the slide room in and out? Are they convenient? Can they be easily bumped? Do you have to hold the control the entire time the slide room is moving or do you push a button and walk away?

Is the slide electric or hydraulic? Hydraulic slide rooms tend to go in and out faster than electric slide rooms. You may wish to time slide rooms as they go in and out. The times will vary significantly, although an extra minute or two to put the slide room in or out will not make a huge difference in the full-timing lifestyle.

Bathrooms

Can you stand up in the shower? Don't be shy, slip off your shoes and try it! Is there sufficient space to pick up the soap if you drop it in the shower? Can you reach the towel bar? You would be surprised how many manufacturers do not even install towel bars. Can you sit comfortably in the tub? Is there a place to shave legs?

What layout do you want in the bathroom? Is a walk through bathroom okay or do you want an enclosed bathroom? If you have an open bathroom will there be enough privacy when you have overnight guests? Will an open or split bathroom mean disrupting your partner, or losing access to the bedroom when the bathroom is in use? Maybe you just want the toilet enclosed. Can you sit on or stand at the toilet comfortably with the door closed?

Be sure there is moisture resistant material around the toilet and shower areas. Is there sufficient storage for towels, linens and toiletry items? Where will electric razors, hair dryers and curling irons be plugged in?

Bedrooms

What size bed do you want? Is the mattress full length? Will you need custom fitted sheets that are hard to find? How hard will the bed be to make? Will one person have to climb over the other to go to the bathroom in the middle of the night?

Is there sufficient storage for your clothes? Remember that most people need fewer clothes on the road. Do you need drawers or will shelves work better? Shelves provide more storage space. Do you need a bedroom slide? Bedroom slides reduce or eliminate under bed storage and add weight.

Will windows provide cross ventilation? If there is a window at the head of the bed, will you be happy with it there?

Where does the TV go? Will it be secure going down the road or will you need to secure it each time you travel? Is it out of your walking path?

Computer Space

Laptop computers are the way to go when traveling. However, if you decide to bring a full-size computer along you will need to find a place for it. Is there a desk or space to build one in? If there is a bedroom makeup table, is there space to sit and use the computer there comfortably? If you plan to use the computer at the dining table, consider mounting a keyboard tray and paper storage tray to the bottom of the table top. In some cases you will be able to mount the CPU to the table leg next to the wall. A printer may fit under the table or a chair. This worked well for us in our first trailer. When you have dinner guests you simply move the monitor and printer.

Do not locate a computer near a converter. Converters have magnets that cause problems for hard drives and floppy drives. Securely mount your computer, especially the monitor, before going down the road. Pedestal style monitors will bounce and break the pedestal if not properly secured.

Lighting

If you plan to boondock, look for 12 volt DC map lights and fluorescent fixtures. They pull less power than other lights. If the bathroom has makeup lights you can remove some of the bulbs to reduce the power pull when boondocking. Try to avoid lights with 1076 light bulbs as our experience shows they burn out quickly. Look closely to be sure there is sufficient lighting where you believe you will need lighting. If possible, evaluate the lighting at night. Make sure there is at least one DC light in each room so you do not sit in the dark when there is an AC power outage.

Floor Coverings

Plan on tracking in sand, dirt, mud and leaves. What floor covering is at the door? How durable is the carpet? Will the carpet show every speck of dirt? How easy will the wheel estate be to re-carpet? Does it have vinyl, tile or real wood floors? Do they have a durable finish? Things dropped on tile and wood floors can easily damage them. Sand and small rocks caught in shoes and moisture can damage wood floors.

You may want to consider simulated wood laminated floors. They are very durable, however, confirm the warranty coverage on this type of floor covering. RV manufacturers are likely to glue it in place, which may void the floor manufacturers warranty.

Window Coverings

Many wheel estates come with mini-blinds. They can block the light while still letting you see out and allow a light breeze through. However, they are hard to clean and they rattle going down the road.

Other wheel estates come with day/night shades. A portion of this shade will let light in, while blocking the glare, the other portion will give you privacy. When you pull these shades you cannot see out and the breeze cannot come in. One way to obtain privacy and a breeze at the same time is to mount day night shades at the bottom of the window instead of the top. This allows you to pull the shades up enough for privacy while leaving space at the top for the breeze to come in. Providing, of course, your window opening is not just at the bottom of the window.

You may want to consider total black out shades in the bedroom. It is not unusual for a street light, the moon or the rising sun to shine in and wake you. If you plan to visit Alaska (hopefully during the summer) black out shades are a necessity.

Wall Construction

There are several types of wall construction for RVs—wood framing, aluminum, steel framing and laminated walls with no studs. All do a good job, so the choice will come down to any personal preferences you have. Remember a salesperson will tell you the type of structure in the RVs they sell are best. Ask them for documentation showing this. If they cannot produce documentation from an independent source think seriously about how important their claims are.

Insulation

Does the RV have foam or batt insulation? Foam insulation has a higher R-value than batt for the same thickness. However, batt insulation does a better job of deadening sound. The more insulation an RV has, the warmer it will be in the winter and the cooler it will be in the summer.

Something we are watching in the RV industry is the front and rear fiberglass caps found on many RVs. The way these caps are installed creates a reverse vapor barrier. This means it is possible for condensation to build inside the wall causing damage to both the insulation and wood studs. While an obvious problem does not seem to exist in the RV industry at this time, we suspect these end caps will shorten the RVs life span or result in major repairs down the road.

Roof Construction

Is the roof rubber, fiberglass, aluminum or something else? If the roof is rubber make sure it has no bubbles or spots that appear to have debris underneath. This could impact the life of the roof. Rubber roofs have a tendency to cause black streaking on the side of RVs following rainstorms. Aluminum roofs are at the most risk for hail damage. We had a rubber roof on our first RV and now have a fiberglass roof, which we prefer.

Wide body

Many wheel estates offer wide bodies, which are up to eight and a half feet wide. The additional six inches of width makes an amazing difference in the floor plan of a wheel estate. There are places where they will be more difficult to maneuver, such as tight camping sites, narrow roads or on a ferry, so consider how you plan to use your wheel estate. Wide bodies may also be wider than some states and other countries allow on the road. While these laws are not currently being enforced, it is something to be aware of before buying a wide body.

Exterior Storage

Most wheel estates have storage compartments with outside access, but the amount of storage will vary widely from unit to unit. Carefully consider what you would store in these compartments so you have sufficient storage. If you need a lot of storage look at motorhomes and trailers that offer basement models. These units have additional space, often extending the entire length of the unit. When selecting a basement model check for ground clearance. You do not want a unit that drags through every dip or when driving on driveways with a slight incline.

Power Systems

AC/DC Power

AC power is what a power company provides and DC power is what batteries provide. All equipment in an RV either operates on AC or DC power. It is important to know what equipment operates on which type of power.

It is not unusual for campgrounds to have power outages, during which time your AC equipment will not work. This may leave you with a half cooked dinner in the convection oven or cause you to miss the most dramatic part of a movie on TV.

Batteries

Many wheel estates come with one 12 volt battery. Unless you plan to be plugged in every night you should have two batteries. If you plan to boondock you may want more batteries.

Most RVs come with 12 volt batteries. However, golf cart batteries (six volt) offer many advantages over 12 volt batteries. Golf cart batteries have heavier plates that can better handle deep discharges and high amperage demands.

DC equipment will not work when your batteries go bad or if you are unable to keep a charge on them. Plugging into AC power will not operate DC equipment. Electronic refrigerators require 12 volt DC power even to run on gas. Both electric and hydraulic slide rooms require 12 volt DC power to operate as well.

It is important to check the water level of batteries monthly. We found our 12 volt batteries needed water added every month. When we changed to golf cart batteries we found they could go two months or longer before needing water. Every battery is different, monitor them closely.

Twelve volt batteries are wired in parallel, so if one battery goes bad the others still provide power. Since golf cart batteries are six volt, two must be wired in series to obtain 12 volts. If one of these two batteries goes bad, neither will provide power. Multiple pairs of golf cart batteries are wired in parallel. In this case, if one battery goes bad, you only lose the capacity from the pair with the bad battery. While golf cart batteries must be wired in pairs, 12 volt batteries can be wired in odd or even numbers.

Converter vs. Inverter

Trailers and motorhomes come with a converter or an inverter. Since converters are less expensive they are typically standard equipment and inverters are considered an upgrade.

A converter will take 120 volt AC power and convert it to 12 volt DC power. This means, as long as you are plugged into AC power your DC equipment will operate even if the batteries are bad. Most converters will also give your battery a slow charge when you are plugged into AC power. A converter, however, will not run your 120 volt AC equipment off the battery.

An inverter converts 12 volt DC to 120 volt AC, allowing you to run AC powered equipment even when you are not plugged in. There are two types of inverters.

One type is plugged into a 12 volt outlet and will run one or two small appliances. They do not offer sufficient power to run hair dryers, microwaves, coffee pots or toasters. This type of inverter gets hot, so be sure you select one with a built in fan. RV stores, truck stops and Wal-Mart are just a few places you can buy this type of inverter.

Some RV manufacturers do not install large enough wiring and fuse to the 12 volt outlet to operate this type of inverter. If you blow a fuse when you use one of these inverters, check the fuse size and the wire size for that circuit in your RV.

The second type of inverter is hardwired into your RV. Most RVers size this type of inverter based on what it takes to run their microwave. Due to the large constant drain on the batteries, air conditioners, water heaters and refrigerators are not normally connected to an inverter. When selecting a hardwired inverter, look for one with a three stage battery charger. This way the batteries receive a quick and proper charge when plugged into a generator or AC power source.

If you plan to boondock and want to use most of your equipment, the investment in an inverter will be well worth the expense.

Most inverters provide a modified sine wave. As a result it is possible, regardless of size, they will not run some equipment. Talk with other RVers to find out which ones work best. If you are shopping for a small inverter you may want to try another RVers inverter to see if it will operate the equipment you plan to use.

If you have expensive equipment you plan to run on the inverter, you may want to check with the equipment manufacturer to see if it will operate on a modified sine wave. Inverters that provide a true sine wave are available, but they will cost you nearly twice as much as those with a modified sine wave.

Tip: If you have an inverter with a modified sine wave sized to run your microwave, yet your microwave will not start, try turning on a hair drier then starting the microwave. Once the microwave has started turn the hair drier off.

Solar Panels

If you plan to do much boondocking you will need a way to recharge your batteries. Solar panels are a quiet way to accomplish this, providing you will be boondocking where the sun shines. Solar panels will not work well in Oregon and Washington during the rainy season. They also do not work well in wooded areas.

To determine the number of solar panels you need you must determine what equipment you plan to use when you are boondocked and how long you plan to operate it each day. Remember to include loads such as the furnace and water pump. The load pulled by different brands and models of the same type of equipment will vary, therefore the most accurate way to determine the load is to put an amp meter in series with the load. A simple way to do this is to remove the blade fuse in the circuit the device is in and put your amp meter in the fuse sockets. These loads will determine how many solar panels and batteries you need.

Do not forget to factor in the constant electrical load some electronic appliances have. In the case of a satellite receiver, computer, VCR, etc. you can eliminate the constant load by unplugging it when you are not using it. For those hard to reach plugs we use a surge protection device that has individual on/off switches for each plug. Office stores sell these boxes for computer systems. There is not much you can do about an electronic refrigerator which will pull electricity, even when running on gas.

There is a general guideline used by those selling solar panels that you should have one battery per solar panel. We do not feel this is necessary. Here is why.

Two batteries, 12 volt or 6 volt, can generally be run down halfway, or about 100 amps. Running the batteries more than halfway down can damage them. Three 75 watt solar panels will realistically provide about 80 amps of charge on a good winter solar day. Therefore, three 75 watt solar panels cannot fully recharge a two battery system in one day. If you had a battery for each solar panel it would take that much longer to fully recharge your batteries.

Our belief is that you should have enough solar panels to recharge your batteries in a day and provide enough excess power to keep up with your power needs during the day. True, with more batteries in a fully charged state, your batteries would last longer in a low solar environment. However, it would take days to recharge your batteries after such a period. So, if your power needs require more than two batteries, you will want to look for an RV that offers enough roof space for more than one solar panel per battery.

There are two other things to consider with the battery per solar panel philosophy. Each battery weighs 65-75 pounds, so how much extra weight are you carrying? And how much does each of those batteries cost?

For long stretches of low solar days we manage either by conserving or by using our Honda 350 generator. At 19 pounds it weighs less than a third of what just one battery weighs. It also runs about 20 hours on one gallon of gas.

RVer's Guide to Solar & Inverters by Noel and Barbara Kirkby is an excellent resource on solar installations. See the **Resource Directory** for ordering details.

Generators

Some people use generators to either power their RV or keep their batteries charged. Some portable brands of generators run quietly, while others are very noisy. Select a quiet brand to keep peace with any neighbors you may have. There are also generators that permanently mount in RVs. Most motorhomes come with one of these. They may run on gas, diesel or propane. Often these generators are large enough to run an air conditioner.

Be sure to determine how you plan to use a generator before you buy one. If you plan to power your entire RV you will need to base the size of generator on your loads. If you will only be charging your batteries you will determine the size based on your battery charger and how quickly you want to charge the batteries.

The air conditioner in the dash on motorhomes will not cool the entire unit when you are traveling down the road. If you plan to stay cool while going down the road you will need to have a large enough generator to run the house air conditioner(s).

When a rainy day or wooded campground comes along we pull out our Honda 350 generator. It will run our computer, printer, TV and satellite receiver all at once on the low setting. Our mixer and vacuum cleaner have larger loads so must be run by themselves with the generator on the high setting. We were even able to run our refrigerator on the generator when the gas mode failed. However, this generator will not run our microwave and is too small to efficiently charge our batteries. While the Honda 350 works well for us, it may not be a solution for you.

Jessica has a laser printer she uses a great deal. To run it she had to get a Honda 1000 generator. That was her unique power need. What are your unique power needs?

Alex and Janis also have a Honda. They say, "The Honda costs more than some other brands, but quietness justifies the price every time we use it." Keep in mind Honda is only one of the brands of quiet generators available.

Heating and Cooling Systems

Furnaces

Most wheel estates come with a small, inefficient household type furnace. They run on propane and have an electric fan. The electric fan will run your batteries down quickly, so it is important that you have a way to recharge your batteries when you use a furnace. Serious boondockers use a ceramic or a catalytic heater, which uses less propane and provides a more comfortable heat than a furnace. Boondockers also look for the version of ceramic or catalytic heater that does not use power. These units are unvented. By code, RV manufacturers can only install vented propane heaters, so boondockers often install their own heaters. For safety, unvented heaters should be operated with a window slightly open.

When selecting a ceramic or catalytic heater be sure it has a thermostat. This will allow you to run the heat while you are gone and return to a comfortable temperature.

Some older catalytic heaters require expensive repairs when they get dust on the element or use propane with a high butane content. New catalytic heaters may not have a problem with either situation. Check with the manufacturer to be sure.

Both catalytic and ceramic heaters may be set up as freestanding units or mounted as permanent units. These heaters do put moisture into the air and can create condensation problems.

For safety do not mount a ceramic or catalytic heater on a wall that will be behind a slide room when it is in. We know one couple whose trailer caught fire when they brought their slide room in and forgot to turn off the heater.

Most campers carry electric heaters to use in campgrounds that include electricity in their fees. Electric heaters will help minimize the condensation problem in damp climates.

Some manufacturers install heat pumps. These units run on electricity and operate more efficiently than other heaters.

They lose this efficiency and do not heat as well when the outside temperature drops below 30 or 40 degrees. One nice feature the heat pump has is it also acts as an air conditioner. You only need one unit to do both jobs, assuming you can count on having power to operate the heat pump.

Adding a heat strip into your air conditioner is relatively inexpensive and provides you with a backup source of heat.

Air Conditioning

Some wheel estates have ducted air conditioning, while others do not. Typically, people look for ducted air conditioning since that is what they are accustomed to in traditional housing. RV air conditioners do a better job of cooling without duct work, however.

Try shopping for your wheel estate on a hot day. Have the salesman run the air conditioner in an RV that is ducted and one that is not ducted. Which do you think is better?

Also listen to how much noise the air conditioner makes. Many are so noisy you may have difficulty hearing anything, including the TV on high volume, when it is running. Some air conditioners cycle on and off. If the air conditioner is a noisy one do you want it cycling on and off? Consider how often you may have to adjust the volume on the TV if the air conditioner is cycling on and off.

Air conditioner thermostats may be wall mounted or on the unit itself. Both will do the job. Can you easily reach the controls on the unit? If the RV has a wall mounted thermostat, make sure it is not located such that the air conditioner blows right on it. This will cause the unit to cycle on and off, never allowing the RV to properly cool.

Ventilation

Ventilation can be important when you are boondocked or in a campground that has insufficient power for your air conditioner. Which windows are operable and will give you good ventilation? Does a window in the back open? Do the windows on the ends of the slide rooms open? The more sides of the RV with operable windows, the more likely you are to catch that breeze, regardless of what direction you are parked. Remember to check the size of the openings in the windows. Some may be too small to give adequate ventilation.

A few RVs have enough ceiling clearance to mount a ceiling fan for additional ventilation. What you are more likely to see in RVs is a Fan-Tastic Vent. This vent fits in the vent openings many RV manufacturers put in the kitchen, bathroom and bedroom ceilings.

The Fan-Tastic Vents may be purchased with a reversing fan feature. This allows you to pull kitchen and bathroom steam out of the RV or pull cool air in. Another option will shut the vent when it rains. A nice feature on those days you are not home and there is an unexpected thundershower.

Look for jalousie rather than slider windows. In most cases jalousie windows will keep rain out, which means more comfort during rainstorms. Pets may also be left at home in comfort while you are gone for the day.

Another consideration is double pane windows. While they are heavier, they do help control temperature and reduce condensation on the windows. The drawback is they generally only come in sliders.

Plumbing Systems

Water Heaters

If possible the water heater should be a combination gas and electric unit. Propane water heaters are noisy, disturbing neighbors when they come roaring to life in the middle of the night. Use of the electric mode saves propane costs when staying in a campground that includes electricity in their fee. Even when you are paying the electric bill it may be less expensive to run the water heater on electric than on propane.

If you end up with a gas only water heater, do not add an electric element that requires removal of the anode rod.

Without the anode rod your water heater will very quickly rust from the inside out.

Turning both the gas and electric water heater modes on at the same time will heat the water in half the time. Most RV hot water heaters have a preset temperature. Water heaters are available with thermostats, so if you have a choice, this is an option to consider.

RV water heaters generally come in six and ten gallon sizes. Both of our trailers have had a six gallon water heater and we have enough hot water to shower back to back. However, if you like long showers or if you have a bathtub you may want a ten-gallon water heater.

To conserve energy we only turn our water heater on once a day, just before we shower. That is also when we do dishes.

Holding Tanks

The wheel estate you select should have at least one of each of these holding tanks: fresh water, gray water and black water. The capacity of these tanks is critical, even if you do not plan to boondock, as some campgrounds do not have sewer hook-ups. The bigger the holding tanks the longer you can wait before you have to go to the dump station. For two people consider a minimum of 60 gallons of fresh water and 50 gallons each for the gray and black tanks. If you plan to boondock consider even larger fresh water and holding tank capacities.

Determine which holding tank each faucet goes to. A shower that drains into a black tank will quickly fill that tank, shortening your stay. If you have the option, install a black tank flusher. Be sure it is mounted at the top of the tank or high on the side. This will make a nasty chore easier.

When an RV has more than one gray water tank check to see if the gray water tanks are plumbed together. Often two gray water tanks will have two dumping points, making dumping a real chore.

Some manufacturers insulate holding tanks, while others do not. Consider where you will be spending your time in the winter. Keep in mind that northern Florida, northern Texas and southern New Mexico can all have freezing weather. If you will be where it is cold you may want the tanks insulated. Additionally, you may want the holding tank compartments heated. Some manufacturers drop a heat duct into these areas. If the drain lines for the black and gray holding tanks are not insulated and heated, they will be the first to freeze. When they freeze you will not be able to dump the tanks. If you find yourself in cold weather without tank and drain line insulation, consider a livestock heater, which will stick directly to the tanks and heat tape for the drain line.

When looking at RVs with insulated tanks determine how easy they will be to access if you have a problem. Paul removed one of our tanks on our first wheel estate and it was a real pain. There were three problems. First the gas line had to be cut and moved out of the way. Next, the way the tanks were sealed for insulating purposes added to the chore and finally the sensor wires and plumbing lines had no excess length.

In the unlikely event we go where it is cold, we will first have our heads examined and second we will install a livestock heater and heat tape on our holding tanks.

When checking out holding tanks also determine what type of sensors tell you how full the tanks are. Internal sensors on black and gray tanks are always dirty and never read accurately. External sensors are very accurate.

Decorating

As you shop for your wheel estate it is very likely you will be appalled by what some decorators have done with RVs. Some will remind you of your great grandmothers parlor! Ugh!

If you are shopping for a new RV, try to overlook the decorating initially. Do allow sufficient time to order your RV rather than buy it off the lot. This will allow you to place your order so you can eliminate some of the decorating disasters you might be stuck with otherwise. As you narrow your selection of RVs talk to the salesperson about the possibility of eliminating decorating items you do not like.

Manufacturers normally offer several different decorating packages which color coordinate the carpeting, wall coverings, valances and furniture. In some cases the manufacturer may be willing to mix and match from these packages, although often they do not mix and match well.

Try to eliminate furnishings and valances to neutralize undesirable decorating packages. Some manufacturers will allow you to select different carpet. If you want different window coverings try ordering the RV without window coverings. If you do not like the mattress for the bed order the RV without it. This is going to be your home, so you should decorate it to please you.

Some manufacturers offer no flexibility in how the RV is ordered, others will do a great deal to please you. Some dealers will not want to work with you on a special order. Other dealers will go to bat for you and either get the manufacturer to meet your needs or do the work themselves.

If you have a lot of special needs you may want to have a custom RV built. We went this route. We eliminated the valances and window coverings. The only furniture we ordered from the manufacturer was the dining room table. We provided the rest ourselves, including the dining room chairs and even the mattress.

Remodeling

Okay, so you can't find the perfect wheel estate. Remodeling can work wonders.

☆ One couple had an old class C motorhome with dark walls. She painted the walls white, then applied a white contact paper with flowers to the walls.

☆ Jessica needed a computer space so her husband took out the dinette and put in a long work surface with file drawers on either end.

☆ Another couple each wanted a computer center. They took out their dining room table and replaced it with the sofa. The living room then had space for two computer centers.

☆ People with cats will put litter pans in the basement and cut an opening for the cat to get to the litter pan.

So if you cannot get the wheel estate the way you want it, consider how you could remodel it to meet your needs. Creativity is key here.

The ultimate story I have heard on remodeling creativity is about a couple who narrowed their search to two trailers. The wife insisted she must have a bathtub. One of the two trailers had a bathtub, but the trailer they liked better did not. So the husband asked the wife if he were to install a bathtub in the trailer they preferred would she agree to that trailer. She said, "Yes." The husband kept his promise installing a bathtub in the storage space under the bed.

Of course remodeling that involves removing walls, adding lots of weight, or impacts the structure of the RV is not advisable. These modifications could cause serious and even dangerous failures of the RV.

Choosing Your Wheel Estate

You now have some idea of what to consider when selecting that perfect home on wheels. If you are still uncertain about what your needs will be, consider buying a used, inexpensive RV first. This way you will be able to evaluate your needs as you experience the lifestyle. Also, if the RV or lifestyle do not work out, you will not be out a great deal of money.

Be sure to read the next two chapters before you fall in love with a particular wheel estate and buy it. They discuss serious flaws that can occur in RVs and what you need to know to buy a safe, durable wheel estate.

7

The Safe and Durable Wheel Estate

Your Role

The next two chapters focus on safety and durability issues which dealerships and manufacturers seldom discuss with customers. Regulation of the RV industry is minimal and an increasing number of manufacturers are showing their inability to build safe, durable RVs. You are about to enter a very exciting time in your life. It should not include spending time at the RV hospital, involved in accidents or watching your wheel estate disintegrate around you.

Fred and Peggy learned this lesson the expensive way. Fred shares:

> *I thought I knew a lot about RVs before we started, but I found there was so much to learn yet. We took off in kind of a thrifty mode because we had this pile of money that was supposed to last us until 94 years old. If we spent any of that, obviously we weren't going to make it. So we took off in this light weight trailer. It was more of a vacation trailer and we found that we were wearing it out. The mattress was going flat, the cushions on the*

dinette were going flat, it just wasn't meant to be used that often.

It didn't have shocks on the axles, it didn't have electric landing jacks, the hole where the shaft went through for the landing jacks started out about an inch in diameter and by the time we traded it off that hole was about 2 inches in diameter. It was never meant to be used in that fashion.

Once you know what type of wheel estate, equipment and features will meet your needs you can shop for the perfect wheel estate. But *do not* take the checkbook along yet! Before becoming emotionally attached to a particular RV you need to determine if it is safe and durable. The responsibility is yours. No one else will do it for you.

Resources

Safety and durability are issues for RVs that have yet to be evaluated by unbiased groups or organizations. For this reason it is important that you read as many articles and books as you can on RVs. Discussing safety and durability with full-timers, not vacationers, is also important. Once you have gathered your data you can determine which is the most valid.

It is very important to know what bias your resource may have when evaluating the information they share. Many RV magazines are dependent on advertisement and other funding from manufacturers and may only give a positive insight to specific RVs. Full-timers may be ecstatic with their wheel estate or they may be very upset with their wheel estate—justified or not. There are two consumer groups: RV Group Wise and RV Consumer Group. RV Group Wise is new, but working hard to compile data. They have a great deal of promise. Follow their growth at *http://www.rvgroupwise.com.* The next section discusses what RV Consumer Group has to offer.

Your job will be to determine which resources provide you with the most reliable information. The best RV evaluation will be based on information from many sources.

RV Consumer Group

Visit your local library and ask to see *The RV Rating Book* put out by the RV Consumer Group. If they do not have it ask if they can obtain it from another library or the RV Consumer Group. If you prefer, you may obtain your own copy by joining the RV Consumer Group. The *Resource Directory* in the back of this book lists their phone number and address.

This book rates over 10,000 RVs for highway safety, durability and value. It also classifies RVs for type of use. For full-timing you should be looking at units with a "snowbirding" or "full-timing" classification. The term "wheel estate" refers to these RV's—the ones durable enough for a permanent home.

As we heard earlier from Fred, this is where they made their mistake. They selected a unit classified for "weekending" or "vacationing." It simply was not built with the durability necessary for full-timing.

The RV Consumer Group is a non-profit, volunteer organization. As a result they are not able to individually evaluate each of the 10,000 models listed in *The RV Rating Book.* It also means they may not have the technical knowledge to make certain observations or recommendations.

Most data comes from the manufacturer's brochure, but when the data is not available estimates are made. Before publication of *The RV Rating Book* manufacturers are asked to correct bad data. However, that data is only as good as the manufacturer's integrity and attention to detail.

The data is then plugged into equations, where assumptions have been made, to establish ratings for each RV. RV Consumer Group has not disclosed the methodology they use in their evaluations. In fact, in the case of one manufacturer, it appears their high rating may be based more on their willingness to do what RV Consumer Group recommends than on safety.

When this manufacturer was asked why they followed a specific RV Consumer Group recommendation the manufacturer said, "Our rating would be lower with RV Consumer Group if we didn't." Later this manufacturer would quote industry standards to us, but could not explain why the standards were what they were. Many of this manufacturer's sales are a result of their RV Consumer Group rating. We asked RV Consumer Group why they made the specific recommendation. They were unable to explain why.

A manufacturer's past performance is also taken into consideration when rating RVs. However, there is no guarantee that they still build to the same standards. Their current standards may be better or worse. Also keep in mind a manufacturer may do an outstanding job building one model and a lousy job building another model. *The RV Rating Book* reflects this.

If you are looking at used RVs the RV Consumer Group can be very helpful. They have compiled data from actual experiences on many brands and models of RVs. You must be a member to obtain the full details they have on file, but the membership fee is an inexpensive investment when buying a used RV. Their data may make you aware of problems unique to specific RVs and give you an opportunity to evaluate the RV you are considering for those unique problems.

The RV Consumer Group and *The RV Rating Book* will help you identify trouble spots with an RV, but they offer no guarantees. A manufacturer's representative for our first trailer made sure we knew RV Consumer Group gave our trailer a high rating. Several years later we found ourselves in a lawsuit against the manufacturer over a defect in our chassis.

We also discovered this defect existed in many chassis' built by this manufacturer during a four year period!

The RV Consumer Group cannot foresee flaws like we experienced. Knowledge can reduce the chance of getting a "lemon," but it will not eliminate them.

If you have an exceptionally good or bad experience with an RV, make sure the manufacturer is aware of your experience. Manufacturers build to meet the consumers demands. It is our responsibility to demand safe and durable RVs. Also, whether you are a member of the RV Consumer Group or RV GroupWise, you can help fellow RVers by reporting your experience to them.

The RV Consumer Group is working to provide rollover information in *The RV Rating Book.* This will be a first in the industry. Since there is no testing of RVs for this situation the data will rely on actual accidents. This will leave holes that must be filled with educated guesses, but it will be a step in the right direction.

Data RV Consumer Group has collected indicates that class-B and class-C motorhomes are relatively safe while class-A motorhomes have a serious problem when it comes to surviving a rollover. Their data also shows more travel trailers are involved in accidents than fifth-wheel trailers. It should be interesting to see where this data takes the industry.

My recommendation at this time is to use RV Consumer Groups data, but use it with caution. Also combine it with a great deal of information gathered from other sources.

Let's take a look at some of the safety and durability things you can check yourself when buying an RV. If you do nothing else, check these items out before you buy.

Motorhome Wheelbase

Wheelbase-to-length ratio is an important safety consideration for motorhomes. While a short wheelbase makes a motorhome feel more like a car, it will be less stable in wind and situations where you need quick response. RV Consumer Group recommends a wheelbase-to-length ratio of 53 percent or greater.

To determine the wheelbase-to-length ratio, measure the distance between the center of the front axle and the center of the rear axle. Then measure the length of the motorhome. Do not assume the motorhome is the length indicated by the model number. Manufacturers do not always use the actual length when assigning model numbers. Now divide the axle measurement by the motorhome length. Here is how the equation works with a motorhome that is 34' 2" and a wheelbase of 20' 6":

$$\frac{\text{wheelbase}}{\text{motorhome length}} = \text{wheelbase to length ratio}$$

Note: feet must be converted to inches

$$\frac{((20\text{x}12) + 6)}{((34\text{x}12) + 2)} = .60$$

or 60 percent

If a motorhome has a tag axle or two rear axles, measure from the front axle to the rear most axle.

Electric Trailer Brakes

Electric trailer brakes do not work as well as brakes on a motorized vehicle. We never felt confident that we would be able to stop in a crisis with our first trailer. On the second trailer we made sure we had bigger brakes. Our travel days are more relaxed now as the bigger brakes can stop both the trailer and truck if need be. However, the truck and trailer still will not stop as fast as a car.

When you are shopping for a trailer find out what size brakes the trailer has. For typical full-time RVs the standard electric brake sizes are 12" x 2" and 12 ½" x 3 ⅜". Allowing for a 25 percent derate these brakes are good for 4,500 and 6,000 pounds, respectively, per axle.

Brakes For Diesel Engines

If you have a diesel engine in your motorhome or tow vehicle you should make sure it comes with an exhaust brake or install one. Have you noticed going down a long hill with a gas engine, when you take your foot off the gas pedal the car does not quickly pick up speed? This is because gas engines provide some engine braking on hills. Diesel engines however, provide little or no engine braking. This can get very scary when you have a house on wheels pushing you down a mountainside!

We were winding our way through Missouri when we knew we had to have an exhaust brake. Driving through woods we started down a hill that did not have a grade warning. As a result Paul did not shift down. We quickly picked up speed and Paul would step on the brakes. Once we slowed down he would let off the brakes, only to quickly pick up too much speed for the winding road. The hill was only a mile long, but when we pulled over at the bottom we could smell the burning trailer brakes. That day we felt lucky to be alive and scheduled installation of an exhaust brake.

Don't wait until it is too late! Installing an exhaust brake is very inexpensive life insurance!

Note: Some pickup truck manufacturers are stating exhaust brakes should not be installed on their trucks. Carefully evaluate the status of this situation before buying a diesel pickup.

Chassis Construction

The chassis is a critical part of the RV construction. Here are a few things you should check. If the chassis has box beams be sure they are not cut to accommodate other parts of the trailer. This greatly reduces the strength of a box beam.

A non-fabricated or solid I-beam (looks like a solid I) will be much stronger and more durable than a fabricated I-beam. A solid I-beam is made of one piece of metal. A fabricated I-beam is made of three pieces—a top and bottom plate welded to a center web plate. Just recently two of our friends told us their fabricated I-beam chassis' failed!

By the way, some chassis are hidden in the construction of the RV. In that case you will have to do a little more investigation to find out what type of chassis the RV has. The best approach would be to tour the factory. If this is not possible, ask the salesperson about the chassis construction. Look to see if the construction is shown in the brochure. Then call the manufacturer and ask them about the chassis construction. Were you told the same thing by each source?

Some manufacturers offer a video tape that shows their entire assembly process. Not only does this show you the type of chassis an RV has, it will show you how the rest of the unit goes together. It is the next best thing to a factory tour.

Some big name RV manufacturers do not use certified welders to build their chassis'. If you find this to be the case on a wheel estate you are considering and it makes you uncomfortable, eliminate it from your choices.

Slide Rooms

Slide rooms make RVs feel spacious. When slide rooms were first offered, consumers quickly became hooked. To meet consumer needs, manufacturers have added as many as three slide rooms to many RVs. Slides add weight that may create safety concerns since some manufacturers have not sufficiently re-engineered their chassis' for the additional weight.

We met one woman whose motorhome had just been bought back under a lemon law. The year she bought her motorhome, a slide was added. In the process the front axle was overloaded, before adding any payload. Unfortunately, the manufacturer did not make this discovery in time to fix the situation and the design of the motorhome did not allow for installation of a heavier duty axle. Fifty motorhomes were built and sold this way. This is one case where weighing the motorhome before buying it would have saved the buyer a lot of stress. We will discuss weight issues in the next chapter.

Here is what we learned as a result of the defect in the chassis on our first trailer. We initially thought we had a problem with our slide room. It was not until later we learned the slide room problem was partially a result of the manufacturer cutting through the box beam chassis to install the slide room. Had we known what to look for before we took delivery of the fifth-wheel we would have been able to walk away from the deal. Instead we ended up filing a lawsuit because of a chassis defect. While the process was educational, it was also very stressful.

Besides chassis failure, slide room operation is another reason to evaluate the chassis as discussed above. Also, checking the following things on a slide room will tip you off to slide room problems, whether they are related to the chassis or not. Here is an evaluation checklist.

From Inside the RV

★ Run the slide room out. Does it sound quiet? You should not hear grinding or squealing.

★ Does the slide room fit tight against the interior wall when it is fully extended?

★ Does the slide room sit straight next to the interior walls and cabinets?

☆ Bring the slide room in. Does it operate quietly and come in straight?

From Outside the RV

☆ Visually inspect the slide while it is in, to determine if it appears to sit straight in the opening. Does it sit square in relationship to the RV?

☆ Run the slide room out. Does it operate quietly? Does it come out smoothly side to side and top to bottom?

☆ With the slide room out determine if the wipers fit tight against all four sides of the slide room. If they do not, expect leaks when it rains.

☆ When the slide is operating, do the wipers act as a squeegee, removing water on the exterior walls?

☆ Step back and look to see if the slide room appears straight when compared to the RV and the opening.

☆ Pull the wipers back on the sides and top and confirm that the spacing between the trailer and slide room is equal all the way around the opening.

☆ Eyeball the underside of the slide from the front or back of the slide. Is it flat, as it should be, or does it have a bow in it?

☆ Run the slide room in. Does it operate quietly? Does it go in smoothly side to side and top to bottom?

☆ When the slide room is in does it fit snugly against the side of the trailer?

☆ Do any of the slide mechanisms go through the beams? Removal of material in the center of a beam is okay. Removal of material near the top or bottom of a beam will significantly reduce the beam's strength. And removal of the top or bottom of the beam should never be done.

If a slide room fails any of these tests the salesperson is likely to tell you, "We can adjust that. Why don't you bring it in next week?" Don't fall for this! Ask yourself why it wasn't adjusted properly before leaving the factory. Maybe they can adjust it, but let them prove it before you give them your hard earned money. That way you do not end up living with a nightmare if they cannot adjust it.

We have looked at many steps to buying a good wheel estate. There is one final step left—evaluation of the weight. The next chapter covers that.

8

Chubby Wheel Estates

This may be the most important chapter in this book, yet some readers will skip it. Reading this chapter and following the advice within could save your life, thousands of dollars and many headaches. If you do not include weight ratings in the selection of your wheel estate you may have problems like John and Janie Anderson did, or worse.

We chose a unit [fifth-wheel trailer] that offered a well insulated shell, with a slide-out room for additional living space. With the advice of the RV dealer, we also purchased a one-ton dual wheel pick-up truck to pull our new home, which had a stated GVWR of 14,000 pounds.

During the course of our traveling we experienced eleven tire failures on the trailer, and spent more than $10,000 on the truck, trying to achieve some minimal towing performance. Shortly after the problems began, we took the trailer to a scale and found out that it weighed more than 16,000 pounds. Unable to believe that we had put that much "stuff" in it, we emptied it out to the same way it came from the dealer and took it back to the scales. Lo and behold, it weighed 14,840 pounds, 840 pounds over GVWR when it was EMPTY! Now we began to understand our problems.

John and Janie's experience is not uncommon, which is why they were able to turn their disaster into a business—A'Weigh We Go. Today they work with RVers, RV manufacturers and dealers and many others to eliminate overloading so RVing can be the safe, fun adventure it is meant to be.

Weight Failures

Weight is one of the most critical items to evaluate when selecting your wheel estate. Sixty two percent of the first 8,000 RVs weighed by A'Weigh We Go exceeded one or more weight limits. Overloading an RV is a mistake that could cost you your life. It can result in expensive repairs to the drive train and brakes on motorhomes and tow vehicles. It can also lead to the failure of springs, tires and even the chassis. All of these failures can cause an accident and some may cause a fire, resulting in destruction of your wheel estate.

Friends of ours were towing their fifth-wheel trailer when a motorist flagged them down. Their trailer was on fire! Their injuries were minor, but their trailer was totaled. They had to go through replacing their wheel estate and many of their possessions. Even with good insurance it was a chore.

Our friends believe the fire was a result of a leaf spring failure allowing the tire to drag against the bottom of the trailer until it caught fire. Were they overloaded? We will never know as they never weighed the trailer.

Besides equipment failure, overloading an RV can void the warranty and may even void your insurance if you are responsible for an accident. Be a responsible RVer. Protect your life, the lives of those who share the highway with you and your bank account. Do not overload any vehicle. Especially an RV.

This chapter has a lot of technical data and uses several formulas. Don't let this discourage you. We will walk through the process together. You, and you alone, must take responsibility for not overloading your wheel estate. The manufacturers won't and neither will the dealers. Only you can make sure you are traveling safely down the road.

Weight Evaluation

There are two steps everyone should take to evaluate the weight of an RV. A third step may be used if you need further convincing. Here are the steps, which we will use shortly in some examples:

1. Look at the data plate and record the weight ratings of the trailer and tow vehicle or motorhome and towed vehicle. Run calculations to determine if you can remain within the weight ratings.
2. When signing a purchase contract include a contingency that requires the RV, full of fluids, be weighed at a certified scale with you present. State in the contract an acceptable payload capacity for the RV. More accurate calculations should be made using the resulting weight tickets.
3. Listen to your intuition! After completing steps one and two, if you still have a strange feeling about the RV, but can't let go of a particular RV yet, take one more step. Find the part numbers on the components that contribute to the weight ratings—axles, wheels, tires, brakes, transmission, kingpin, hitch, etc.—and contact their manufacturer to determine each component's weight ratings. The RV weight rating should be based on the component with the lowest weight rating. For example, an axle may be rated at 5,200 pounds, but if the two wheels have a combined rating of 5,000 pounds the axle system ultimately has a rating of 5,000 pounds. This third step may save you a lot of grief and convince you to walk away from a bad RV.

Weight Ratings

All motorized vehicles and trailers are required to have labels displaying certain weight information. Generally you will find this label for cars and trucks in the door jamb on the driver's side of the vehicle. The label is on the wall near the driver's seat in most motorhomes and on an exterior wall or hitch on trailers.

These labels include the following weight information:

* ☆ The GVWR (Gross Vehicle Weight Rating) is the maximum any vehicle should weigh—be it a car, truck, trailer or motorhome.
* ☆ The GAWR (Gross Axle Weight Rating) is the maximum weight each axle should carry.

In September 1996, RVIA (Recreational Vehicle Industry Association) implemented a labeling guideline for their members. Some manufacturers who are not members of RVIA also post RVIA's recommended label. Generally you will find this label in a bedroom closet or kitchen cabinet, although some manufacturers make the label hard to find. The following information can be found on the RVIA label:

* ☆ GCWR (Gross Combined Weight Rating) is the maximum combined weight for the motorized vehicle and the towed vehicle or trailer. Trailers do not have a GCWR. GCWR may not be readily available for an old motorhome or a tow vehicle, but it is important that you obtain the number. To find the GCWR for motorhomes, without the RVIA label, check the chassis manufacturer's manual. For tow vehicles see the manufacturer's towing guide or brochure. If you do not find it, ask the manufacturer to provide the GCWR in writing. If you cannot easily obtain this information, eliminate the motorhome or tow vehicle from your shopping list.

☆ GDW (Gross Dry Weight) or UVW (Unloaded Vehicle Weight). GDW is the term used prior to September 1996 and UVW is the current term. GDW and UVW are the weight of the RV when it leaves the factory. For motorhomes, this includes a full tank of fuel. Water, propane and generator fuel is not included in this figure. Many manufacturers do not have a scale to weigh the RVs they build. Therefore, the GDW/UVW is an estimate based on the weight of a small sample of units built by the manufacturer. A GDW rating may or may not include the weight of manufacturer installed options. Guidelines for the newer UVW rating requires the weight of manufacturer installed options be included in the weight. In most cases the weight of manufacturer installed options is also an estimate. Be aware that modifications to a used RV and dealer additions to a new RV may drastically change the weight calculations you are performing from labels.

RVIA labeling also provides the GVWR and the GAWR for the RV. Also listed is the water tank size and weight when full.

The RVIA label also lists the NCC (Net Carrying Capacity). This is the available payload without exceeding the GVWR. However, it does not tell you where you can place your payload. What if the only storage space is over axles that are fully loaded or even overloaded by the weight of the RV itself?

A quick look at one of these labels may give the impression that there is no need for making weight calculations. We will soon see how easy it is to miss a problem when weight calculations are not done. If you plan to buy a motorhome do not skip over the truck and trailer calculations. There is some overlap in the calculations, so reading the truck and trailer sections will be worth your time.

Pick-up Truck Weight Ratings

We will look at pick-ups here. Similar calculations should be made for all tow vehicles.

When we upgraded from our 1992 Dodge pickup to our 1999 Ford pickup, we were shocked to learn there was a 700 pound difference in similarly equipped trucks. That 700 pound difference amounted to 700 pounds less payload. You cannot assume one truck weighs the same as another truck.

Data given in the brochure text will make the truck sound like a real power horse, but find the weights and ratings for the truck you are looking at and you may find a completely different story. Do your homework before buying your tow vehicle, or you may be out a lot of money for a vehicle that doesn't do the job.

If you are buying a used truck or a truck from a dealership lot, the easiest and most accurate way to determine whether it will meet your needs is to take it to a certified scale and weigh each axle separately. If you are ordering a truck you will have to dig numbers out of brochures to run the necessary calculations. Actual weights will be more accurate than brochure weights so weigh the truck, if you can, before buying it.

To make sure you buy a truck that can tow your trailer you will need to take the following steps. Obtain the manufacturer's vehicle brochure and their towing brochure. Even if you are buying a used truck you will need these brochures. If the brochures are not available contact the manufacturer for the missing information. If you have weighed the truck, use actual numbers in the calculations, otherwise find the numbers in the brochure.

The brochure for our example shows a maximum loaded trailer weight (MLTW) of 13,800 pounds. However, this assumes a stripped basic truck and does not take into consideration things like the weight of passengers, options, hitch, fuel and stuff you will carry in your truck. Forget this number, it has no real meaning.

Step One

First determine how heavy the truck really is. Find the GCWR in the manufacturer's brochures for the truck you have selected. Normally there is a difference in GCWR based on the type of transmission, engine and rear end ratio the truck has. Select the highest GCWR for the model truck and engine type you are considering. At this time ignore the impact different transmissions and rear end ratios have on the GCWR. If you will be working with numbers from a weight ticket skip to step two now.

While the MLTW is useless to us, it can be used to determine the weight of the truck. Find the highest MLTW for the model truck and engine type you are looking at. Again ignore the impact different transmissions and rear end ratios have on the MLTW. If there is a difference in MLTW for fifth-wheels and travel trailers, use the MLTW for fifth-wheels at this time, regardless of the type of trailer you will pull.

For our example the GCWR is 20,000 pounds and the MLTW is 13,800 pounds. Now subtract the MLTW from the GCWR to determine a base weight for the truck.

20,000 lbs.– 13,800 lbs.= 6,200 lbs.

Check the tables to see if the manufacturer's weights assume a passenger weight. In our example the manufacturer made the following notation in their table:

"Maximum loaded trailer weight assumes towing vehicle with any mandatory options, no cargo and driver (150 pounds) only. Chassis cabs also assumes 1,000 pounds second-unit body weight."

Subtract any allotted driver weight from the base weight.

6,200 lbs.– 150 lbs.= 6,050 lbs.

This is the base truck weight we will work with.

Next we must add the weight of any options. These weights will not be in a brochure and will be based on your best guess. Our example includes options such as a spare tire, stabilizer bars, extra leaf springs, rear bumper, power windows and locks and air conditioning. For our example assume 375 pounds for these options.

6,050 lbs. + 375 lbs.= 6,425 lbs.

The brochure and scale verified weight of the truck in our example is 6,425 pounds. Since the manufacturer does not provide the weight of options it will be necessary to weigh the truck to determine the actual weight. At this point you are in the ball park and can determine if the truck is worth further consideration.

Step Two

Before we go further, if you have come across the shipping weight of the truck you are looking at, ignore it. For our example the shipping weight was 5,668 pounds, 757 pounds less than the above calculated and verified weight. Next you need to determine the weight of what you plan to carry in the truck. This includes passengers, pets, fuel, hitch, leveling boards, tools, etc. This amounted to 1,000 pounds for our truck and is probably a conservative number for most full-timers. The best way to determine this weight is to weigh the empty truck, then weigh it again loaded as you plan to go down the road. The difference is the weight you have added. For consistency always weigh the truck with a full tank of fuel.

For our example we will use 1,000 pounds of "stuff" which gives the loaded truck a weight of 7,425 pounds.

Now find the GVWR for the truck in the manufacturer's towing brochure. The GVWR for the truck in our example is 8,800 pounds. Subtract the weight of the loaded truck from the GVWR to get the payload capacity of the truck.

8,800 lbs. − 7,425 lbs. = 1,375 lbs. payload capacity

This is the maximum tongue (hitch or kingpin) weight for your trailer. Those familiar with fifth-wheels of full-timing quality know they will have king pin weights which greatly exceed 1,375 pounds. However this *may* be a good tow vehicle for a travel trailer.

If you are within the GVWR it does not mean you have not overloaded the truck, however. You will have to take the loaded truck to the scale and see how much weight is on each axle.

For our example the GAWR for the front axle is 4,550 pounds. The actual weight on the axle is 3,270 pounds. The difference of 1,280 pounds is the payload for the front axle. The GAWR for the rear axle is 6,084 pounds. The actual weight on the axle is 4,155 pounds. The difference of 1,929 pounds is the payload for the rear axle.

Most, if not all, the weight from a fifth-wheel kingpin will transfer to a truck's rear axle. With a travel trailer the front axle of the truck will be a little lighter and more than the hitch weight will transfer to the rear axle. A weight distributing hitch for a travel trailer will cause the hitch weight to be distributed more like that of a fifth-wheel's kingpin.

Earlier we found the highest GCWR for the truck used in our example, including the engine, but ignoring the transmission and rear end ratio. The next step is to find the actual GCWR for the truck you are looking at, including the transmission and rear end ratio. Subtract the loaded weight of the truck from this GCWR to get the actual MLTW for the specific truck you are looking at. If you expect or know your loaded trailer will weigh more than this amount then your options include selecting a different transmission, engine, rear end ratio, model truck or a lighter trailer.

For our example the GCWR is 20,000 pounds and the weight of the loaded truck is 7,425 pounds. The difference of 12,575 pounds is the actual MLTW for this truck. This is 1,225 pounds less than the MLTW of 13,800 pounds stated in the truck brochure!

While the MLTW in the brochure did not tell us anything of value regarding the truck's capacity, it is a weight that should not be exceeded. For our example the MLTW was 13,800 pounds for a fifth-wheel. A trailer weight of 12,575 pounds is well under the MLTW. For the same truck towing a travel trailer the brochure lists a MLTW of 10,000 pounds. A travel trailer weighing 12,575 pounds exceeds this and would create an unsafe towing situation.

Do not take short cuts in making your weight calculations. Here is an example of how far off these short cuts can be.

The maximum payload number in the brochure is based on the lightest truck available, probably not the truck used for towing. For our example, if we subtract the maximum payload weight of 3,520 pounds from the GVWR of 8,800 pounds we would believe the truck weighs 5,280 pounds. But this is over 1,100 pounds lighter than the truck's actual weight! This 1,100 pound difference amounts to 1,100 pounds less payload than you would have calculated from the numbers in the brochure.

Data Collection

You will find blank copies of the tables used in the following examples in *Appendix B.*

If the RV has a generator, be sure to include the amount of fuel it can hold when calculating fuel capacities. Also make note of any data the label(s) provide, even if the tables do not have space for it. The information may be useful later.

We will look at two weight calculations—one for trailers and one for motorhomes.

Trailer Weight Calculation

First you will need to gather data off labels on the trailer. Table 8.1 shows the weight ratings for the fifth-wheel trailer and tow vehicle, which we will use in this example. You will find these weight ratings on the labels discussed earlier. Please note the tow vehicle in this example is different than the one used in the previous example.

TABLE 8.1 Weight Ratings—Trailer Example

	TOW VEHICLE	TRAILER
GVWR	8,510	11,560
GAWR		
Front	4,000	5,080
Middle		
Rear	5,450	5,080
GCWR	16,000	
GDW/UVW		8,920

Table 8.2 on the next page shows what different liquids weigh. The *Gallons* and *Weight* columns have data for our fifth-wheel trailer example.

Let's see how the weight works out for this trailer. We will work with the "wet weight" of the trailer, which allows for the weight of all fluids, fresh water, propane and if you have a generator the weight of fuel for it. This will assure sufficient payload when there is water in the fresh water tank. Even if you plan to camp at full hook-up campgrounds, the day will come when you travel with water. Be safe. Include the weight of water in your calculations.

TABLE 8.2 Fluid Capacities—Trailer Example

FLUID	WEIGHT/ GALLON	GALLONS	WEIGHT
Water	8.34 lbs/gal	60	500 lbs.
Propane	4.0 lbs/gal	20	80 lbs.
Diesel	7.1 lbs/gal		
Gas	6.2 lbs/gal		
Total Weight			580 lbs.

To determine the "wet weight" the GDW/UVW is added to the weight of the fluids.

$$8,920 + 580 = 9,500 \text{ lbs. wet weight}$$

Next determine the trailer payload by subtracting the wet weight from the GVWR.

$$11,560 - 9500 = 2,060 \text{ lbs. payload}$$

What does one consider sufficient payload? That depends on what you plan to take with you. We feel we travel light with less than 2,000 pounds of "stuff". We have met others that don't bat an eye at carrying 4,000 pounds of "stuff". RV Consumer Group suggests the payload capacity be 20 percent of the GVWR for motorhomes and 30 percent of the GVWR for trailers. A'Weigh We Go has found full-timers tend to carry 2,000 to 3,000 pounds of "stuff," including the weight of water.

What you are trying to determine at this point is if a particular RV is worth further consideration. If you calculate a negative payload at this point, remove the RV from your choices. If the payload is less than 2,000 pounds you should also give serious consideration to eliminating the RV from your choices.

Once the trailer has passed the payload test you can go to step two, weighing the tow vehicle and trailer. Remember to do this with full fuel and water tanks on both the tow vehicle and trailer. This step will tell you if the weight is properly spread across the axles and if all weight ratings can be met.

The best way to weigh a tow vehicle and trailer is tire by tire. Weighing this way, before loading the RV, can uncover design errors. One gentleman told us how his motorhome handled poorly. One day a friend was following him down the road and asked if he knew his motorhome sat lower on one side than the other. His research showed the manufacturer had placed much more than half the weight of the motorhome on the low side.

The manufacturer's fix was to add an additional leaf spring to the low side. This may or may not have been a good fix. For example, the tires may have been rated to carry their share of the entire weight of the motorhome. But, were they rated to carry the load when more than half of the load was on one side of the motorhome?

When an RV is built it should have the necessary equipment to carry the weight of the RV, plus your payload. With proper construction both sides of the RV should weigh nearly the same. When one side weighs a great deal more than the other side the equipment—axles, tires, springs, wheels, etc.,—should all be rated for the weight of the heavier side. A'Weigh We Go weighs RVs and tow or towed vehicles tire by tire just because of cases like this one. It is best *not* to buy an RV that is a great deal heavier on one side than the other. The heavier side is going to have more wear, leading to more maintenance. More importantly the imbalance of the RV could lead to handling problems or even an accident.

You can make a good guess at whether an RV is heavier on one side than the other. Look at the equipment in the RV. If all of the cabinets are on the same side as the slide room chances are that side of the RV is going to be heavier.

Scales weighing tire by tire or even side to side are hard to find, but are your best choice when you can find them. The next best thing is to find a certified scale with several platforms that will allow you to weigh each axle separately. Many truck stops have these scales.

It is especially important for tandem or triple axle trailers to be level with the road. Otherwise, the rear axle will be carrying more load than the front axle, if the front of the travel trailer is high. Conversely, the front axle will carry more load if the trailer is low in the front. Either situation can lead to overloading of an axle. Interestingly enough, A'Weigh We Go has found that fifth-wheel trailers generally carry equal load on the axles when the front of the fifth-wheel trailer is slightly nose high. This is because there is substantially more unit in front of the axles.

Some axle systems have equalizers, which are meant to equally load the axles. However, A'Weigh We Go has found weights still vary from axle to axle. Be sure to weigh all axles on a separate scale platform!

Travel trailers with weight distributing hitches should have their spring bars properly connected when on the scale. Spring bars shift the weight distribution on the tow vehicle. If the spring bars are not connected when you obtain your weights, the results will not be accurate.

Ensure the RV is level when you weigh it. The low side of an RV will have increased weight while the high side will have reduced weight. Weighing an unlevel RV could indicate weight problems you do not have or cover up weight problems you do have.

When weighing RVs and tow or towed vehicles, passengers and pets should be in the vehicle where they will ride going down the road. If you have an 85 pound dog, that rides in the trailer, that is where it should be when you weigh the trailer.

You will need to cross the scale twice—once with just the tow vehicle and once with both the tow vehicle and trailer. If you weigh at a truck stop tell the attendant you need to do a re-weigh for the second trip across the scale. Often the charge for this is less and sometimes there is no charge.

Table 8.3 on the next page shows the weight ratings from the labels and the weight ticket weights for our fifth-wheel example.

The gross weights on Table 8.3 are determined as follows. For the tow vehicle add the axle weights. For the tow vehicle and trailer together add the axle weights for both the tow vehicle and trailer. Since a portion of the trailer weight rests on the tow vehicle you must calculate the trailer only gross weight. Subtract the tow vehicle gross weight from the gross weight of the tow vehicle and trailer together to get the trailer only gross weight. In this case the gross weight of the trailer is:

$$15,780 - 6,280 = 9,500 \text{ lbs.}$$

What does this information tell us?

Table 8.4 summarizes the capacities available in comparison to the weight ratings. We will walk through the calculation of each of these numbers.

TABLE 8.3 Ratings and Weights—Trailer Example

	TOW VEHICLE RATING	TOW VEHICLE ONLY WEIGHT	VEHICLE & TRAILER WET WEIGHT	TRAILER RATING	TRAILER ONLY WEIGHT
GVWR	8,510			11,560	
Tow Vehicle AXLE					
Front	4,000	3,520	3,480		
Rear	5,450	2,760	4,210		
Trailer AXLE					
Front			4,045	5,080	4,045
Middle					
Rear			4,045	5,080	4,045
GCWR	16,000				
GDW/ UVW				8,920	
Gross Weight		6,280	15,780		9,500

TABLE 8.4 Capacities - Trailer Example

	TOW VEHICLE	HITCHED TOW VEHICLE	TOW VEHICLE & TRAILER	TRAILER
Payload Capacity (GVWR—Gross Weight)	2,230	820		2,060
Axle Payload Capacity				
Front	480	520		1,035
Rear	2,690	1,240		1,035
Total				2,070
Combined Payload Capacity (GCWR—Combined Gross Weight)			220	

First, evaluate the payload capacity based on GVWR minus the actual gross weight.

Truck only (data from Table 8.3):

truck GVWR - front axle weight - rear axle weight
= unhitched truck payload

8,510 - 3,520 - 2,760 = 2,230 lbs. of payload remaining.

Truck payload with trailer connected (data from Table 8.3):

truck GVWR - front truck axle weight - rear truck axle weight
= hitched truck payload

8,510 - 3,480 - 4,210 = 820 lbs. of payload remaining.

Trailer only payload (data from Table 8.3):

trailer GVWR - trailer gross weight = trailer payload

11,560 - 9,500 = 2,060 lbs. of payload

When the trailer is hitched to the truck the truck's payload drops to 820. Will this be enough capacity by the time you load your belongings into the trailer? When you load a trailer your things are spread throughout the trailer, therefore the weight is also spread throughout the trailer. This means the trailer axles are carrying a portion of the added weight and the tow vehicle carries the rest. In this case the trailer has an available payload of 2,060 pounds. As long as you do not exceed the 2,060 pounds of trailer payload, you probably will not exceed the 820 pounds available in the truck.

Next we evaluate the available axle capacities by subtracting the actual weights from the GAWR. The formula is:

GAWR - axle weight = available payload

Truck only (data from Table 8.3):
    front axle: 4,000 - 3,520 = 480 lbs.
    rear axle: 5,450 - 2,760 = 2,690 lbs.

Truck with trailer hitched to it (data from Table 8.3):
    front axle: 4,000 - 3,480 = 520 lbs.
    rear axle: 5,450 - 4,210 = 1,240 lbs.

Trailer only (data from Table 8.3):
    5,080 - 4,045 = 1,035 lbs. payload per axle
    or 2,070 lbs. payload total for both axles

You may have noticed the available capacity on the front axle of the truck goes up when you hitch the trailer to the truck. You might envision what happens here by thinking back to your playground days. When you sat on a teeter totter and a playmate sat on the other end you were pretty well balanced. But if an adult sat on the other end you found yourself up in the air. In this case the weight of the trailer is the adult sitting on the back of the truck. The result, of course, is to decrease the load on the front of the truck.

Another important weight to evaluate is the GCWR. In this case the truck has a GCWR of 16,000 pounds. If we subtract the 15,780 pound gross weight for the truck and trailer, we find we only have 220 pounds of capacity left.

Until now everything looked good, but this number should cause the sirens to go off. This calculation says you can only take along 220 pounds of "stuff"! What are the chances you can reduce all of your worldly belongings and food to 220 pounds? While the trailer can carry 2,060 pounds of payload, if you exceed 220 pounds you will cause excessive wear on the tow truck. Your options include finding a truck with higher ratings, or eliminating this trailer from your choices.

Motorhome Weight Calculations

The calculations for motorhomes are similar to those for trailers, with a couple of differences. We will not make calculations including a towed vehicle in this example. You can do this using the same steps used in the trailer example. However, we will look at what a towed vehicle can weigh.

When figuring payload for a motorhome do not forget the weight of passengers. The passengers should be in their seats when weighing the motorhome. This will allow you to calculate the payload capacity for your possessions. Tables 8.5 and 8.6 give label data for this motorhome example.

TABLE 8.5 Weight Ratings—Motorhome

	Motorhome
GVWR	17,000
GAWR	
Front	6,000
Middle	
Rear	11,000
GCWR	25,000
GDW/UVW	15,200
NCC	1,800

TABLE 8.6 Fluid Capacities—Motorhome Example

FLUID	**WEIGHT/ GALLON**	**GALLONS**	**WEIGHT**
Water	8.34 lbs/gal	90	751 lbs.
Propane	4.0 lbs/gal	30	120 lbs.
Diesel	7.1 lbs/gal		
Gas	6.2 lbs/gal		
Total Weight			
			871 lbs.

We start by determining the wet weight—GDW/UVW plus the weight of the fluids. You will recall, for motorhomes the UVW includes the weight of a full tank of fuel.

$$15,200 + 871 = 16,071 \text{ lbs. wet weight.}$$

To this weight we add the weight of passengers. We will assume a low figure of 300 pounds. This increases the wet weight to 16,371 pounds. Now determine the payload capacity by subtracting this number from the GVWR.

$$17,000 - 16,371 = 629 \text{ lbs.}$$

Do you hear the sirens? No way can you reduce your worldly possessions and food to 629 pounds! Quickly remove this motorhome from your shopping list.

Let's look at a couple more calculations. Remember NCC (Net Carrying Capacity) being mentioned earlier? The label for this motorhome gave a NCC of 1,800 pounds. How is it possible to have a NCC of 1,800 pounds when we calculate only 629 pounds of payload? Simple, the weight of fluids and passengers has not been considered. How likely is it that you will not have passengers and fluids on board when you use your motorhome? Not very likely. You can get the same number yourself by subtracting the weight of fluids and passengers from the NCC.

NCC rating - weight of fluids - weight of passengers
= payload capacity

$$1,800 - 871 - 300 = 629 \text{ lbs. payload}$$

Run the numbers. Don't just accept NCC as the bottom line.

To determine what size vehicle or trailer you can pull, subtract the actual weight of the fully loaded motorhome from the GCWR. In this case we will assume the RV weighs in right at the GVWR of 17,000 pounds. This means you could tow a vehicle or trailer weighing 8,000 pounds.

GCWR - actual weight of motorhome
= maximum weight of towed vehicle

25,000 - 17,000 = 8,000 lbs.

That is a good number. If you really want this motorhome you could get a light weight vehicle to tow and load all of your worldly possessions into it. Not likely! Don't forget towed vehicles have GVWR and GAWR's also.

In our example the GCWR says this motorhome can move 25,000 pounds down the road, but the GVWR says the motorhome can only hold up 17,000 pounds. The axle capacity is the weak link here.

When you reach the point of weighing a motorhome be sure each axle is on a different platform. Some motorhomes have a third axle, generally know as a tag axle. The tag axle normally has a different weight rating than the middle axle. The towed vehicle may be weighed on one platform. However, if you will be towing a car on a tow dolly you should have the tow dolly axle on a platform by itself, to determine if the tow dolly axle has sufficient payload capacity.

There are a couple of things to keep in mind about towed vehicles. If the towed vehicle travels with all four tires on the ground, there should be no weight transferred to the rear motorhome axle. If, on the other hand, the vehicle is on a trailer or tow dolly, or you tow a trailer, there will be weight transferred to the rear axle of the motorhome.

If you are already short on payload capacity, select a tow vehicle that can be towed with all four wheels on the ground. If you are towing a trailer behind a motorhome you will need to determine the impact it has on payload.

Regardless of what you are towing, run the same calculations we did in the trailer example, using weight tickets. To accomplish this, weigh the motorhome by itself and again with the towed vehicle or trailer attached.

Keep in mind that even if a motorhome is rated to tow a vehicle over 1,500 pounds, you should still install separate functional brakes. Not only will it give you more peace of mind, in some states and provinces it is the law!

Other Weight Considerations

Here are several things to keep in mind as you analyze whether a particular RV and tow or towed vehicle will remain within the weight ratings when you add your possessions.

★ For motorized vehicles, including motorhomes, the GAWR can never be less than the GVWR. For trailers, however, the hitch will carry a portion of the load, so the GAWR for all axles can be less than the GVWR.

★ Where you place load in an RV will determine how that load is shared between the axles on a motorhome, or the axles and hitch on a trailer.

★ The different weight ratings—GVWR, GAWR and GCWR—are all based on capacities of different components. If you find the GAWR of the axles is greater than the GVWR that does not mean you can ignore the GVWR, which also factors in the rating of the drive train, hitch and chassis. While the logic behind individual weight ratings is not obvious to us, they exist for good reasons. Stay within all weight ratings.

★ Be aware some trailers have a heavy hitch weight that could exceed the GAWR or GVWR of your tow vehicle before you even load the trailer. Keep your eyes open for this.

✰ Hitches and tow bars also have weight ratings. In some cases they may have a different rating for each component. Don't overlook these ratings.

Alive To Tell

I cannot emphasize how important it is to not overload an RV. Pat and Shelia feel lucky to be alive to tell their story. They put a contract on a used motorhome with the contingency that the motorhome be weighed, full of fluids and that it have a minimum of 2,000 pounds payload. The label stated the GVWR was 22,500 pounds. When the wet weight came in at 22,600 pounds—with two people and no "stuff"—they walked away.

The next day the salesperson contacted Pat and Shelia and asked that they talk with a management person at the motorhome chassis factory. The manager explained that the motorhome actually had a GVWR of 26,000 pounds and that it had been labeled with a GVWR of 22,500 pounds for marketing purposes. The company wanted to create an incentive to buy their higher end models.

While the explanation bothered Pat and Sheila, they loved the motorhome and took the bait. At less than 30,000 miles the rotors required turning. They also experienced abnormal tire wear and the smell of the rear brakes overheating. They were careful to use their exhaust brake to slow them down, minimizing brake wear.

Later Pat and Shelia had the actual components compared to those listed in the brochure. They learned the rear axle, plus the rear rotors and wheels were all lighter weight components than shown in the brochure.

Pat and Sheila followed the right steps, but ignored their intuition. The motorhome manufacturer provided bad information, which led them to buy a motorhome they ultimately felt put their lives at risk. So they filed suit against the manufacturer. They eventually settled out of court and bought a bus conversion, which they feel safe driving.

It is in situations like Pat and Shelia experienced that the third step in evaluating an RV should be used. Listen to your intuition. If something does not feel or seem right evaluate the weight ratings component by component. And do so before you buy!

Tires

Tires are a very important component in the overall weight picture. Here are some tire tips from A'Weigh We Go.

★ An overinflated tire may not provide adequate contact with the road during braking, particularly on wet roads, causing loss of control of the vehicle.

★ Overload and/or under inflation, over a period of time cause the majority of tire failures. In other words, the majority of tire failures are from progressive damage.

★ The correct pressure for a tire depends on the load that a tire carries. This can only be evaluated by weighing the loaded RV or vehicle tire by tire and using the correct tire chart to determine the pressure.

★ Most highway tires are designed to do their job, mile after mile, day after day, between 56 and 65 miles per hour, sustained speed. Driving faster decreases the load capacity of the tire, while driving slower increases the load capacity of the tire.

★ Incorrect leveling can shorten the life of a tire. Be sure the foot print of the tire is fully supported and not hanging over the side of the leveling board. In the case of duals, both tires should be fully supported.

Getting Assistance

If you would like to know more about weight issues or you would like some help making sure you do not start out overloaded, contact the experts in the field—A'Weigh We Go. They offer seminars and weighings nationwide. Check their web page or contact them for their current schedule to see when they will be near you. They also have a handbook that covers these weight issues in more depth than we covered here.

A'Weigh We Go
211 Mae McKee Road
Chuckey, TN 37641
(423) 257-7985
awwg@rvamerica.com
http://www.aweighwego.org

John takes pride in responding to every letter and e-mail they receive. However, a SASE (self-addressed stamped envelope) would be greatly appreciated with letters.

Shopping Time

Congratulations, you now know more about buying an RV than 99 percent of RV buyers and most RV salespeople! It is finally time for serious shopping. The most important thing to remember, as you select your wheel estate, is to listen to and trust your intuition. Take time out to ask yourself, does selecting this RV feel right? Set aside any personal attachment that may have developed for the RV. If something doesn't feel right, even if you cannot pin point what it is, walk away from that particular RV.

When working with a salesperson, remember to find out what their personal experience with RVs has been. If they don't own an RV, or are not familiar with full-timing, they will not understand your needs and probably do not know the product very well. This is okay. You now know to rely totally on your research and not to allow the salesperson to influence you. Don't forget to remind yourself of this when the salesperson tells you how great this doo-dad or that gadget is.

If there are any questions in your mind about a particular unit, walk through local campgrounds, looking for the same model, built within a year or two of the one you are considering. Knock on the door, tell the owners you are looking at the same model they own and ask what they think of it. While RVers love to share experiences some will hesitate to tell you the bad things. If they do not share anything bad about the unit, specifically ask them about their worst experiences with the unit. Others may have nothing good to say about their RV. Get the specifics, it may not be as bad as they indicate.

If you cannot find similar units in the local campgrounds ask the dealer to give you the name of others who bought that model in the last year or two. Call and ask them what they think of the unit. Specifically ask them if they have weighed it. Check with the RV Consumer Group (and RV Group Wise) for the latest data on the unit, even if it has a good rating in *The RV Rating Book,* as new data may have come in since it went to press. However, do not base your wheel estate selection solely on these ratings.

When you eliminate an RV for safety or durability reasons, explain why to the salesperson. This not only educates the salesperson, but gets the word back to the manufacturer that they are dealing with informed buyers. This is the first step toward improving the safety and durability of future RVs.

Many RV manufacturers go bankrupt. Be sure to ask the dealer if the manufacturer is in bankruptcy—even if the manufacturer has been around for a long time. If they are in bankruptcy, cross that RV off your shopping list. The workmanship is likely to be poor and the warranty becomes questionable. It would be worthwhile to double check with either or both the RV Consumer Group and RVIA to determine if the manufacturer is in bankruptcy. You might even check with the bankruptcy court in the manufacturer's state, just to be sure.

Ask the dealer's service manager if the manufacturer has been good about paying them for warranty work they have done. If not, chances are you will have difficulty getting warranty work done.

If you find you must cross several RVs off your list don't panic. There are more travel trailer, fifth-wheel and motorhome manufacturers than you can even imagine. Even after shopping for over three years, being on the road for six years and visiting 47 states we still see manufacturers names we did not know existed!

Plant tours are fun and interesting. Most RV manufacturers are pleased to give you a tour of their facilities. Did you know most RVs are built from the inside out, just the reverse of a house? If you can incorporate some tours into your buying process you will learn a lot and be able to check out the construction for durability and safety.

Still can't decide what you need in an RV? Visit with others in campgrounds and at RV shows about what they feel is most important. While everyone's needs are different, you are sure to find a few people with similar needs or desires.

Alex and Janis share these shopping tips. "Shop for your wheel estate in the rain when possible. Leaks are a common problem with RVs, so why not check it out before you buy? Also, take a pair of overalls along for when it is time to check out the chassis and holding tanks. Imagine the salesperson's surprise!"

Finally, a note on purchase price. "We were leaning toward a fifth-wheel trailer," Jessica says. "We had selected one and sent letters to many dealers asking the price. It was amazing as those prices varied by $12,000 for the same trailer!" So once you select a specific wheel estate, shop around for price.

The information in the last four chapters is by no means complete. Read everything you can get your hands on about RVs and how to shop for them. Gather as much information as possible from current full-timers on the subject. As long as you are a well-informed buyer, you have little to fear when you shop for your wheel estate. Happy shopping!

9

Have Bus Will Travel

Bus conversions are another type of wheel estate you will see on the road. The first image that may come to mind is of luxurious accommodations for the famous singer traveling from city to city for performances. This image represents only a handful of bus conversions on the road, however. You certainly do not need such deep pockets to afford a bus.

We know one couple that bought and converted a bus for $30,000. Their secret? They did it themselves with left over materials, which they got for nothing from a family member in the construction business. They did an outstanding job and you would never guess their bus is full of scrap! It is a beautiful home on wheels.

If you are shopping for a new bus conversion, you should expect to spend several hundred thousand dollars, but you may be able to find a used bus conversion for under a hundred thousand dollars.

Bus conversions make great homes on wheels. They are, however, a totally different type of RV. As a result, evaluation of a bus conversion is totally different from evaluation of other RVs. We will not look at the evaluation process for bus conversions in this book. You will find resources to help you with this process in the *Resource Directory.*

The following are tips, observations and experiences that owners of two bus conversions offer to those of you considering the bus conversion option. Pat and Shelia recently moved from a motorhome to a bus conversion.

> *The advantages to owning a bus over an RV are safety, durability and a very smooth quiet ride. Buses are built to travel a minimum of five million miles. Repairs are similar to RVs in cost, but buses can last up to ten times longer.*
>
> *The obvious disadvantage is price. New bus conversions can cost between $500,000 and $1,000,000. Shopping for an older conversion requires lots of research and takes a lot of time, but there are some out there for under $100,000.*
>
> *It [selecting a bus conversion] was a disadvantage for us with no mechanical background, but we are finding the routine fixes to be very simple and have learned most of what can be done with our small supply of tools.*

Pat and Shelia offer these seven important tips to those shopping for a bus conversion:

1. *Learn all you can about buses; where to look for unusual wear, rust, how to determine engine condition, suspension, steering. Have a good bus mechanic to consult with.*
2. *Drive as many different buses as you can in order to experience differences in size and brand.*
3. *Unless you are mechanically skilled and don't mind getting dirty, buying a bus, which was converted, after a few million miles of service can be risky.*
4. *Whether the bus was converted professionally or by a private individual, electrical diagrams must be*

available. If not, repairs can be very costly and fire risk could be high.

5. *Attend bus conventions and talk to bus owners. Remember nobody knows all there is to know about bus conversions. Gather all the information you can and you'll gain confidence in your ability to choose the right bus.*

6. *It is like buying a house—every one is different. The longer you take to make your choice, the more satisfied you'll be.*

7. *You may want to convert your own. This is usually the least expensive way to go; however, it usually takes between one and five years to complete. Talk to at least ten people who have done their own before you decide to take on such a task.*

Obviously Pat and Shelia did their homework. Paul and Cheryl, owners of the WanderingStar, have even more experience with bus conversions and share the following:

At the time of this writing my wife and I have lived full-time in a bus conversion for three years. We love it and would be hard pressed to consider other forms of RV liveaboards. But we do not hard sell the bus option. There are many considerations on the choice of any conveyance and the laundry list of each individual's desires and needs differ greatly.

Like others, we have progressed through the ranks from pick-up camper to class A motorhomes. We loved them all and all for different reasons. For example, the full sized pick-up camper, which we used for months at a time on photo safaris, was on a 4-wheel drive power wagon. Extremely versatile, we took it to remote regions in all types of weather.

As we began to use motorhomes we enjoyed them all, but did begin to realize weaknesses that only a bus application seemed to solve. The number one reason was on the road security and handling. Their weight and load restrictions are far superior compared to regular motorhomes. This makes the bus a very fun vehicle to drive. Busses were invented to haul many people in comfort. With just two, it's extreme comfort. On the open road it is a sheer joy to ride or drive a highway bus. City driving is of course more demanding, due to the size and the care of your "space."

The commercial bus frame is just that, a commercial/industrial grade product. Interior finishing aside, the core product is meant to endure for millions of miles, day in and day out for years. They are designed to meet incredibly tough maintenance standards and service. They are not planned obsolescence, but have readily available upgrades to take them through the decades of service for which they are designed.

Properly maintained they hold value and looks. We are continually sought out in RV parks (while surrounded by the latest of motorhomes) and complimented on our bus. Her aluminum sides are in good order and her paint topside is kept up. She is 33 years old.

As a 1966 over the road, or "Inter-city" bus with over 1,000,000 miles, she is only in her mid years of road-mile use. She could easily outlast two more owners after we part with her. We can make additions or changes inside without fear of needing a new frame in a couple of years.

Nor is weight an issue. We carry 150 gallons of diesel, another 30 [gallons] in reserve and 30 [gallons] more in gasoline for the 6 kW generator. There are 120 gallons of fresh water in a stainless tank and two 70 gallon tanks for gray and black water. Our propane is in two 20 gallon tanks.

One might wonder why we are supporting three fuel systems. Herein lies a potential problem of a used conversion. You inherit the design of those who have worked on the unit (not necessarily professionals) before yourself. In this case it would have been wise to stay with all diesel and installed a diesel or propane generator. But we bought the bus as is and have come to appreciate the gas powered unit. In a factory engineered unit, I suspect a diesel generator would have been used in the first place.

We have one bay nearly seven feet square by 40 inches high. It is used for nothing but storage. In a second bay we have over 50 cubic feet of storage shared with the utilities of ten deep cycle batteries and inverter, along with the water works. The generator and fuel systems are in another service bay.

The engine is a Detroit Diesel V-8 designed in the late 1950's. While it has a continual line of successors in the Detroit line, it is not only still made today, it is used widely in military motorized guns. These are amazingly tough engines. Every bolt and spring is available and they [the engine] can be upgraded. Nearly every town has its diesel pro who can adjust and change until you're pulling the same horses of the most modern of units. All at a price, of course.

Age has its price, however. No matter how well made and maintained the miles take their toll and repairs are needed. Here is where the pros and cons begin and never end of what is the best deal.

For my part I have yet to see the rig, at any price or age, that didn't demand attention. These are rolling homes with complex mechanical systems.

Start with the core vehicle, the bus frame and works. Over the course of four total years ownership and nearly 200,000 road miles, repairs have been needed, but always available. From drive shaft to alternator to air bags to transmission, every part is very much the same as trucks. Trucks are kept on the road by a huge network of truck and diesel shops across the country...and Canada and Mexico. There simply has never been a part that couldn't be found and usually with one day's total service. The windshield on our bus lists for $129 and is often available at the local Greyhound Station. On consumer grade products one can wait a long time for parts that are no longer available because of model changes.

Inside is another story. The market is rather small for the brand-new never been owned bus conversion. My guess is that less than two hundred are produced a year and then, like the larger custom yachts, by special order. They are by nature a custom product. So I speak of the used conversion and that means the insides are yours to solve, if you're the owner. The vendors who will back up the products and warranties are few.

Again, arguments will persist, but I do not find this a real problem because of the stories I've heard of name-brand motorhomes with appliance problems that couldn't or wouldn't be solved.

This becomes an individual choice. If you feel comfortable with a name brand motorhome and the service offered by the dealer and parent company, you would be wise to pursue that course of action. Some of the benefits include a "blue book" guide on most production motorhomes. This not only gives the buyer an idea of dollars, but allows a banker ease in financing.

With a bus conversion a banker is at a loss on value and the hopeful buyer trying to finance a long term loan will need to do his/her research. Likewise, insurance can be a bit tricky. There are only a few vendors who offer coverage in the bus conversion market. However, they seem to me to be fairly reasonable...if one can call insurance reasonable.

The end result? We are very pleased with our decision of a bus conversion. We feel they are a bargain in the long run. They are not for everyone and there is a learning curve after the purchase. But isn't there always?

The person bitten by the bus bug needs to soak up any and all information that they can find and then visit every bus person and talk. I've seen few that won't share what they know and like all RVers, they all know something different. Happy trails!

Here are some additional pluses for a bus. The interior of a bus is spacious, offering many ways to layout the living space. As Paul shared, buses have a great deal of exterior storage. A few even manage to carry a car in the storage compartments. The drawbacks include their weight and ground clearance. These factors may limit campground and boondocking opportunities.

As you can see, there is a great deal to consider when deciding whether or not a bus conversion is for you.

10

Residency and the Role it Plays

Chances are you have never considered the impact state of residency plays in your life. Sure, you may have complained about one state tax or another, but have you ever considered the tax laws when determining where you will work and live? You may not even be aware of how different tax laws are from one state to the next.

Residency is a primary concern for many full-timers. Since states collect their taxes in different ways, full-timers look for the states that will have minimal tax impact on their budget. Some will look for a state with no income tax, while those buying an expensive RV may look for a state with no sales tax. Those living off investments will look for states that do not tax investments. However, if you own a house or have health insurance that requires you live in your current state, you may not be able to re-establish your residency.

The information in this chapter gives you some idea of what residency options are available today. While we will look at why some people have gone with multiple state residencies, I **do not** recommend this. If you have multiple states of residency and the states decide to come after you, look out!

Your best choice will be a state of residency that meets most, if not all, of your needs.

What Is Required For Residency

Residency requirements vary from state to state. Things that typically help establish residency include driver's license, vehicle registration, insurance, wills and voter's registration. The more you transfer to the new state, the better off you will be if one of the states decides to look into your residency. You may wonder why a state would care where you reside. It all comes down to your money and how they can get their hands on it.

Check the residency requirements for each state you are considering. Also check to see what steps are necessary to discontinue residency in your current state. If you are leaving a state that collects income tax, be sure to file a partial year tax form, even if you leave in late December. You may even want to go a step further and send a letter to the state notifying them your residency has changed.

Selecting Your State of Residency

There are several things full-timers should consider when selecting their state of residency. Each individual or couple should base their decision on their unique needs. Most will select a state based on financial impact, while some will consider other things. Be sure to consider the convenience or inconvenience of rules and regulations in the states you choose. For example, will it interfere with your lifestyle if you must return to your domicile each year?

The following are some items you may want to consider when selecting your domicile. Since laws and regulations change it is important for you to check the current laws and regulations before selecting your domicile.

No State Income Tax

Alaska, Nevada, South Dakota, Texas, Washington and Wyoming have no state income taxes. Florida, New Hampshire and Tennessee are limited income tax states, taxing only special income, like interest and dividends. If you will be living off investments you may not want to be a resident of one of these three states. If you will be working on the road, keep in mind that state income tax is paid to the state where the money is made.

Vehicle/RV Registration

Depending on the state, license plates for the same vehicle may range from $50 to $3,000 or more. Title and transfer fees are generally nominal. Find out if you can obtain your license renewal fees over the phone. Also determine if the state will mail your plates to wherever you are, using a general delivery address if necessary.

Some states require vehicle safety inspections. Others may require smog testing in some or all of their counties. Determine how frequently these tests must be done and if they are a requirement for license renewal. What impact do these regulations have on your lifestyle?

Sales Tax

Sales tax on a vehicle or RV purchase may run from as little as nothing to as much as seven percent or more, depending on the state. Vehicle and RV sales tax laws will vary from state to state and even county to county. States with higher taxes than you originally paid on a vehicle may collect the difference from you when you register your current vehicle with them. When you trade a vehicle some states will only tax you on the difference in value between the vehicles. These states may also tax you on the full value of the new vehicle if you sell the old vehicle yourself.

Vehicle and RV Insurance

Insurance can vary a great deal from state to state. The states with fewer people tend to have lower insurance rates. Insurance costs also vary from county to county within a state. We found the same coverage on our truck and trailer would cost us 41 percent more in Texas than in South Dakota. Full-timing insurance companies will be happy to quote you rates for the two or three states you are considering.

Health Insurance

Health insurance costs vary from state to state for the same coverage. Each state has unique health insurance regulations, which make it hard to compare the same coverage from one state to the next. Also, most insurance agents hold a license for only one state, so you will have to work with several agents to evaluate policies in different states.

Voter's Registration

You may wish to register in your new state to establish additional intent of domicile. You can then request an absentee ballot in advance of an election. Ask what the absentee ballot process is when you register.

Most states require a physical address, so a post office box will not work for your voter's registration. When we went to register in South Dakota, the only address we had was a post office box. This was not acceptable, but the Voter's Registration Office said the campground address where we were staying was acceptable.

Driver's License

Determine how much a driver's license costs and how long it is good for. Can it be renewed by mail? Will you need to take a written and/or driving test to get the new license? Most states will not accept a post office box address for your driver's license. In South Dakota they had no problem using the campground address on our voter's registration.

You will also need to determine the licensing requirements for RVs in each state you look at. Some, like Texas, require different licenses based on the gross combined weight rating (GCWR) of what you are driving and towing. For example, in Texas, a vehicle or combination of vehicles that exceed 26,001 pounds requires a Class A or B license. If you are towing a trailer with a gross vehicle weight rating (GVWR) in excess of 10,000 pounds a different type of license may also be required in Texas.

Wills

If you have a will you should have it reviewed in your new state of residency. If the text in your will states "is to be interpreted by the laws of _____ state" you will definitely need to have it revised for your new state of residency.

Estate and Inheritance Tax

Be aware of what the state inheritance and estate tax laws are. At some point this may cause you to re-evaluate your state of residency.

There is a booklet that will assist you in selecting a state of residency. ***Selecting an RV Home Base: State Tax & Registration Information*** that provides sections, by state, on financial responsibilities, vehicle licensing and registration, voting as well as additional sources of information. Use this booklet as a starting point, keeping in mind that the laws may have changed since the booklet was published.

Many full-timers select the following states for residency:

- ☆ Texas because of the Escapees RV Club mail service. Also, the community accepts full-timers, making it easy to establish residency.
- ☆ Florida because, while there is an intangibles tax, there is no state income tax and it is in the Sunbelt.
- ☆ Nevada because there is no state income tax.

☆   Oregon because there is no sales tax on vehicles and expensive RVs.

Oregon has been making it more difficult for full-timers to claim residency there. Recently, a full-timer whose domicile is Oregon, told me Oregon now expects residents to spend at least six months a year there. This does not mean you should rule out residency in Oregon. It is just something more to investigate.

Many people seem to have overlooked what we believe is the best domicile—South Dakota. This may be because the state is in snow country and not a place most full-timers travel to often. However, once you become a resident the state will take care of just about everything by mail, meaning no special trips home.

Carol, a fellow South Dakotan said, "South Dakota is totally in tune with what we are doing, they are totally civilized, totally helpful and have made things a lot easier."

When state employees were asked if something could be done a certain way, they told her, "Of course you can do that. Of course we can do that." So do not overlook this gem in your search for a domicile.

Once we had narrowed our research to a handful of states we sent a survey memo, similar to the one in *Appendix C,* to the states we were seriously considering. If you do this be sure to include a SASE (self addressed stamped envelope) to encourage a reply from each state. Add any additional questions you may have to the survey. We sent our survey to six states. Some did not respond. One state took several months as they processed the survey through three departments to answer all the questions. We were pleasantly surprised when South Dakota responded, with answers to all the questions, in exactly one week!

One state could not give us an exact license fee for our truck. We called them three or four times and never received consistent information, so we crossed them off our list of possible domiciles.

We continue to learn new things every day on the road. We learned that besides the cost of license plates, some states have personal property taxes that affect RVs. One weekend camper told us how they registered their motorhome in the neighboring state because in the state where they live it would cost them $2,500 a year for motorhome property taxes. This is risky business and could result in huge fines being assessed. We will look at one such episode that occurred in Washington shortly.

Janis, whose domicile is Florida, told how Florida is now enforcing their intangible tax on equities, such as money markets and stocks. She pointed out that other states have intangible taxes on the books, although not all are enforcing them. This could change at any time.

Once you make a decision, continue to ask questions. Nothing in this lifestyle is in concrete and a time may come when you want to make changes.

Full-timers As A State Asset

Some states, like South Dakota and Texas, recognize how full-timers and the states can help each other out. Full-timers want an inexpensive domicile in a state that understands their lifestyle.

The states enjoy revenue brought in by taxes on vehicle and RV purchases, licensing fees, insurance premiums, etc. Full-timers also increase the census, which increases federal funding and representation, yet they cause little wear and tear on the state as they spend their time traveling elsewhere.

Not all states are so receptive, however.

Precautions

If you decide to change your residency, be aware that you must do it properly or you may face large fines. To properly change residency you must understand the residency requirements of the state you currently live in and your new domicile.

Many full-timers have had no problem licensing their RV and vehicle in different states. Some may even have their drivers license in yet another state. It may only be a matter of time before they run into trouble, however. Some states take residency very seriously. Oregon has a $2,500 fine for falsely claiming Oregon residency. And consider how far Washington is willing to go.

At an Escapade (educational rally for full-timers and wannabees) I learned of a couple who had lived in Washington, which has a sales tax. The couple had a legitimate business in Oregon, which does not have a sales tax. The plan was to claim Oregon as their domicile when they started to full-time. They bought their motorhome and took it to Oregon to register it, only to learn they could not do so without the original Bill of Origin. They returned to Washington while they waited for this document. In the meantime the motorhome spent a month in the motorhome hospital. They also had an illness in the family that required attention.

Somehow the state of Washington got wind of this and charged them with a penalty of $44,000, for not registering their motorhome in Washington. Washington's investigation produced a one inch stack of documentation establishing the couple's Washington residency. Among these papers was documentation of no mileage on the motorhome, that they still voted in Washington, that they still received mail in Washington and the fact they had used a Washington address to sign up for an RV rally after buying the motorhome. While they were not able to get out of the penalty, they were able to negotiate it down to $28,000.

More recently Oregon and Washington requested the FBI investigate the vehicle sales records of an RV dealership in Oregon. One result of the investigation was a charge of vehicle registration fraud against a Washington couple. They used a friend's address to register their motorhome in Oregon for $250, instead of paying Washington's registration fee of $38,000. To avoid jail time they paid court costs, fines, penalties and registration fees totaling $101,568, plus they performed 40 hours of community service.

Washington takes the loss of revenue seriously. Since Washington has no income tax, a large part of their revenue comes from vehicle sales tax and licensing fees. Washington has a large full-time staff that checks license plates. If a vehicle with Washington plates is towing a trailer with a different state's plate, or a motorhome with out of state plates is towing a car with Washington plates, watch out!

After three days in Vancouver we were stopped because an officer had seen our truck with South Dakota plates two days in a row. He was just checking vehicles with out of state plates for residency! Most states are not this stringent, although this may change in the future.

Intent plays an important role in establishing domicile. If a state can establish that you are claiming residency in another state or states just to avoid taxes, look out! Those with vehicle plates, driver's licenses and insurance in different states may someday face severe consequences. If you own a house in one state, it may be hard to convince that state that you have residency in another state. Also if you have insurance in a state that otherwise is not your domicile, it is possible the insurance company could deny you coverage just when you need it most.

Residency can have positive financial benefits and is worth serious consideration. However, for your own financial security, establish your domicile with care.

11

Wheel Estate and Vehicle Insurance

Unless you still own property, insuring your RV and vehicle will be more challenging than you might expect. Certainly it will be more challenging than insuring a house. Here is one concern Janis had about insuring her fifth-wheel trailer as a full-timer.

> *We had very good coverage with an excellent company. I was concerned about them understanding that we did not live in Florida but traveled full-time across the country. I explained what we were doing and they told us it would be okay for six months. I kept checking back with them and they kept telling me it was okay, but I was still concerned. I asked them to put in writing that our coverage was good for full-timers. When they would not put this in writing I decided it was time to find another insurance company.*
>
> *We selected a company that insures full-timers. Their policy clearly states that it provides coverage for full-timers.*

Janis was cautious, possibly avoiding a problem. I recall what our State Farm insurance agent told us when we hit the road.

We were happy with our agent and the coverage received in the past, so we asked him if he could provide insurance for our trailer and tow truck. He made a real effort, working with people high up in the company, to see if there was a way to cover us. He came up with four separate policies to cover our truck and trailer.

It seemed a little bizarre to need four policies to cover two vehicles, so Paul asked him if he felt this would provide adequate coverage. We were lucky. We had an honest insurance agent who put his clients ahead of the bottom line. He told Paul that he honestly was not sure we would have complete coverage. His suggestion was to go with a company offering full-timing insurance.

Does your insurance agent really have your best interest at heart, or do $$$ signs come first? If you plan to approach your current insurance agent about coverage in the full-timing lifestyle, be sure you know exactly what coverage you need. Let's take a look at what that coverage should include.

Insurance Components

What do you look for in insurance? A typical automobile insurance policy will include the following:

- ☆ Bodily Injury/Liability
- ☆ Property/Liability
- ☆ Medical
- ☆ Uninsured motorist
- ☆ Under insured motorist
- ☆ Collision
- ☆ Comprehensive

Full-timers' insurance also looks at the higher cost of an RV. The need for special repair facilities and personal possessions in an RV must also be considered. These are just a few differences full-timers' insurance companies must factor in when determining their rates.

CPL Coverage

Full-timers' RV insurance should include CPL, or comprehensive, personal and liability coverage. CPL provides liability coverage outside the RV. Some people feel they can obtain this coverage with a renter's insurance policy, but this assumption is risky. A renter's insurance policy does not factor in your home moving around the countryside.

Some people still own a home and believe they obtain this coverage by adding their RV to their homeowner's policy. Is this coverage in effect when you are away from home for long periods of time? Is it in effect when someone else is living in your home? Check your homeowner's insurance policy to see if it specifically states you must live in the home.

Personal Effects

Another consideration is coverage on your personal effects. Do you carry everything, or almost everything you own with you? Homeowners' policies typically cover only ten percent of your personal effects when you are away from home. If you tie your RV insurance to a homeowners' policy, and carry all your possessions with you, then you will not have adequate coverage. Full-timers need full coverage on their possessions.

When evaluating different policies look for those policies that give you full replacement or actual cash value of your possessions. For example, if you have a twelve-year-old computer and software that meets your needs and your RV burns to the ground what will the insurance company give you for your loss? Will they reimburse you on depreciated value—nothing in this case—or will they provide you with sufficient funds to replace your computer and software with today's technology?

Documentation of your possessions will increase your recovery if you do file a claim. Written documentation is sufficient, however, photos and videos will remove many questions that may otherwise arise. Review your inventory periodically and store it some place other than your RV.

How much coverage do you need on possessions? Do you have $5,000, $10,000 or more worth of possessions with you? Most full-timers' policies give you the flexibility to declare the value of your possessions.

Will you have some possessions in storage? Find out if your full-timer's policy will cover those items or if you need another policy to cover them. Also, if you have jewelry you will want to check into additional coverage for that. Full-timers' policies normally limit coverage on jewelry and musical instruments.

Replacement Coverage

If your house were to burn to the ground you would expect your insurance company to rebuild your home. This is not automatically true with full-timers' insurance. First you must determine if you can obtain replacement insurance on your RV. If you can, what are the requirements? One insurance company will only provide this coverage if you buy a new RV and obtain your policy from them when you buy the RV. Another full-timer's insurance company does not offer this coverage at all. Some insurance policies insure based on an agreed value that is set by a periodic appraisal.

The best policy we found gives full replacement of your RV, regardless of cost, for the first five years of the RV's life. You can even buy this coverage if your RV is a few years old. This means you can buy a three-year-old RV and still receive this coverage until the RV is five years old, which will be when you have owned it for two years. After year five the insurance rolls into replacement value of the RV, based on your purchase price. This company, for an additional charge, then provides replacement value coverage up to year 20.

Travel in Other Countries

Generally, full-timers' insurance will provide coverage when you travel in Canada. Mexico is another story, however. The Mexican government is the only provider of liability insurance in Mexico. It must be purchased through agents specializing in Mexican insurance.

If you plan to travel outside the United States, regardless of what countries you travel in, be sure to determine whether your RV and vehicle will have coverage in those countries. Some full-timers' insurance companies will keep your comprehensive insurance in place if you obtain liability coverage for the full duration of your visit in another country.

Check the Policy

Some companies offer a disappearing deductible. For every year you do not place a claim, your deductible goes down. A savings, if you do have to file a claim.

Check each policy you are considering for roadside assistance coverage. Some provide good coverage while others provide limited coverage. Does the coverage include both the RV and tow or towed vehicle? Also find out if it includes a rental car when your vehicle is out of service.

If your RV needs repairs for an insurable claim and you cannot live in it while repairs are being made, you will be faced with food and lodging expenses you may not have budgeted for. Some full-timers' insurance policies have an allowance for this situation. What situation must exist for you to use this clause? What is the allowance? What does the allowance cover? How long can you use it? Are there limits on the number of times you may use it? How are you reimbursed?

If your RV catches fire and you call the fire department, there is likely to be a fee for their response. Will your policy cover this fee?

Most companies will provide discounts on your insurance for installation of theft devices, graduation from safe driving courses and memberships in associations such as Escapees RV Club or Good Sam.

Recently some friends bought a motorhome. When checking insurance quotes they could not believe what one company told them. The insurance coverage was good only when the RV spent the nights in a campground! Even if you do not plan to boondock or stay in parking lots, at some point you may want to park in a family or friend's driveway. A driveway is not a campground so what coverage would you have? Be sure to ask what requirements and limitations the insurance policy has.

State of Residency

Companies dealing with full-timers are familiar with the lifestyle. If you have not selected your state of residency, ask the insurance companies to provide quotes for two or three different states. They should have no problem working with you. If they do, you can call several times and ask for a quote in a different state each time.

You may not be able to buy full-timers' insurance in every state, so investigate your options before choosing your domicile. Also, talk with full-timers to find out which insurance companies they use and why.

Keep in mind that the cost of insurance varies from state to state and community to community within a state. Avoiding large cities should help hold insurance costs down. We found we could save $500 per year by insuring our tow truck and fifth-wheel trailer in South Dakota instead of Texas.

Our State Farm agent made us aware of something else. He said, "Select any state but Texas for residency. Their insurance laws are different." Texas laws make it difficult for full-timers to obtain the right coverage.

Many full-timers claim Texas as their home and most feel they have adequate coverage. A couple of companies provide full-timers' insurance in Texas. Another gets around the insurance laws by insuring Texas full-timers in other states. I am told this **is not legal.** If you go with a company like this you may find yourself in a real bind down the road. If Texas is one of your domicile choices, learn all you can about Texas insurance laws.

Other Coverage

Depending on your net worth, you may want higher liability coverage than your full-timer's policy provides. An umbrella policy will provide additional coverage, however, not all insurance companies offer umbrella policies to full-timers. But don't give up, a few agents working with full-timers have seen the need for this coverage and can provide it for you.

Some full-timers' insurance companies will be able to insure your tow or towed vehicle while others cannot. If you select a company for your RV and find they will not insure your tow or towed vehicle, do not panic. This may be in your best interest if you are later responsible for an accident with your vehicle. When the same company insures both the RV and vehicle both rates may go up following an accident. However, if different companies provide coverage for the RV and vehicle, the second company is not likely to raise your insurance rates.

Before filing an insurance claim consider how it will affect your insurance rates. Some accidents will cause your insurance to go up for three years. If there is little damage would you be better off to pay for repairs out of your own pocket? One insurance agent said he would tell his clients, if asked, whether filing or not filing a claim would be less expensive for them.

Insurance Cost

Full-timing insurance is expensive. We were shocked to learn the insurance for our 28 foot fifth-wheel trailer would cost as much as insuring our 3,000 square foot home in Denver, Colorado. Of course a wheel estate has risks a traditional home does not. Especially when it bounces down the road. Maybe the insurance rates are not so bad after all.

When shopping for insurance talk directly to both agents and insurance companies. The following experiences explain why this is important.

When a friend decided to change insurance companies he called an agent for a quote. Feeling it was too high, Paul called the company directly and was able to get our friends a lower rate for the same coverage.

We experienced just the reverse when we looked into changing companies. This time, Paul called a different company directly. When they were unable to answer basic questions about the policy we decided not to change. A few months later we spoke to an agent who provided coverage from the same company. The agent was able to answer all of our questions. The coverage was better and less expensive than what we had, so we changed.

You will find a list of several full-timers' insurance companies in the **Resource Directory.**

12

Health Insurance and Medical Care on the Road

Health Insurance

Health insurance is a big concern for young full-timers. Unless you are retired military, or have a pension that includes it, health insurance is likely to throw a kink into your budget. If you have a pre-existing condition, you may have difficulty finding health insurance coverage at all. Unfortunately there are few easy answers to these dilemmas.

To Buy or Not To Buy

The first thing you will have to decide is if you can afford to be a full-timer without health insurance. What would happen if you do not have health insurance and discover one day that you have a major illness? Chances are you could get treatment, but you would also use up your life savings very quickly. Not only that, you may find that once you recovered you would have to go back to work to pay off the bills. Could you ever financially recover from this? And is the risk worth it?

These are questions Jessica and husband Sam pondered:

We decided we would not get health insurance when we hit the road. We thought that the risk of us getting sick wasn't that great at 47 and so we just decided we would take our chances. After all, we were both healthy.

We talked about it during the four years we had been on the road. I would check into health insurance periodically, but every time I found it to be prohibitively expensive. We thought we could do better with our money and did not feel good about the large deductibles.

This last summer I grew increasingly uncomfortable when a young full-timing friend discovered she had cancer. She was even younger than me, which makes you think, "What if something like that happens to me?"

A few months later I had a mammogram and a follow-up exam was necessary. The follow-up indicated I needed a biopsy. I met with the surgeon and he explained the procedure to me. I then asked him what the biopsy would cost, thinking maybe a couple of thousand dollars. When he said four to six thousand dollars I felt like I had been kicked. After all, this was just a biopsy, a simple procedure to find out if there was a problem. And what would it cost if it was cancerous? It dawned on me that something like this could be catastrophic and just totally wipe us out!

I had been told, by different people, that there was a 10-30 percent chance that the spot on the mammogram was cancerous. So it was not a high risk situation, but if I fell into that 30 percent I could lose my life if I did nothing.

We told the doctor that we were low income and had no insurance. Utah, where we were living and working at the time, had covered my mammograms since I was over 50. They also cover mammograms for low income women. The doctor referred us to both Utah state aid and Medicaid. The Utah state aid had such low financial limits for qualification even owning a car would put you over the financial limits.

With Medicaid the requirements included being disabled for more than 12 months or having a terminal illness. Obviously we were on our own. The billing department at the hospital did say they would work with us, at no interest, to pay the bill off over time. We were also told we would not be turned away because we were low income

In the end the bill was about $4,500.00 and I did not have cancer. I had met a lady who did have breast cancer and she thought the removal of the cancer, lymph nodes and radiation treatment she went through cost between $100,000.00 and $150,000.00. If I had to go through that I would have been paying for it the rest of my life. I do have health insurance coverage now, although my husband has still chosen not to have health insurance.

Jessica's story is the one that nags us in the back of our minds. She got lucky and did not have cancer, but will you be so lucky? That is the question each individual must weigh as they decide whether to pay for health insurance or not.

Health Insurance Options

Major medical insurance offers a financial shield for those who cannot risk their life savings. With this coverage, your health insurance pays the bills that could otherwise bankrupt you. You pay the smaller bills, such as doctor's visits and prescriptions.

Your insurance kicks in after you have met a deductible of $1,000, $2,000, or higher. The higher your deductible, the lower the cost of your insurance. Since young full-timers are normally in good health, the cost of doctors and prescriptions should be minimal. This reduces the risk to taking a short term job to cover the cost of the deductible.

How else might you find insurance coverage? DeAnna tells how she and Al have dealt with the insurance issue:

> *When we first started full-timing we were not able to get health insurance. This was a real problem. Al's head injuries required he be re-evaluated by a neurologist every six months, which was a major expense.*
>
> *Then we spoke to a disabled veteran who suggested that Al check into medical care with the military. He had been in Viet Nam and received a minor injury. That injury did qualify him for health coverage by the VA, which has relieved a lot of financial burden for us. I still have no health insurance, however.*

In Al's case, insurance coverage was there for the asking. Are you eligible for insurance through the VA or some other organization?

If you belong to a group that offers group health insurance, check their cost. Often, group plans are more expensive than other options available to you. Don't overlook the option however, as you may find one that is less expensive.

For those with pre-existing conditions, check individual state insurance regulations. Minnesota does not allow their residents with pre-existing conditions to be turned away. Health insurance may be what ultimately determines your domicile.

Things To Consider

Domicile will have an impact on your insurance costs. With our South Dakota residency we find our health insurance premiums among the lowest compared to our friends. A Texas agent told me they would not be able to beat our insurance cost, as health insurance in South Dakota costs less than in Texas. So, be sure to factor health insurance into your domicile selection.

Contact two or three different companies or agents in each state to find out what health insurance coverage will cost. Be sure to compare apples with apples by asking for the same coverage on each quote.

When you review quotes you should be sure you know what coverage they are providing. Do they cover emergency room visits and surgery or do they just cover the actual hospital stay? What about transplants? Be doubly careful in reviewing the coverage on those plans with low costs. Are they too good to be true?

Janice and Gabby took a different approach to health insurance and, as Janice tells us, learned they did not have the coverage they thought they had.

> *We had a cancer care insurance policy, a hospitalization policy and a couple of other policies, including a Medicare supplement policy, since Gabby qualified for Medicare when we started full-timing.*
>
> *Then one day Gabby had to have surgery, so the bills were submitted to the supplemental policy. We were shocked at the absolutely ridiculous amount they paid. At that point we decided we would be better off to set aside a certain amount, instead of paying them, earn interest on the account, and hope for the best. We then canceled all the policies. While we do not have much in this account so far, we do have enough to pay our medical, dental and pharmacy bills from the account.*
>
> *I do have mixed feelings about what we are doing. If something catastrophic was to happen to me I don't know what we would do. At least with Gabby, Medicare covers just about everything.*

Janice does periodically check health insurance policies, but has yet to find one that meets her needs and fits her budget.

Another consideration is whether you, or the insurance company, picks your doctor. Traditional plans allow you to select the doctor. This gives you the most flexibility. PPO plans often pay a higher percentage of the bills when you go to doctors and hospitals they have selected. HMO's generally require you to go to their doctors, except for emergencies.

Be sure to check the policies you are considering to see if they cover you across the United States. Where can you receive treatment? Is this acceptable? What coverage will you have outside the United States? Does the insurance company pay the bills directly or reimburse you? What conditions must you meet?

HMO's and PPO's may require you return to a specific region for care, if you want to minimize your out of pocket expenses. However, don't rule these plans out based on this alone. They may provide better coverage for the same cost, or less, than other health insurance options. Consider how often you plan to return to the HMO or PPO region. What is the worst medical situation that could happen while you are out of the region? How would you deal with it?

I know several young full-timers who have Kaiser health insurance, an HMO plan. None of them have run into problems obtaining care when out of their region and a couple of these friends have had major health problems. Some have told me they even obtain routine services at Kaiser facilities across the country.

Do not rule out policies with a PPO option either. Many of these policies encourage use of PPO doctors by covering a larger portion of your expenses when you see a PPO doctor. These doctors may only be in a few states and possibly states you do not travel in a great deal. You will have to weigh your out-of-pocket expenses if you are not in their PPO region against what you are willing to pay. Maybe the PPO region includes states you plan to spend a great deal of time in.

Nicole dealt with cancer while on the road and out of her PPO region. She found the best way to find doctors is to contact the PPO provider for the region she is in. They can provide a more complete listing of doctors in the region she is visiting than her own PPO provider can. By doing this she has been able to use her PPO insurance out of her region. If you plan to go with PPO insurance, ask if using PPO doctors in other regions will give you the same coverage as using PPO doctors in your region.

Nicole also learned that you need to know what kind of doctors you should be seeing and ask your PPO provider to provide you with those doctors. The PPO provider is not likely to make life easy and you may have to press them to get what you want and need.

People in Nicole's cancer support group told her how some managed care plans are cut to the bone. For example, they will provide the surgery to remove the cancer and send you on to radiation. However, they will not provide an oncologist unless you insist on one.

Experiences like these could happen with any type of insurance. If your insurance company denies you things you feel you need and have paid for, stand firm, do not back down. It is unfortunate that when we are at our weakest we have to fight our hardest, but this seems to be the way some insurance companies hold their costs down.

When your insurance requires that you be in their region for medical care, emergency medical air transportation insurance may offer a solution. Some of these policies will return you to your region for medical care. You will find these companies advertised in RV magazines. You may even have the opportunity to attend one of their presentations in a campground.

A word of caution. **Be sure you know what you are getting** if you buy one of these policies.

Because of her health situation, Susie bought one of these policies. Then one day her vehicle rolled three times. The paramedics said she was lucky to have survived and felt she may have broken a leg in two places and broken her neck. They loaded her in an ambulance and moved her to an air ambulance that took her to a large city. Evaluation at the hospital determined she had deep bruises and no broken bones. That was the good news.

The bad news came when the bills started coming in. Susie's air ambulance bill was $6,000. She submitted this bill to her emergency medical air transportation insurance company and was denied. It seems they only cover transportation from the hospital to home. So, read the policy and make sure you understand what it covers before you buy.

Finally, does the insurance company you plan to go with have a problem with you traveling full-time? One person with cancer told their agent they would not be back in state for over a year. The agent said their insurance would probably be canceled. This is something you do not want to hear when your life is on the line!

She explained to the agent that while she was out of her state of residency, she still paid taxes in that state, had her will there, registered her vehicle there and voted there. As a result nothing came of the cancellation threat.

Find out up front what requirements the insurance company has regarding residency. You can also check with the state licensing board to determine if there are residency guidelines the insurance companies must follow.

Some states do not allow insurance companies to cancel individuals, but they do allow them to cancel groups. As a result, some companies will make each individual policy a group of its own. This makes it easy for an insurance company to cancel you if you become too expensive for them. Know how the company you are working with handles their groups.

Tips For Selecting Health Insurance

Alice Zyetz wrote an article entitled **Medical insurance for Boomers: Does it really exist?** which was published in the September/October 1996 issue of *Escapees* magazine. Alice included these tips from Dave Loring and Roger Thomas, Escapee RV Club members and licensed insurance agents.

☆ Make sure your policy has lifetime coverage of at least one million dollars per person.

☆ Buy a quality plan that provides you with coverage everywhere you travel.

☆ Find out the insurance company's A.M. Best rating. A.M. Best provides an impartial assessment based on a company's financial stability and ability to pay claims. This information may be found at the library.

☆ Be a shopper. Compare the different plans. Make sure the coverage is in plain English. Ask questions.

☆ Don't pay a "policy origination" fee to an agent. Normally, there might be a small dollar fee to process the paperwork, but nothing else.

☆ If you travel outside the country, be sure you have coverage in the countries you travel in.

☆ Be careful of how the deductible is written. Some companies may have it start over for each new illness. Instead it should start over each year.

☆ Be clear about the definition of pre-existing condition. A good company will describe it as a condition "for which you've received treatment, medication or advice in the past six months." A bad company may define it as a condition that manifested itself for a particular time before the policy began. For instance, consider that you had a new policy commencing on January 1. When you visit a doctor on January 2 you discover you have a cancer that may have been growing for more than six months. The plan could label this a pre-existing condition, even if you had no knowledge of it.

★ There is no free lunch. Insurance is based on statistics. If you have a relatively low premium, you're probably not being covered well. Evaluate the policies closely.

★ When shopping for insurance carefully evaluate the coverage. Is just hospitalization covered or is true all-inclusive medical coverage provided? Is the policy guaranteed renewable and non-cancelable? What is the quality of the company and its claim turnaround time? These are just a few things to consider.

As I said earlier, there are no easy solutions for young full-timers. Do plan to do a great deal of shopping if you want to find a health insurance plan you can live with and afford. Also keep in mind the above information only provides you with a basis for starting your research. You are likely to find other interesting factors to consider as you do your homework.

Obtaining Medical Care On The Road

Seeing a doctor on the road is a challenge on the best day. Our first year on the road Paul, who never goes to doctors, had a problem that required attention. We asked at the campground where to go and they referred us to a hospital clinic. Mistake number one! Never go to the emergency room or a medical clinic tied to an emergency room unless it is an emergency. They charge an arm and a leg for their services!

When we arrived at the hospital clinic Paul asked if they could take care of his specific problem or if there was a specialist in the area he should see. He was assured they could take care of the problem. After seeing him they told him not to worry, the problem would clear up. Paul went home, in pain, with just the name of two specialists in the area.

The next day Paul was in so much pain we tried to contact those specialists. Neither one was available. I then called the state medical board. While they could not make referrals, they did give me several names of doctors to contact.

The doctor Paul saw said the hospital should have taken care of his problem. With a quick procedure, this doctor had Paul more comfortable. The charges—less than the hospital had charged just to see him.

Returning to the hospital, we spoke to the administrator. The discussion ended in a refund of what we had paid. But the story doesn't end here. We soon had a bill from the doctor, whom Paul never saw. Hospitals and doctors bill separately. We sent a letter back explaining we had met with the hospital administrator and they had refunded our money. The doctor's response was to send a refund check for money he had not received. We returned the check.

A year later we were at the opposite end of the country when I went to see a doctor. My experience was also bad. Among other problems I received a bill for lab work. I had obtained a quote for the work I was having done and it did not include the cost of the lab work. I wrote a letter to the doctor's office and they ended up paying the lab bill.

So what have we learned? Always ask for a quote and hold them to the quote. If you receive unsatisfactory treatment, don't pay for it or ask for your money back. If you have a specific problem it is likely to be less expensive and save you time to go right to a specialist.

Carry your medical records with you. If you need to see a doctor it will help them become familiar with your medical history and better serve your needs.

Some say it is easier to get an appointment if you make it in person. It is easy for the receptionist to turn you away when they do not have to look you in the eye. If you are short on funds, discuss payment options with the receptionist when you make the appointment. Before you make the appointment discuss whether you will be able to have a copy of any records, tests and x-rays.

Susie has rheumatoid arthritis and needs lab tests done monthly. Here are her tips for dealing with hospitals, especially on a routine basis.

We are very fortunate as our insurance plan is tied to a network of PPO providers across the country. While I need lab work done monthly, I will not allow my disability to control our travel plans. We are pretty spontaneous and don't know where we are going to be next.

I have 100 percent coverage when I go to a PPO provider, however they tend to be in large cities and we tend to travel in small communities. When I obtain service from a non-PPO provider my insurance pays 80 percent and I pay the other 20 percent. Whether I have full or partial coverage from my insurer I try to keep the costs down.

I have found you really have to shop for medical care to minimize the costs, as they vary a great deal depending on where you are in the country. For example, my husband had a malignant skin cancer removed in the Los Angeles, California area. They charged $1400 for the procedure and pathology. Later we were in Alaska and he had to have exactly the same thing done, however, that time he was only charged $65.

I do carry my records with me and when I have new tests or x-rays done I want those records as well. Some hospitals will balk at this, although if you are paying for them, technically they are yours. Others will say they will mail them to you. Then, once you are gone, it becomes very difficult to obtain them, so I am adamant that I want my records before I leave. If necessary I will pay the hospital myself, then obtain reimbursement from my insurance company.

My rheumatoid arthritis specialist at home has given me two prescriptions for lab work I need to have done. One includes an extra test if I am having a particular problem. It is important to watch for hidden expenses. There have been times I have had lab work done, only to discover when reviewing the bill that tests other than those on my prescription have been done. Once, when my doctor received my lab results, he asked why I had several tests done. I had not asked for these tests and they were not on my lab prescription.

So now I have certain steps I take to avoid these hidden costs and unnecessary tests. While it is a bit of a hassle up front it saves my insurance company and myself money. It also saves me aggravation and time in the long run.

I start by going into a hospital and asking to meet with the hospital administrator, if it is a small hospital, or the head of the billing or insurance department in a larger hospital. These people have different titles in different hospitals. Usually the person at the front desk will assure me they can help me. I tell them I am sure they can, but insist on speaking to one of these people. Often they are not immediately available to see, so I go a day ahead or call ahead for an appointment.

When I meet with this person I have a list of questions I go through with them. I make sure that written or stamped on my admission form is a statement that there will be no other bill or that this is the final payment for lab work. In other words, I want my admission form to state what my costs are and that there will be no additional costs. I tell them if there are any hidden costs that we need to talk about those up front. I ask them if they charge for specific things.

They don't care to go through all this work of course. Some become a little aggravated with the extra work. But if they would not put in hidden costs and if the PPO providers would comply with their PPO contract this process would not be necessary.

When I am not near a PPO I will negotiate the cost of the services being provided. I tell the person I am working with what my insurance will pay and provide them with an 800 number to contact my insurance company to confirm this. Sometimes this takes a day. I explain that if I have my tests done at a hospital that is a PPO provider my expenses will be completely covered, but that I am sightseeing and camping in their area and would prefer they do the tests. I am up front with them that I am bringing them business that I could take elsewhere. Often this negotiation results in the hospital being willing to split my 20 percent of the bill, so instead of paying 20 percent I pay only 10 percent.

While Susie has major health problems her tips are useful even for a one time visit to a hospital.

Dental Care

Obtaining dental care on the road is another concern. My experience in obtaining dental care has been better than with medical doctors. I do, however, try to return to my own dentist once a year.

Many full-timers will go to a Mexican border town for dental work because they believe it is less expensive. Those that do this have indicated it works well for them.

I discussed Mexican dentistry with one dentist in the United States. He told me that Mexico has many good dentists. What one must watch for, however, is the quality of work. For example, while crowns are significantly less expensive in Mexico, the materials used are not as strong and often they will not fit properly around the gums. This results in a shorter life for the crown. The question becomes, are you really saving that much?

One full-timer told us about his visit to a Mexican dentist. He said the dentist had worked on him with gloves covered in blood from other patients. In the United States dentist follow strict hygiene procedures. In Mexico you should make sure the dentist you use has good hygiene procedures, which includes sterilized equipment and even a clean office.

Paul and I decided to check out Mexican dentistry ourselves, so we went to a dentist that friends recommended. I knew I needed to have two fillings replaced. The Mexican dentist told me I needed 5 fillings, but his preference was to put in three fillings and two crowns. I had no crowns, so I was uncomfortable with this advice.

Paul on the other hand has no fillings in his mouth at all. He did have some dimples that had shown up on the exterior of his teeth, however. This dentist said he had brushed through the enamel and recommended fillings on five or six teeth.

Our cost would be over $600 if I had fillings and more if I had the two crowns. We did not have the work performed.

Later that year I had x-rays and a filling in Oregon. That dentist told me I did not need any other work. A few months after that we both visited our own dentist. She replaced the second filling I needed replaced, and also said I did not need any additional work done. In Paul's case she suspected his problem was from grinding his teeth, not from brushing them. She took a wait and see attitude and did nothing.

The cost of my filling at my own dentist was about $15 more than it would have been in Mexico, but I saved the unnecessary cost of a filling and two crowns. In Paul's case we saved the cost of five or six fillings and the ongoing replacement of those fillings every five years for the rest of his life.

We will not use Mexican dentists, but it works for others. Be an informed shopper and do what works best for you.

Finding Doctors and Dentists

The Yellow Pages help you locate doctors and dentists, but do not tell you how good they are. A combination of computer phone directories and mapping programs will help you locate doctors and dentists before you reach a community.

If time allows, ask around to find out who the best doctors and dentists are in a community. You can ask campground employees, visitor's center staff, waitresses or the Wal-Mart clerk. Anyone from the community is likely to have a recommendation. When you get the same recommendation two or three times, chances are you have found a good one.

With luck you will not need to seek out too many doctors and dentists on the road. If you do, add to the tips above by visiting with other full-timers to see how they manage.

13

You Are Going To Do What!

One of the largest hurdles you may face is how your friends and family view your plan to become a full-timer. Most people are likely to support your lifestyle change. However, be prepared for those who may not support your choice.

Telling friends and family what you plan to do can and should be fun. I will never forget the look on one of my co-workers faces when, at the age of 36, I told him I was going to retire and travel full-time. He looked straight at me and in all seriousness said, "You're kidding!" As I shook my head his mouth dropped open. My announcement left him speechless. For four years Paul told his co-workers we were going to become full-timers, but until he set the date no one believed we were really going to do it.

We were lucky, all of our friends were supportive of what we were doing. They had seen us work full-time jobs, plus spend all of our free time building houses. They knew we had worked hard to become full-timers. And while many were envious, some also commented full-timing was something they did not think they could do. Which is okay. Full-timing is definitely not for everyone.

Carol recalls the reaction from her friends and family. "It was amazing! No one said we were crazy. Half of our friends and family members said, 'Oh, I always wanted to do that.'

But none of them ever did. I was amazed at how many people said we were living their dream!'"

"My parents were thrilled to death because they wanted to travel this way part-time, but were not able to do it," Kathy said. "Now they live their dreams through us. My sister, however, was upset because I was leaving my nieces. While Gene [Kathy's husband] was concerned about leaving his Mom, she is glad we are doing what we want to do. Our friends still don't understand, but none of them own an RV either. We get questions like, 'Don't you get tired of traveling?' and 'What do you do all the time?'"

Gene spoke of leaving his Mom. "My Mom was getting older and I felt like I was abandoning her, but everything worked out all right in the end. I call Mom twice a week and often spend the summer near her. I try to remember that it is not like wagon train days when family traveled across the country and never saw the family they left behind again. I can always jump on an airplane and be with Mom in a few hours."

One of the concerns some people express about the full-timing lifestyle is never getting to see their family. Janice says:

They don't realize that it is so much easier to visit family in your RV. You can come and go as you please. You have everything with you. Of course they will say 'Come in the house and sleep in a real bed.' They don't understand I have a real bed and this is my house.

My parents accept what I am doing now, although they didn't always. While they are happy that I am happy, they feel I want to run away from home. They feel this is a result of them doing something wrong when they raised me. Actually, the thing that helped them adjust to my lifestyle shows what a small world we live in.

We were at a Boomerang, a gathering of full-timing baby boomers, and I was visiting with one of the guys at the campfire. We started visiting about where we had worked and it turned out we had both worked for the same company. This led to him asking what my name had been at the time. Since it was before I was married I told him my maiden name.

He got the strangest look on his face and said, 'I know that name, but you are not the person I know.'

I explained that when I left my mother had taken my job and it turned out that was who he knew. We had missed meeting each other by a couple of weeks. It turns out he worked with my mother for a number of years.

The morning after this conversation I called my mother and asked if she remembered him.

She said, 'Well of course. I also remember his darling little wife's name.'

I said well, I met them last night and they are out here full-time RVing as well.

She says, 'You mean that sales engineer is out there RVing with you? Oh, I feel so much better. I'm so glad you are enjoying yourself!'

All of a sudden I had the stamp of approval.

Sue, the "darling little wife" Janice's mother knew, also had some stories to share about family and friends accepting her new lifestyle.

Our children thought it was a great idea. They told us to go ahead and have a great time. My husband's parents do not understand what we are doing, however. They have a hard time understanding that when we are in Arizona they should still send our mail to our mail service in Texas. They also will send stuff for us to family members they believe we will be visiting soon, when actually we may not visit them for months.

One Christmas we were parked in front of my in-laws and staying in their guest bedroom. One evening I said, 'I'm going to go home.'

My mother-in-law looked at me real funny and said, 'Well where are you going?'

I said, 'I'm going home, out to the coach.'

She responded, 'Oh, that's really funny. Ha, Ha.'

I thought, 'No, it's not. It's my home. What's so funny about me going home?' But then she asks questions like, 'Do you have blankets in there? What do you do about food?'

My father is a free spirit and has no problem with our lifestyle. I believe my mother is envious in some ways. She and my father talked about living this lifestyle when they got older. But then their marriage did not last and she seems kind of jealous that we are able to full-time. My mother, of all of our parents, copes the best with writing to us at our mailing service.

Sue goes on to tell about how her best friend reacted to the news of her new lifestyle.

I was very close to my next door neighbor. We were the same size and had even gotten to the point [where] we combined our wardrobes. When I told her about our change in lifestyle she was aghast at the whole thing.

She said, 'You can't leave. You can't move away. I need you here next door.'

I told her she did not need me next door and reminded her that they were planning to move themselves.

She responded, 'Yeah, but that is just a mile or two. That's not a big deal.'

When my friend saw our daughter she told her, 'You have to stop your parents from doing this. This is a terribly, terribly wrong thing for them to do.'

Our daughter told her, 'No, I think it is a great idea.
I think they will have a good time and they should go.'
At this point my friend wrote us off as friends. She
didn't even say good-bye. It really hurt to lose a friend
this way. Our other friends were very supportive. They
are happy to see us when we come to visit and anxious to
hear our adventures.

If you receive the kind of response Sue did from her friend, Jessica's thoughts may help put things in perspective. "My philosophy on life is that you are led to things when you are ready for them. If you are not ready, or you need to have some different experiences, it is not going to appeal to you. That is okay."

"The other surprising thing," Jessica says, "is that you think you have such good friends in your life, but gradually it seems you lose what you have in common with them, unless you can somehow renew your friendships."

Janice looks back to when they started full-timing. "We really did not know what to expect and we kind of thought we would be alone out there on the road. We did not know others full-timed as well. It wasn't long before we found out there are thousands of people living this lifestyle. Acquaintances quickly become friends in this lifestyle because the time before moving on is short, so relationships are intense."

This doesn't mean you don't see the same people again. Often you will see them time and time again, just by coincidence. "We met one young full-timing couple early in this lifestyle," Janice said. "Over the years we have met them in 29 different places, some planned and some just happy coincidence."

Finally, carefully consider when you will announce your plans to become a full-timer at work. While you are excited about your new lifestyle it may be wise to wait until the last minute to share your plans at work.

I had a close call. My immediate boss was wonderful and very supportive of my plans. Upper management was a different story, however. I waited until two months before departure to make my manager aware I would be leaving. His response was to not give more than two weeks notice as he could not protect me longer than that.

After obtaining the money from the closing on our house I felt secure enough to give my two weeks notice. This meant my last day was two days into the new year. My manager wanted me out of the job before the end of the year because he did not want to pay for a month of benefits when I would only be working two days. With people on vacation over the holidays, it would not be possible to make a smooth transfer of my projects. As the lead person on a major program for the company, I had four or five years of background to pass on to others.

It was disappointing to know my manager was willing to throw everything I had done out the window to save a few dollars on benefits. The thing that really hurt, however, was that we had started at the company together. I thought he was my friend, yet he didn't even make an effort to say good-bye.

You can never be prepared for the pain resulting from unexpected reactions like those of Sue's friend and my manager. It is hard to accept these people are not the true friends you believe them to be. On the other hand, you never know when something out of the blue will cause someone to accept your lifestyle, as Janice found with her mother.

Choose the lifestyle that is right for you. While a transition into the full-timing lifestyle may carry some pain, nothing worth going after comes easily. In the next chapter we look at services for the full-timer, including how to stay in touch with friends and family.

14

Services for Full-timers

Services you take for granted today, will become challenging when you become a full-timer. Receiving mail, staying in touch with friends and family when you don't have a phone, paying bills and getting cash are some of the most important items you will have to deal with. Through advancements in technology and the efforts of full-timers on the road before us, most of these challenges are easily overcome. Here's how.

Mail

Mail service is one of those things you cannot live without. Even if your friends and family don't write, you can't avoid a few bills!

The first question you must answer is can you obtain an address for your domicile other than the one you will use for your mail. We currently use a campground address for our domicile and keep a mail forwarding card on file at the post office with our mailing service address. We give the domicile address only for things related to domicile—vehicle licensing, voter's registration, health and vehicle insurance companies, etc. While these agencies and businesses need your domicile address, others, including the state, may send mail directly to your mailing service. The use of a mailing service, and its location, will not affect your domicile.

Some full-timers opt to have a family member or friend forward their mail. They may even have that person pay their bills. This may work for you, but consider it carefully. Mail forwarding is a big responsibility. The person needs to sort the mail and only forward what you want sent. You may need to do this over the phone with them. Then they need to package the mail and take it to the post office to get postage.

How frequently do you plan to have your mail forwarded? What kind of time impact will it have on the friend or family member? Are they reliable? Will they get the mail out when you ask them to send it? Or will you find yourself waiting for them to get around to going to the post office, calling them repeatedly to remind them to send it? Are you going to pay them for the service? How will you reimburse them for the mailing charges? Is the person forwarding the mail planning to move in the future? You sure don't want to have to change addresses again!

Postal regulations allow a private individual to forward your mail. To do this; cross off the address, but **not the name,** and put the new address on the envelope. Also cross off the bar code on the envelope or the letter will come right back to the first address. Then drop it in the mail. This procedure only works on mail with first class postage.

How will you know you have received all your mail? If a letter is lost, how do you know which one? What if the lost letter contained a check, charge card or other important documents?

If you decide to try this method and you have 16 pieces of mail, the person forwarding the mail should label each envelope 1 of 16, 2 of 16, etc. They should also make a list of each envelope, tied to the number assigned, with the return addresses so if the mail is lost you can contact the originator of the letter to have a duplicate of what is lost sent to you.

If having a family member or friend forward your mail sounds risky at best, what other options do you have? In small communities, and I do mean small, you may be able to talk the postmaster into forwarding your mail. Often small community postmasters consider you a friend and look forward to hearing about your travels.

For a while we rented a post office box, using it as our legal address in South Dakota. The only things mailed there came from the state. We filled out a form to have all mail forwarded to our mail service. While we had no problems doing this, it has come to my attention that in 1975 the postal rules made it illegal to rent a post office box simply to forward the mail.

If working with your postmaster is not an option there are mail services available. There are three different types of mail services available:

★ Those offered by RV clubs such as Escapees RV Club, FMCA (Family Motor Coach) and Good Sam.
★ Those offered by businesses specifically for RVers.
★ Those serving businesses and individuals.

All of these services act as an agent for you and by Postal Regulations they must affix new postage to any mail they forward to you.

How do you find these mail services?

★ Check with RV clubs you belong to or are considering joining.
★ Check advertisements in RV magazines.
★ Look in the telephone directory for "Mail Services."

Also ask full-timers what mail service they use. They can tell you who is reliable and answer your specific questions.

Be sure to evaluate different mail services to determine if they can really meet your needs. Also try to determine if they will be around for the duration. Mail services occasionally go out of business, leaving you without mail service. The following is a list of things to evaluate when looking at different mail services. You may have additional questions of your own.

★ What are the fees? We learned about this the hard way after using our first service several months before uncovering hidden charges. Obtain all costs in writing, which any reputable mail service should have no problem giving you. Hang on to this paper in case there are any questions about charges in the future. Fees to ask about include:

- Box rental fees.
- Enrollment fees.
- Annual fees.
- Service fees and how much they are.
- Is the postage charged at the postal service rate or is there a service charge added to the postal service rate?
- Is there a charge for sorting your mail?
- Are there fees for package handling and forwarding? How much are they?
- Can mail be requested by calling an 800 number?
- Does the 800 number service include Alaska, Hawaii, Canada, Mexico and other countries?
- Are there any other charges?
- How will you be notified of increases in fees?
- How does billing take place?

- Must you keep money on deposit with the service? How much?
- Will the service provide you with a statement of expenses? Must you request this or is it automatically provided? How frequently will you receive a statement?
- Can you pay your bill by charge card?
- What forwarding requests will generate additional fees? What are these fees?

☆ When will your mail be forwarded? The same day requested, the next day or are you restricted to your mail only being sent on a certain day of the week?

☆ Can you request your mail be forwarded by phone or must it be requested in writing?

☆ Will mail be sorted and only what you request forwarded? Is this done each time over the phone or can guidelines be kept on file?

☆ Do they accept packages?

☆ What methods of forwarding are available? Priority, overnight, UPS, Federal Express, etc.

☆ If you urgently need one piece of mail will the service determine if it has been received and forward it by the method you request?

☆ If you are in one place for several weeks can you request your mail be sent to a certain address on a set schedule?

When you start using a mail service and pay to receive your mail you will want to quickly eliminate junk mail. You may be able to accomplish this by simply not leaving a forwarding address.

If you have a lot of junk mail to eliminate you may want to use one mail service for a few months, then change to another one. When you sign on with a mail service provider you sign an agreement required by the U.S. Postal Service. This agreement states the U.S. Postal Service will not forward your mail. It does require your mail service provider to forward your mail for six months, at your expense. Once these six months are up your mail service provider will return first class mail to the sender and dispose of all other mail. This means you will only receive mail from those you have notified of your new address.

Once you change to the second mail service be careful who you give your address to and your junk mail should remain at a minimum. When ordering anything, even magazines or financial newsletters, be sure to write across the order card **"No Mailing Lists Please."**

To save on address changes later you might start with two mailing services, a temporary one and a permanent one. Give out the address of the permanent service only to friends, relatives and those who send you bills. Forward the mail from your previous address to the temporary mailing service. After receiving your mail from the temporary service for a couple of months, determine who else needs to receive your permanent mail service address. Then discontinue the temporary service.

Regardless of who sends your mail, you will usually have it sent "General Delivery" to a post office where you plan to be. Often only one post office in a big city will accept general delivery mail and chances are it will be the post office across town from where you are. To minimize confusion and make the experience of obtaining your mail more pleasant, have your mail sent to small town post offices. To determine the closest general delivery post office and its zip code call (800) ASK-USPS (275-8777).

Receiving packages on the road can be a challenge until you figure out the tricks. UPS requires an actual street address. Sometimes you can use the campground office. Local mail service businesses will usually accept a package for you, for a small charge. In a small community you may be doing business in a store and find they will accept a package for you.

Check with carriers like UPS or Federal Express. You may be able to use their address and pick your package up in their office. Our printer needed repair and the warranty only covered shipping by Federal Express. We went right to Federal Express to ship it, then picked it up at their office a few days later.

One couple we know gets their medication by UPS. They normally pick their medication up at the UPS office, however, twice UPS has found them in the desert first. They were in a small community and UPS had a general idea where they might be.

Another person spoke to the UPS office before placing his order. Explaining where he was camping he asked if they would deliver a package. UPS was happy to deliver to his door, using an address of "1 Hitchhiker Trailer," for shipping the package.

Toll-Free Calls? Not From Pay Phones

In 1997 the Communications Act, which requires the FCC to take actions to promote competition among pay phone service providers, went into effect. The intent of deregulating the pay phone service providers (PSP's) is to provide the PSP's with fair compensation for their services and encourage widespread placement of pay phones.

Many campgrounds do not have enough pay phones, so the possibility of more in the future is good news. The bad news comes for the full-timer who uses toll free numbers.

If the billing for a toll free number is in your name, your bill will include a PSP charge each time the number is called from a pay phone. This means, if you use a calling card at a pay phone and dial a toll free access number, you will have a PSP charge added to your bill. If your message service has a toll free number, you will find a PSP charge on your bill for every message left from a pay phone and for every time you call to pick up your messages. Some businesses with a toll free number will block calls coming from a pay phone so they do not have to pay the PSP charges. This means reaching these businesses will be more difficult for you.

The FCC put a rule in place that requires long distance telephone companies to compensate PSP's 28.4¢ for each toll free call placed from a pay phone. This rate is a default rate that may go up or down at any time through an agreement between the long distance companies and the PSP.

Some companies face additional costs to process the PSP charges. In this case they will bill you more than 28.4¢. This additional cost may push your PSP charges as high as 35¢ per call. Before signing up for a toll free service that you will pay the bill for, ask what the PSP charges are. Some companies do not have a way to track the calls from pay phones. In this case you should know how they bill you for the PSP charges.

Message Service

When Paul and I first hit the road one concern our parents had was how to reach us if there was an emergency. We thought we had the bases covered with a mailing service that would take messages for us. We would keep the mailing service notified of where we were staying and they could pass this information on if necessary. We would also provide our itinerary to our parents.

Ha! That was back in the days when we did everything on a schedule. It did not take long to learn we could not live with an itinerary. We would get someplace and want to spend more time or not like another place and want to move on sooner. Then came the day we mailed our parents our itinerary and all the mail sent from the campground that day was never received. It took two weeks to determine that our itinerary was lost. Of course, by then our plans were different anyway.

Our mail service had never taken messages before and we found it did not work for us. Now what? We finally decided to call one of our parents each week, telling them where we were and where we planned to be. If one of our parents needed to reach us and they did not have the latest itinerary they would call the other parents to track us down.

It became a hassle to spell the names of towns and provide addresses and phone numbers over the phone. It also generated big phone bills on our calling card as we found ourselves gabbing away about things that could be shared in letters.

In our second month on the road we bumped into someone that was using a message service. They explained how it worked and how affordable it was, so we signed up. That particular message service has gone by the wayside, but we have since learned there are many message service options available.

On our message service we leave a greeting that tells family and friends where we are staying. Our family and friends can leave us a message to get in touch with us and in case of an emergency they immediately know where to reach us. Campgrounds will normally deliver a message to your door if there is a real emergency, otherwise they will post the message for you to pick up. Our friends on the road can and have found us from our greetings. What a wonderful surprise to be someplace where you know no one and have friends knock on your door!

One decision you will have to make is whether you will use a toll or toll-free number for people to call. Some people feel their message service is like their home phone, which was a toll number in traditional life. Others do not want to discourage phone calls by forcing friends and family to pay to speak to a machine. They believe this results in not hearing from or connecting with friends and family, so they use a toll-free number. Most full-timers we know have chosen the toll-free option.

To find a message service check the phone book, check with phone companies, check RV magazines, check with mail forwarding services and visit with full-timers in campgrounds.

There are several types of message services:

- ☆ Automated services that record the voice and play it back on demand.
- ☆ Non-automated services where a message is dictated to a person who writes it down or places it in a computer to be read to you later.
- ☆ Semi-automated services where the message is left on an answering machine, written down later and read to you when you call in.

Things to keep in mind when deciding which type of service to go with include:

- ☆ Is hearing the voice of the person leaving the message important to you? Sometimes the actual voice can tell you how critical a message is.
- ☆ Will you get enough detail if the message is dictated to someone or recorded and written down later?
- ☆ If a person takes the message or reads them back will they make the experience a pleasant one?

We started with a service where the message was dictated, typed into a computer, then read back to us. The service providers made this a pleasant experience. However, we found these messages were often less detailed than we currently receive on an automated voice message service. Questions to ask when selecting a non-automated or semi-automated service include:

★ Can messages be left or picked up 24 hours a day, 7 days a week?

★ What are the charges?

★ Are there PSP charges?

★ How long a message can be left?

★ How many messages can be left in a month?

★ How many times a month can you pick up messages?

★ Can a greeting be left?

★ Can messages be left on your service for a specific person, other than yourself, to pick up?

★ How many people are on staff to take messages and read them back to you?

★ Are the messages recorded on paper or in a computer? If in a computer, how many hours was the computer down in the last year?

★ Are messages left on an answering machine and written down later? How long until a message is written down?

When you compare automated services the following are some of the questions you may want to ask.

★ Can you leave a greeting?

★ Is there a monthly charge? Does this charge include any minutes of usage?

★ How much is the per minute charge?

★ When do the charges start accruing?

    ♦ Is listening to the greeting included in the chargeable time?

    ♦ Is leaving a greeting included in the chargeable time?

    ♦ Does the chargeable time include both leaving and picking up the message?

- For example, if there is a 20¢ per minute charge and you have a one minute message will you be charged once (20¢), or will you be charged for both someone leaving the message and you picking up the message (40¢)?
- Will you receive a statement? What information will the statement include?
- Can you pay your bill by charge card? Will they automatically bill your charge card?
- Can you put a maximum dollar amount on your monthly message service?
- Is there an enrollment fee?

☆ What additional charges are there?

☆ Is access to the service via a toll or toll-free number?

- If toll-free is it good in Canada, Mexico, Alaska and Hawaii?
- If toll-free are there any charges associated with use of the number?
- Are there PSP charges?

☆ Can you get your own personal phone number or will it be a general number with an access code?

☆ How long a greeting can you leave? Time a typical greeting you would leave to determine how much time you need.

☆ How long can the message be? A minute is often too short, but two minutes will meet most of your needs. To prevent running up a huge bill you may want a cap on the length of messages.

☆ Is there a limit on how many messages you can receive or retrieve in a month?

☆ Can you save your messages? This feature is useful when you do not have paper and pencil to write down information in the message.

✭ Can you forward messages and responses to others using your same service?

✭ How many times and for how long has the service been down in the last year?

If this type of message service is not ideal for you there are other options for receiving messages. Having a relative take messages for you is one option. You must decide if that relative and everyone in the household can and will take a detailed message. Will you pay them for this service?

Often relatives taking messages will not have a note pad by the phone or are not willing to write down the details. As a result, I will seldom spend the money to call and leave a message for people whose families take the messages.

Another option might be to have a separate phone line going into a friend or relative's home. You can either attach an answering machine to this line or use the local phone company's answering service. The number for this line can be a toll or toll-free number. The drawback with this method is it will probably cost more than having a message service.

Useful Tools

There are two tools you will find useful when making phone calls or picking up messages on the road. One is a "phone amplifier," which Radio Shack sells. This is a hand held speaker box with a volume control that attaches to the hand set of a phone with a suction cup. It allows a second person to listen to a phone conversation or messages.

The second tool is a small tape recorder. Plug the phone amplifier cord into the microphone jack, on the recorder, and you are able to record your messages. This allows you to delete your messages right away, write down important information when you get home and not be charged to pick the messages up a second time. It also allows your spouse to hear the messages. Radio Shack sells this cord separately also.

Pagers also provide a way to receive messages. Some pagers show text, which is entered by a person with the proper computer equipment. These messages are very short. Some message services will page you when a message is received. You then go to a phone to pick up the message. Some pagers work nationwide, but like cellular phones, there are areas the signal will not reach. At this time very few full-timers have found pagers to be a solution for their communication needs. As technology changes, this too may change.

Calling Cards

Rates vary a lot with calling cards. Since the phone industry changes daily we will just take a quick look at how to select a calling card.

Many phone companies offer calling cards. Call the big name companies as well as those listed under "long distance carriers" in the phone book. You may also want to check with these companies to see what message service options they offer. We have found some of the best calling card rates in brochures we picked up at campgrounds.

Organizations like the Escapees RV Club, Good Sam and Coast to Coast also offer calling cards. You may be a member of another organization that offers calling cards as well. Before signing on with one of these organizations find out who their carrier is and what rate they offer. Then check directly with the carrier to see if you can get a calling card for less from them. One of our calling cards is from the same carrier as one of the organizations mentioned above and by getting it directly from the carrier we save several cents a minute. Obviously some of these organizations make a profit on calling cards.

Remember to ask full-timers what they use for their calling card. These people have the time and often take pride in finding the best deal possible.

You may also want to consider having more than one calling card. The same goes for charge cards. Paul and I carry different charge cards and calling cards. This way we always have a back up if our charge card or calling card are lost or stolen. This minimizes the inconvenience of losing these cards.

When you speak with calling card providers the following are just some of the questions you may wish to ask.

★ What is the per minute charge? Do you bill in seconds or minutes?
★ Is the billing flat rate or based on the time of day you place the call?
★ Is there a monthly minimum?
★ Is there a charge for the calling card?
★ Is there a charge for using the card at a pay phone?
★ What other charges are there?
★ How long after the call does billing take place? It may take a membership organization a couple of months to process the bill for your calling card with them.
★ What information is on the bill?
★ How long do you have to pay the bill?
★ Can the billing date be changed to coordinate with when you receive your mail?
★ Do they offer a service where you can have an 800 number put in to the numbers you call frequently?

Another option is pre-paid calling cards, which are available in many stores. Things to check here include the cost per minute and any flat charges per call. Some of these cards are only good for a limited time. If you don't use it within that time your money is gone. Your money is also gone if you lose the card. Remember, most prepaid calling cards will deduct the PSP charges from your time, reducing the minutes available on the card.

Cellular Phones

Cellular phones are becoming increasingly attractive to full-timers. As of 1998 AT&T's One Rate made it possible to have a cellular phone with nationwide service, no roaming charges and no long distance charges. The drawback is you have to buy a set amount of time and the lowest amount of time is more than many full-timers need.

Sprint, GTE, Bell South and Bell Atlantic all offer nationwide service providing you are in the right community. Be sure you know what nationwide coverage means before you buy. Some are only nationwide in cities and communities where the provider has service. You will need to have an address in the community where you plan to get the phone, which may increase the challenge of signing up for the service. Another thing to check is what the state taxes are on phone service. I have heard some states charge as much as $20 on a $90 phone bill.

Even if these rates are too expensive you may still want to carry a cellular phone for emergencies. You do not have to have cellular phone service to call "911." You can also use your charge card to place phone calls from a cellular phone. However, keep in mind this type of cellular phone call can be very expensive.

Other Phone Options

Are there phone numbers you plan to call frequently? Some companies will assign a toll-free number to your frequently called numbers. Your cost for these calls is normally less than your calling card rate. Toll-free numbers also save dialing all the numbers on your calling card for these frequent calls. There is no impact on the phone service of the person you are calling.

Be sure to check the rates before using these toll-free numbers when you are out of the country. Sometimes a calling card is less expensive. You may also have to activate a toll-free number for use out of the country before you can use it.

Internet Access

While it is rapidly changing, it can still be a challenge to access the Internet while on the road. The good news is campgrounds are starting to put in pay phones with RJ jacks and some have phone lines to the sites. Others will allow you to use their phone line if you are using a toll free number and only picking up e-mail.

With the new cellular phone rates cellular phones are becoming an economical way to access e-mail. You will need a special modem that works with the individual cellular phone, if you plan to access the Internet this way.

If you plan to use the Internet or e-mail you may want a laptop computer. This gives you the flexibility to go to the communication link. Some Internet services allow you to upload and download e-mail in a couple of minutes. There are also rates for people who only use e-mail. Look for phone lines to access the Internet at stores where you are making purchases, copy centers, visitor centers, hotels, truck stops, etc. Be creative in finding a phone line.

There is now a service called PocketMail for those who just want to access e-mail on the road. The device to access PocketMail has a keyboard to type messages in, although the keyboard is small. One of the devices you can buy does have a limited ability to transfer data back and forth with your computer. The neat thing about the devices for accessing this service is you just hold it up to a phone handset. No cables!

The Internet has become a key research tool at many libraries. Some will restrict use to only those with a library card, but most do not have this restriction. You simply go to the library and sign up for Internet time, generally a half hour or an hour. If no one is waiting to use the Internet, you usually can stay on the computer longer. We have found many libraries do not allow e-mail access on their computers.

Colleges and universities are another place to look for Internet access. Many communities have Internet cafes, where for a fee you can use their computers to access the Internet.

Getting Money

Obtaining money on the road can be easy, providing you set it up in advance. Writing checks is not a feasible option since many businesses will not take an out-of-state, or even an out-of-community check.

Make sure the financial institution you deal with offers both a debit card and an ATM card. Generally these features will be on the same card. If you already have an ATM card check it for a VISA® or MasterCard logo. If it has one of these symbols your card has both features.

The ATM card allows you to obtain money from thousands of ATM machines around the world. Only once in six years have we found an ATM machine hard to come by and then it was only 15 miles away. Unfortunately, the use of these cards often carries charges from the individual's financial institution and from the institution who owns the ATM. These charges are the same regardless of the amount withdrawn, so large, infrequent withdrawals will cost less than small frequent withdrawals.

At this time you may be able to get around these charges if you do not mind spending a little time standing in line. Most banks will give you a cash advance on your debit card and not charge you for the service. Before doing this check with your own financial institution to see if they charge for cash advances.

Some people will use their debit card, instead of a charge card, so they do not have to deal with charge card bills. This simplifies life if you are not able to receive your mail at the right time for billing. If you use a charge card, call the charge card company and schedule your billing period to align with when you expect to receive mail. Charge card and calling card companies are normally happy to adjust your billing date to meet your needs.

Another way to handle money on the road is to use traveler's checks. Most places charge for traveler's checks. However, since they are insured, you can recover your money if the checks are lost or stolen.

While the everyday services we take for granted are a bit of a challenge on the road, they are becoming easier to obtain. If you do your homework and have the necessary services in place when you hit the road, your transition into full-timing will go smoothly.

Don't be too concerned about getting just the right service providers arranged in advance. Technology is changing rapidly. Also, as you visit with other full-timers you will learn of new options. Your service needs are even likely to change with time, so expect to make changes down the road.

On the Road

15

Selecting Your Yard: Determining Your Style of Camping

Personality and lifestyle often determine where a person lives. Some choose to live downtown in a large city to be near the action. Others live in the suburbs where malls and grocery stores are convenient, there is less traffic and they know their neighbors. Those who wish to escape the hectic life move to the country or the mountains for the tranquil beauty.

The same process takes place when full-timers select their yard on the road. Some want interaction with others and a campground umbilical cord—water, electric, sewer and cable hook-ups. Others prefer the tranquillity of nature, so they put money into their wheel estates, adding solar panels, inverters and even wind generators, which make them completely self-sufficient. Most full-timers enjoy a variety of yards.

Types of Yards

There are many yards for full-timers to select from:

Private Campgrounds

These campgrounds are privately owned. Some are very expensive full hook-up resorts that offer golf, tennis and many other activities. Others may be nothing more than a dirt site that may or may not have partial hook-ups. Most private campgrounds fall between these extremes, often offering swimming pools and sometimes a clubhouse. Private campgrounds all have a fee.

Public Campgrounds

These include BLM (Bureau of Land Management), National Forest Service, Corps of Engineers, national, state, county and town campgrounds. The services at these campgrounds range from absolutely nothing to occasionally full hook-ups. Some of these campgrounds may be free, while others will charge a fee. Many of these campgrounds are in beautiful areas and generally RVs park further apart than in private campgrounds.

Organization Campgrounds

Escapees RV Club has full hook-up and boondocking sites at their Rainbow Parks and SKP Co-Ops. Most of the Rainbow Parks offer long term lease lots, while all the SKP Co-Ops offer lots for sale. Fraternal organizations, such as the Moose and Elks, often have campgrounds or a place for members to park at their lodges nationwide. The military has campgrounds that retired military personnel can use. Do you belong to another organization that has campgrounds?

Membership Campgrounds

In the past these parks have been for members only. Now some are open to the public. These parks generally have a swimming pool, club house and laundry facilities. Some also offer planned activities and meals. To join a membership campground you generally pay a one time fee, with annual dues thereafter. Belonging to a membership park may make you eligible to join other organizations such as Coast to Coast or RPI (Resorts Parks International), which gives you guest privileges at campgrounds across the nation. AOR (American Outdoor Resorts), CCA (Campers Club of America) and Passport America are just a few of the other membership organizations you will come across. We will focus on Coast to Coast, RPI and the parks affiliated with these organizations. However, what we discuss should be considered when evaluating other membership organizations.

Boondocking (camping with no hook-ups)

Boondocking may be a function of getting from one place to another, a need to save money or just a desire to enjoy nature. Some will boondock at a rest stop, truck stop or a Wal-Mart parking lot while they get a few hours sleep as they make a quick trip across country. Those who enjoy nature and being by themselves will find a mountain stream or a southwestern cactus to park next to for several weeks or months. In the past, boondocking has been free, making it easier for those on tight budgets to manage. That is changing as the government and others start to charge for the use of some boondocking sites. Other full-timers are a great resource when it comes to finding wonderful boondocking sites. Boondocking sites may include BLM land, National Forest, state and county parks, property you own, as well as driveways of friends and family. Creativity is the key to great boondocking sites.

Property Sitting

These opportunities may range from boondocking to full hook-ups. Property sitting can include homes, ranches, construction sites, resorts off season, and other types of businesses.

Camping Discounts

Many organizations offer discounts to their members. Good Sam, Escapees RV Club and Coast to Coast are among the organizations offering discounted camping for their members at private or public campgrounds.

Fairgrounds

Fairgrounds often have campgrounds. Services will vary from boondocking to full hook-ups. Avoid these campgrounds at fair time since the sites are booked far in advance. Sometimes several years in advance!

Does the Yard Meet Your Needs?

What you plan to do in an area will help determine where you want your yard. If your options are to stay at an expensive campground nearby or commute from a less expensive campground, which will you do? We found we prefer to spend the money rather than commute.

Would you like to participate in planned activities or do you have plenty to keep you busy? Do you like to be by yourself or do you prefer people around? How much and what kind of interaction would you like with others?

What type of neighbors will you find in a particular campground? People staying in private campgrounds may be passing through the area, on vacation, camping with friends and family or may even be permanent in the park. Those on vacation are likely to have an agenda that includes twice as much as they can accomplish. The permanent people in the park will have an established lifestyle and friends. These neighbors will have little interest in visiting, playing games or making new friends.

When you stay in an organization-sponsored campground, you and your neighbors have your membership in common. This provides a basis for building wonderful friendships.

Throughout the year membership campgrounds are full of full-timers, generally seniors. In the summer families use membership campgrounds as well.

You may choose to boondock alone or with friends. During the winter, communities of boondockers are found near places like Quartzsite and Yuma, Arizona or Niland, California. Boondockers stay in these areas for weeks or months at a time. Some of these areas do require a BLM permit.

The yard you select will have an impact on how many other young full-timers you are able to hook-up with. We stayed in membership campgrounds our first 22 months on the road and can count on two hands the number of people we met near our age. We enjoyed meeting and building friendships with seniors during that time. Then we met up with a group called Boomers and realized we missed friendships with people our own age. The Boomers also made us aware of how many young full-timers are on the road.

After visiting with many Boomers we came to understand why we had met so few full-timers our own age. The majority spend the winter in southern Arizona where there are plenty of boondocking sites and the weather is normally warm. We were not boondockers at the time and had only briefly passed through Arizona the first winter.

Independence runs high among young full-timers. Besides wanting to stand on their own feet, they enjoy a new found freedom from "stuff." This is not to say they go without. Many carry their satellite dish, computer and cellular phone with them. However, they do not take along the "stuff" that never gets used.

We also learned most young full-timers wheel estates are very comfortable without an umbilical cord tied to it. And with their limited budgets, they prefer to spend their money on dinner out or entertainment, rather than campgrounds.

What type of yard do you prefer? As you travel it is likely your type of yard will change. We started out staying mostly in membership campgrounds. Now we like to boondock, but we also go into private campgrounds for longer stays.

Don't be afraid to try different types of yards. You may just surprise yourself with wonderful new experiences!

16

Membership Campgrounds:
To Buy or Not to Buy

If you are considering joining a membership campground there are a few things you should know so you find the best deal possible.

Why Campgrounds Offer Memberships

First you might wonder what motivates campgrounds to join membership systems. Campgrounds are able to raise money up front by selling memberships. Affiliations with organizations like Coast to Coast and RPI enhance the membership package these parks have to offer potential buyers. The opportunity for the camper to visit hundreds of campgrounds across the United States, Mexico and Canada, for a small nightly fee, increases what people are willing to pay to belong to a membership campground. In addition, membership parks can count on the income from annual dues. Non membership campgrounds, on the other hand, must *hope* they have a good camping season.

Who Owns the Campground?

If you decide to join one or more campground organizations, like Coast to Coast or RPI, remember they do not own the campgrounds. They are only a clearinghouse to bring campers and campgrounds together. In exchange, they receive annual dues and some receive a portion of the nightly fee charged.

Do not confuse these organizations with membership parks that have multiple campgrounds, such as Thousand Trails, NACO and Western Horizons. Some of these "home park systems" offer camping across the United States by themselves. They may or may not have an affiliation with one or more campground organizations.

What's in it for You?

Why would you want to join a membership campground or park system? A home park in an area you plan to visit frequently may save you money. Joining one or more campground organizations may open the door to inexpensive camping in many of the places you travel. Most of the campgrounds affiliated with campground organizations have desirable amenities—like swimming pools, clubhouses and Laundromats.

We have noticed membership campgrounds often offer a camaraderie you do not find in other campgrounds. People visit with neighbors like they are long time friends. When you put your vehicle hood up the men come running to help troubleshoot your problem. Many of the occupants of membership campgrounds are full-timers who enjoy visiting and learning from others.

As we traveled from one membership campground to the next we noticed many of our neighbors were our neighbors in the previous campground. We were living in a moving community, where our yard changed weekly, but many of our neighbors remained the same for several weeks at a time.

Selecting a Home Park

Before selecting a home park for the first time visit several membership campgrounds. This will give you an opportunity to see how they work and determine what you get for your money. Membership campgrounds are all different and some are a much better value. Most membership campgrounds are happy to have you stay for a couple of nights to become familiar with their park. In exchange they will probably ask you to attend a sales presentation.

If you prefer to visit the parks you have an interest in, without listening to a sales presentation, Coast to Coast has a program they call Hook Up To Luxury For Less. In this program you buy coupons to visit many of the parks within the Coast to Coast system. Be sure to ask if the parks you wish to visit are in this program before buying the coupons.

Do you really expect to use the home park, home park system or visit campgrounds in the membership system? There is no point in throwing your money away on something you will not use, although it is surprising how many do.

We considered buying into one home park system until we looked at the locations of their parks. The parks were either not where we would be traveling or other campgrounds in the area could meet our needs. So why spend the money?

Another thing to consider before buying into a membership park is how much you plan to use it. If you do not plan to visit your home park, you will not have a concern about restrictions on your visits to the park. However, if you plan to visit family in the area every summer, or you want to winter in your home park, you should look closely at restrictions pertaining to the length of stay.

Some home parks have rules that limit your stay and require that you be out of the park for a certain period before returning. Others may allow you to "buy" your time out so you never have to leave. Some may charge you for any stay. Then there are those parks that only allow you to visit a set number of days or weeks per year. Other parks may charge a monthly or seasonal fee for a stay of several months. Home park systems may or may not allow you to go right to another park in their system without a week out. The combinations are endless, so know your needs and check it out when you shop for a membership park.

If you plan to join a campground organization you should verify the membership campground you are considering has an affiliation with the organization you plan to join. You will also want to be sure the campground organization offers what you need. For example, Coast to Coast and RPI allow members to stay two seven-day periods per year in each host campground. Coast to Coast requires these seven-day periods be separated by at least 30 days, while RPI only requires they be separated by seven days. Coast to Coast also has a program called Coast Deluxe, which offers longer stays. Fewer parks participate in this program. For you to belong to the Coast Deluxe program, your home park must participate in the program.

With Coast to Coast or RPI another thing to consider is their 125 air mile rule. This means you cannot use your Coast to Coast or RPI privileges at other parks within 125 air miles of your home park. Some parks have reciprocal privileges with the parks within this region. If you plan to spend much time in the area around your home park, determine if your home park has reciprocal privileges with the other parks. If they do, this may work out very well for you. If they do not, you may want to select a home park outside the 125 air mile radius so you can visit the parks in the area you wish to spend time.

Doing Your Homework

You will be in control of the sales presentation if you go in with a pre-determined plan. Consider the following when preparing for the sales presentation.

Know if you are ready to buy or not. A salesperson will make their campground membership sound like something you cannot live without. Also, be prepared for a hard sell and be pleasantly surprised if you get a soft sell instead.

No matter what you hear, leave the sales presentation and evaluate the package overnight. Frequently salespeople will tell you, "This offer is only good today." When you hear this a siren should go off in your head, telling you to look for something amiss. Why do they need to push so hard? Do you really believe they will give up a sale tomorrow if you return and offer to pay their price? What kind of business person would throw away a sale? Stand firm and don't let your emotions interfere. If you decide to buy and they tell you the price has gone up, walk away. Salespeople are hungry. When they recognize you won't back down, they will come back with the original price.

After you hear a sales presentation, ask to take the contract home and review it overnight. Do this even if you do not plan to buy. It will give you a chance to become familiar with membership campground contracts.

We once asked to take a contract home and the salesman said no, so we walked out. In less than 15 minutes the salesman was at our door handing it over. The next day we told him we did not want the membership. He complained that nine out of ten people who read the contract did not buy a membership. Chances are, like us, they found clauses in the contract that were unacceptable.

Here are a few things to look for in contracts, based on our experiences and those shared by others. To legally protect yourself, seek an attorney's advice before signing a contract.

There are several things to look for in membership campground contracts. One thing is a clause that says something like, the park can change anything at anytime. A clause like this means exactly that—the owners of the campground can change anything at any time. For example, they could change how often you can visit your home park and how long you can stay. Or they could start charging you to visit your home park. There is nothing you can do to prevent these changes if a clause like this is in the contract. This does not mean you should not buy that membership. If there are certain things you do not want to change, try writing in a clause that will satisfy your concern. Be sure you and the campground representative initial any changes to the contract.

What does the contract say about severing your tie to the park? Does it say you must pay your dues for life unless or until you sell your membership? Do you have to get the park's approval before selling the membership? Be sure the contract is clear on how to sever your ties with the campground and make sure you are comfortable with the terms.

Is the salesperson telling you the truth? One way to test this is to see if what they have told you is in the contract. If not, write it in. This includes things that may not be important to you today, but could be important to you in the future. If they will not sign a contract that includes their major selling points you would be wise to pass on that membership.

Is the membership campground you are considering part of a multiple home park system? If so, what privileges do you have at other parks in the system? And how soon after leaving one park in the system can you visit another? Is all of this spelled out clearly in the contract?

A salesperson told Tom and Nicole that the home park system they were buying into would be establishing parks in the western half of the United States. They wrote this into their contract. When the parks did not appear they were able to cancel their membership and recover most of their investment.

By visiting with members before the sales presentation you can learn what the park considers negotiable before you strike a deal. You may also learn if a park or park system is about to go under. Ask the members if they wrote any special clauses into their contract or if they know other members who did. What were those clauses? This is also a good time to find out what they paid for their membership.

We have spoken to people who bought a membership with another couple. They share the usage, up front cost and dues. There was no limit that only one couple could use the membership at a time. While this is a wonderful deal, be aware that it is a sign of an unhealthy campground or home park system. We know two couples who bought one of these memberships. By the time they made it to their first home park many of the campgrounds in the system were closed.

The contract should state how long you can stay, how long you must be out of the park before returning and how often you can visit the park. If this is not in the contract, write it in.

Be sure the contract states the annual dues. Are they frozen? If not, make sure the contract states the maximum increase per year. Look for any clauses that state you may be responsible for special assessments, such as a new electrical system for the park, along with your dues. Are you willing to be responsible for major expenses?

Another item to add to the contract is a statement such as: *Owner will provide a Coast to Coast and/or RPI letter of release, at no charge to member, on request.* If you decide to change home parks in the future, Coast to Coast and RPI will require a letter of release from your current home park before transferring you to a new home park. Often parks will charge you for this letter, some as much as $500.

You will find a contract check list in *Appendix D* to help you with this process.

The Good and the Bad

As with anything you buy, there are good and bad campground memberships. I wish I could tell you these parks and their sales staff are honest, but some have never heard of honesty. That doesn't mean you should rule out membership campgrounds. While we are on our third home park in six years, we continue to feel membership campgrounds are a good value and meet our needs. You just need to be aware of the potential problems so you can ferret them out before you spend your money.

Often you will find campgrounds encouraging volunteers to help make the park better. In the majority of cases this improves the RVing experience. However, when you hear a membership campground say there is not enough money to run the park, so we need volunteers to help, it is time to start asking questions. This is a signal that the membership campground is in financial trouble or that they are pocketing your money instead of putting it back into the campground where it was intended to go. Take a minute to run the numbers yourself. You will probably find the annual dues alone provide as much money, per site, as many non membership parks receive in a year. Most membership parks have a goal to sell 10 memberships per site. Let's assume a membership park does sell 10 memberships per site and collects dues of $200 per membership. On an annual basis the membership campground would make $2,000 per site.

10 memberships x $200 per site = $2,000

A non membership campground that charges $20 per night, has a season of four months and an 80 percent occupancy would make $1,920 per site annually.

$20 x (120 nights x .80) = $1,920

Realistically, few parks will have 100 percent occupancy, or a season of more than four months. If a campground has a long season and high occupancy, they will not have an interest in becoming a membership campground. They can make more money on their own.

So, how do you protect yourself from a bad or financially unstable membership campground? Visit with members of the park you are considering joining. Do they talk about the park being run by volunteers? Be sure to ask why volunteers are running the park. This is not always a bad sign. Do members talk about increasing dues or decreasing services? What do they feel the campground's financial position is? Are members being offered lifetime memberships? Any of these can indicate financial difficulties.

How many memberships per site is the park selling? Ten memberships per site is typical. This allows the campground to make enough money on dues to operate. You may have difficulty getting into your home park if they sell more than 10 memberships per site. If you plan to visit your home park frequently, ask the members if they have trouble getting into the park.

Is the park in good standing with Coast to Coast and RPI? We bought our first membership and learned the hard way that Coast to Coast had the park in suspension. As a result, Coast to Coast would not issue us a membership card.

If the salesperson tells you they own the park, you may want to check with the county to see who owns the property. Did the salesperson tell you the truth? You may also check with the county to see if the taxes are being paid. If not, shop for another home park. We have never checked things out with a third party. We do, however, protect ourselves by buying low cost memberships so we do not lose much if we make a bad deal. Because many membership parks go out of business or drop out of affiliated membership organizations you should make sure you can recover your costs in one year, two at the most.

Your Costs

Your costs will vary depending on the membership campground you join. Most membership campgrounds charge a fee to become a member. This fee can run from zero to several thousand dollars.

Most parks have annual dues that run from $100 to $400 a year, although they could be more. We decided to take a risk this time and joined a campground that has no dues. Instead they charge their members the same nightly fee they charge Coast to Coast and RPI guests.

We recognize this park cannot survive for the long term this way. As a new park they needed funding to establish the campground. We anticipate they will increase the cost to become a member and implement annual dues once the park is complete. Sometimes it is worth the risk to get in on the ground floor.

If you join a campground organization there will be annual dues for each organization you join. Coast to Coast's annual dues for 1999 were $70 while RPI's annual dues for 1999 were $55.

Finally, there is a nightly fee to visit a host park. The 1999 fees were six dollars per night for Coast to Coast and five dollars per night for RPI parks.

It is not necessary to have memberships in multiple campground organizations. Often the same campgrounds belong to more than one campground organization. At first, when you leave the traditional lifestyle behind, you may find you are more comfortable having a set itinerary. During this phase you will probably want reservations at campgrounds. Most RPI host parks require reservations and RPI has a good reservation system to accommodate this.

Eventually most full-timers prefer not to travel by a schedule, but as the mood strikes them. If you reach this point you will want a campground organization where you don't need to make reservations. This has been the case with most Coast to Coast host parks.

Some people have told us they can never get into a Coast to Coast park. In six years on the road we have only found four Coast to Coast parks that were unable to accommodate us. In all four cases they were full. We believe the reason we have been successful while others have had difficulties has to do with our approach to the system.

When we call a park for reservations and they tell us they have no space, we generally will drive up anyway and, with one exception, have always gotten space for a few days this way. We also make sure we have reservations before going to a tourist area during peak season. In the winter we avoid Coast to Coast and RPI parks in the south.

Finally, before you buy into a membership campground, you will want to analyze what it will really cost you. Consider the number of nights you will use your home park and host parks. If you do not know your travel plans yet, run your numbers with several different combinations of home park and host park stays. This will help you determine the number of nights it will take for you to feel the investment is worthwhile.

Let's look at two examples, one for an expensive membership and one for an inexpensive membership. We will base our decision on total investment so we will look at cumulative costs. We will then convert these figures to nightly costs for easy comparison with other camping options.

The first calculation is for an expensive home park system with multiple home parks. The original cost is $3,000 and the annual dues are $200.

First Year Costs

Initial Investment	$3,000
Home Park Dues	$ 200
Total	$3,200

Nights spent in the home park system   100

Cost per night at the end of the first year:

$3,200/100 nights = $32.00/night

Second Year Costs

Investment in first year	$3,200
Second Year Home Park Dues	$ 200
Total	$3,400

Annual nights in the home park system	100
Total nights first and second year	200

Cost per night at end of second year:

$$\$3,400/(200 \text{ nights}) = \$17.00/\text{night}$$

Now let's assume you also plan to use host parks. For this example we will assume dues are paid to both Coast to Coast and RPI.

Annual Membership Dues

Coast to Coast	$ 70
RPI	$ 55
Total	$125

Assuming you spend 100 nights per year in a host park at six dollars a night your costs go up $1,200 for the first two years.

$$200 \text{ nights x } \$6/\text{night} = \$1,200$$

Your nightly costs at the end of the second year are now:

$$\frac{(\$3,400 + (2 \times \$125) + \$1,200)}{(200 \text{ home park nights} + 200 \text{ host park nights})} = \$12.13 / \text{night}$$

Depending on your typical, non-membership, camping expenses, a nightly cost of $17.00 may not justify joining a membership campground system. If however, you can use both home and host campgrounds, joining a membership system may be justified.

What happens if you invest less up-front in a home park? In this case we assume an initial investment of $500. Since less expensive memberships are generally single parks you are not likely to stay in the home park for as many nights a year. Let's assume you stay 30 nights a year in your home park. All other figures remain unchanged.

Second Year Costs

Initial Investment	$500
Dues: first and second year	$400
Total	$900

Nights spent in the home park per year   30

$900 / (2 years x 30 nights) = $15.00

Again we add membership dues for Coast to Coast and RPI.

Annual Membership Dues

Coast to Coast	$ 70
RPI	$ 55
Total	$125

Spending 100 nights per year in a host park at six dollars a night, increases your costs by $1,200 for the first two years.

200 nights x $6 / night = $1,200

Now your nightly costs work out to:

$$\frac{(\$900 + (2 \times \$125) + \$1,200)}{(60 \text{ home park nights } + 200 \text{ host park nights})} = \$9.04 / \text{night}$$

Let's make one final calculation. In the first example we had a total of 400 membership park nights in the first two years. Let's use the same 400 membership park nights in the second year, but since you are not likely to spend 100 nights a year in your home park, we will leave the home park nights at 30 and increase the host park nights to 170 per year.

$$340 \text{ nights} \times \$6/\text{night} = \$2,040$$

The nightly costs work out to:

$$\frac{(900 + (2 \times \$125) + \$2,040)}{60 \text{ home park nights} + 340 \text{ host park nights})} = \$7.98 / \text{night}$$

As the last two calculations show, some campground memberships can be very cost effective. You will find a worksheet to make your own calculations in *Appendix D.*

Often membership fees and dues are negotiable. One or two years of free dues is something many people are able to obtain through negotiations. Knowing your financial limits, you can quickly counter back and test the waters. **Always** make any agreement to buy a membership contingent on your review and approval of the contract.

There is one final thing to be aware of about membership organizations. When we hit the road in 1994 it only cost a dollar per night to visit a host park. Now it is up to five or six dollars per night. Coast to Coast and RPI have also experienced a decline in membership campgrounds. On the other hand they have experienced an increase in Good Neighbor and Enjoy America parks. Good Neighbor and Enjoy America parks are private campgrounds that host Coast to Coast and RPI members for a set nightly fee. However, this fee is higher than that at the membership campgrounds.

No one knows what the future holds for membership organizations. However, with this in mind, it would be prudent to minimize your investment in membership campgrounds and membership organizations.

There is one way to avoid the risks with membership campgrounds. Coast to Coast has a Good Neighbor Park program separate from their membership park program. This program does not require membership in a home park thereby eliminating contract hassles, investments in a home park and annual dues to a home park. The nightly camping fee will be higher than with membership parks, but your cost in the long run may be less.

Now you have the tools to stay in control of a membership park sales presentation! Happy shopping!

17

Comfort in Boondocking

I remember the first time I realized what boondocking was all about. We had made a day trip to Quartzsite, Arizona where thousands of RVs boondock during the winter. I took one look at the boondocked RVs and said, "Why would anyone want to camp without hook-ups?" Two years later we gave boondocking a serious try. We loved it and the flexibility it offers. Now we enjoy boondocking a third to one half of the year.

Finding Boondocking Sites

If your yard selection includes boondocking, there are a few things to consider. First, where can you boondock? When it comes to locations Biker Chuck says, "Finally it dawned on me, it's not that you have to know where they are, it's just that you have to have in your mind that they are there." With practice, finding boondocking sites will become second nature.

Word of mouth is always helpful, but this resource will take time to develop. Escapees RV Club has a "Day's End" column in their magazine that lists boondocking sites. Some Escapee members keep a list of boondocking sites on their computer. Most are happy to share their data for either a small fee or a floppy disk.

BLM offers many sites for boondocking, some free and some for a fee. Write or stop in at a BLM office to obtain details about camping on BLM land.

The National Forest Service also offers many wonderful places to camp. We have boondocked on mountainsides watching the aspen change and within hiking distance of beautiful waterfalls. The National Forest Service even has some campgrounds with little or no fee. As long as there are no signs posted stating otherwise, you can camp anywhere in National Forests. In some tourist areas, like near Yellowstone and Glacier National Parks, the National Forest Service only allows you to camp in their campgrounds. Here we found that local full hook-up private campgrounds were only a few dollars more than the no hook-up National Forest Service campgrounds.

Boise Cascade has some wonderful free campgrounds in Washington and Idaho. These are popular on summer weekends, so arrive Sunday through Thursday if possible. Washington Department of Natural Resources also has great free campgrounds.

Often boondockers will park on vacant land, even if they do not know whom to ask for permission to stay. Some will pick up trash in the area, leaving it in a bag by their door. If someone comes knocking on the door they explain they would like to spend a night or two, but did not know whom to ask for permission. They also point out that they are trying to help by picking up trash in the area. In most cases they are welcome to stay.

Friends and family's yards are a wonderful place to boondock. It gives you a chance to visit, yet you are able to go home when the visit starts to wear on you and your hosts.

Property Sitting

If you wish to stay in a town for a few days or weeks, check with construction sites or other facilities that may experience vandalism. Explain to the site manager that you are looking for a place to park your RV for a while and your presence at their site should deter vandalism. Do not lead the site manager to believe you will act as a security guard, putting your life on the line for the property. Do ask if they would be willing to provide a phone line after hours so that you can call the police if something does happen. If you have a dog who is likely to hear unusual noises let them know. Some of these sites will provide power and in some cases you may even be able to negotiate a salary or fee for your service. When you leave one of these sites you may wish to obtain a letter of reference for future opportunities.

Along with construction sites you may be able to property sit for homes or other types of businesses. Check with ski resorts, summer and church camps, dude ranches and homeowners. A Bed and Breakfast may have room for you if you will keep their place running, or take care of the yard while the owners are away. The only limit is your imagination for creating a boondocking site that works for you.

Overnight Stops

If you are looking for a place to get off the road for a night consider truck stops, closed weigh scales, scenic overlooks, historical markers and gravel pits along the road. In town try parking lots of any type. Be sure to park in these lots after business hours and depart before business hours. Parking lots may include banks, churches, gas stations, medical clinics, police stations, museums, post offices, schools, RV stores, tourist attractions and vacant lots or buildings.

Select a restaurant with a large parking lot for dinner and ask the waitress or waiter for permission to spend the night. Often city parks will allow you to spend a night, sometimes several. Some will even provide hook-ups for little or nothing. If you need to do laundry, find a Laundromat with a large lot.

If you would like to see a movie, try spending the night in the theater parking lot. Shopping centers will often let you spend the night. Stores such as Wal-Mart have always been RV friendly, although they are being pressured by the powers that be to eliminate boondocking in their parking lots. If you see a sign that says "No Overnight Parking" it doesn't hurt to check with the management anyway. Often those signs are for semi trucks and not RVs.

Appreciation and Etiquette

You can show businesses your appreciation for being allowed to stay by making your purchases at their business. At other sites you can show your appreciation by helping with chores. Picking up trash is one thing property owners appreciate. When the opportunity exists, thank the property owner or their representative for allowing you to stay. By giving something back to the property owner, boondockers build a support system within communities that will help defeat community efforts to eliminate boondocking.

When possible, ask for permission to stay. Most of the time you will be welcome. Do not put your awning down or leave things around your wheel estate when parked in a parking lot. It should not look as if you have taken up residency. Also, limit your stay to one night unless you make special arrangements. Taking advantage of a good situation may eliminate the boondocking opportunity for the next person.

Security

When you pick your boondocking site you will want to consider security. Some places, like malls and Wal-Mart, will have their own security people who will look after your safety.

The first hand stories we have heard about security problems have been about campgrounds where vehicle break-ins or people coming to the door occur the middle of the night. We have not heard first hand stories about people having problems when they are boondocking. This could be because boondockers are more in tune to their location when selecting where they stay.

In six years on the road we have not met anyone who has had their life threatened. Maybe this is because it is common knowledge that many RVers carry guns, a personal decision for you to consider. Or maybe, what little is in an RV is not worth the trip to boondocking sites miles from anywhere. What I do know is that I feel much safer in my wheel estate, when I am boondocked, than I did during the last couple of years I lived in Denver, Colorado.

When selecting a boondocking site, familiarize yourself with what is in the area. Listen to your intuition and if you feel even slightly uncomfortable look for another site.

Boondocking Equipment

While RVs are self contained, they seldom provide comfortable boondocking for more than a couple of nights. Two things are necessary to make boondocking for long periods work; having the proper equipment and making a few lifestyle modifications. Much of the equipment for boondocking—solar panels, batteries, inverters, generators and heaters—was covered in *Equipment for the Wheel Estate.* Here are some additional equipment options to consider.

Some boondockers have wind generators as an electrical source. Of course you must be where there is wind for this to work. The best place to gather more information on wind generators is in Quartzsite, Arizona, late in January or early February. You can visit with boondockers using wind generators. If you decide to take advantage of this source you will find vendors in the area during this period.

Holding tank sizes are very important to boondockers. While you want to carry as much water as possible, do not overlook the weight factors. Water weighs 8.34 pounds per gallon. This equates to 417 pounds for a full 50 gallon water tank and 834 pounds for a full 100 gallon water tank.

If you need water you can always haul it rather than move your wheel estate. Water bladders the size of water beds are available for hauling large quantities of water. Water tanks in some wheel estates can only be filled under pressure. If this is the case you will need a pump to transfer the water into your RV water tank.

So what is a reasonable size for your fresh water tank? While it can be done with less, a 60 gallon fresh water tank is the smallest you should consider. Many boondockers have 100 gallon fresh water tanks. You will have to balance the weight issue with comfort and length of stay without moving.

Next, consider the black and gray tanks. The black tank collects your toilet water and sometimes your bathroom sink water. The gray tank will collect your shower and kitchen sink water. It is very difficult to boondock if these tanks do not have adequate capacity.

If you really want to boondock, you will find a way as Ron and Sharon did. Their GMC motorhome has a combined black and gray tank of only 40 gallons. A 40 gallon gray tank would be a challenge for any boondocker, unless you are in an area that allows gray water on the ground. However, when one tank catches both the gray and black water you are not able to dump the contents on the ground.

In our first trailer we managed well with 50 gallon gray and black tanks. Our second trailer has 100 gallons of gray capacity and 50 of black capacity. With the first trailer we found it very helpful to stay in an area where dumping gray water was possible. In our second trailer we have no need to dump gray water at all and our black tank now determines when we must move.

Some diehard boondockers may take their furnace and water heater out of their wheel estate. They believe they add unnecessary weight. These people use the sun to heat their water. Some will heat water by painting a milk jug black and setting it in the sun on a cardboard box with only the bottom and two sides remaining. The interior of this box is covered with aluminum foil. It faces the sun and the water jug keeps the box from blowing away.

There are also solar showers. This is one of the things that help Ron and Sharon manage with their limited gray/black tank capacity. Some people will use their solar showers inside. Due to their limited tank capacity Ron and Sharon set up a curtain and use their solar shower outside, so the shower water never goes into the tank.

I can hear you now, "I'm not going to live that way!" Don't worry! You don't have to go to this extreme to boondock! At least you won't if you obtain the appropriate creature comforts in your wheel estate.

Finally, if you are really into boondocking and the equipment that makes the lifestyle easier, you may want to check out solar ovens. When you want to bake you simply set this box in the sun and let it preheat for a little while, then pop the food in the oven. No propane needed and no additional heat in the RV. One couple even found the oven quickly heated up to 350 degrees while sitting in snow on a cold day. Solar ovens are a little larger than a 13 inch TV, so you do need to be creative to find space to carry them.

Water Conservation

When we first started to boondock we were lucky if we could go 3 days before we had to find a dump and fill up with water again. Then we hooked up with some serious boondockers and they helped us stretch our stays with a few easy lifestyle changes. We now can go a couple of weeks with 60 gallons of water, which means we still have a lot of gray and black tank capacity as well. The following are some tricks we apply to save water:

☆ Put a shut off valve on the toilet so you can flush it with jugs of water. This reduces the amount of water going into the toilet.

☆ Take navy showers every other day. Shower with a dish pan. This will catch about half the shower water, which you can then use to flush the toilet.

☆ Use paper plates and only wash dishes when you run out of silverware. For us this works out to every other day when we run the water heater for showers.

☆ Turning the water on and off in an RV shower provides cold bursts of water. Adjusting the water temperature takes time and wastes water. If you have a thermostat on the water heater, set it on the lowest setting. Otherwise time the water heater. Then shower with just hot water. Experiment with how long you must run the water heater to get just the right temperature to turn on only the hot water. The time will vary depending on the temperature outdoors and when you last ran the water heater. This method will eliminate the cold bursts of water and reduce your water consumption.

Just being aware that there is a limited supply of fresh water will make you stop and think before turning a faucet on.

There are other tricks, like the solar water discussed above. One is to use the rinse water from doing dishes to wash dishes the next time, a third time to flush the toilet.

Some people go as far as not putting toilet paper down their toilet, feeling this saves valuable black tank space. You need not go this far, however. Considering the size of a roll of toilet paper, not putting it down the toilet is unlikely to extend the capacity of your black tank by even a day.

Energy Conservation

There are things you can do to reduce energy consumption also. Everything should be shut off when not in use. This includes the inverter, which pulls power when it is on. Things, like computers, TVs and satellite receivers pull power, even when you shut them off, so they must be unplugged when not in use. If you cannot reach the plugs, especially in an entertainment center, pay a visit to your nearest office supply store. They sell boxes that act as surge protectors and also allow you to individually shut the power off to equipment run through the box. Our TV sits on one of these boxes. In our case we can individually turn the power off to our TV, VCR, satellite receiver, and computer.

If you have an electronic refrigerator with a high humidity setting, turn it off. It pulls enough power to make the effort worthwhile.

Remember that on cold nights furnaces pull a great deal of power. If you plan to boondock where it may be cold consider a ceramic or catalytic heater which will pull little or no power.

Sharing ideas is a key part of the full-timing lifestyle. Visit with other boondockers to learn how they manage the lifestyle without giving up their creature comforts. Before long you will have some tricks of your own to share.

18

Community:
As Big As You Make It

One of Coby's concerns when they hit the road was the loss of community. "I've got guys to go fishing with and play golf with and we have people we get together and socialize with. [Now] I'm going out there on the road where I'm not going to know anybody, I'm not going to have any friends [and] I'm never going to see anybody. Just Sue [his wife], Forbes [the dog] and I and the motorhome in this desolate country where there is nobody else. I was really concerned about that," Coby said.

"[Now] I will readily admit," Coby says, "that anytime we are on the road we will have more social contact, see more friends and do more things in two weeks than if we were home for three months."

As Coby found, there are many opportunities to become part of a community on the road. However, it does not happen without some effort on your part. Since you will often find yourself among people you have never met before, your ability to walk up to a stranger and start a conversation will be essential. If you are a wallflower, unable to make this first move, finding community in the full-timing lifestyle will be very difficult.

Creating Community

You never know when and where you will make a friend for life. You could be helping with a shared campground meal, doing laundry or participating in campground activities.

Community goes hand in hand with involvement, the more you participate the more you become a part of a community. If you belong to a group that has rallies, your attendance and assistance at the rallies will make you a welcomed member in the community. The success of rallies depends on volunteers. As a result, your involvement not only brings friendship, but a more rewarding rally experience.

Some groups have a roster listing members and their interests. If you find someone with your interests, write to them and see if you can get together. Some organization newsletters share member's travel plans. If you will be in the same area as another member, leave them a message on their message service, or if you know far in advance, write them a letter and suggest getting together. Be bold, the worst they can say is no thanks, which isn't likely when they have written into the newsletter to say they will be in a certain area. Membership in the same club offers a foundation to build what may become a lifelong friendship.

Some of our most rewarding Boomer visits have been when we contact Boomers we have never met before. After a wonderful visit we part, looking forward to seeing each other down the road.

The first couple of years on the road we made new friends during activities at membership parks. Most of these friends were seniors who endorse our belief that we should enjoy the full-timing lifestyle while we can.

Once you create a community you will need to maintain it. You can stay in touch by using mail, message services, phones or e-mail. Since we live in a mobile community you can make plans with your new friends to meet them in new locations.

Where To Look For Community

If you stay in one area for a while or return to a favorite spot year after year you can participate in traditional communities. Every community has churches and they often have a fellowship hour after the service. This is a prime opportunity to meet people and learn about ways to become involved in the community while you are there.

Several Christian groups welcome RVers in their efforts to build and refurbish churches and other church property nationwide. They generally even provide RV hook-ups for their volunteers. While doing something good for others, these volunteers are forming friendships that will last long beyond the project they are working on.

There are many different volunteer organizations where you may find community. One many RVers participate in is Habitat for Humanity. A group known as RV Gypsies has their own newsletter—*Care-a-vanner*—and schedule for Habitat projects. Some Habitat affiliates will host RVs, welcoming you at anytime. Habitat's RV Gypsies can provide you with a list of these affiliates and phone numbers.

Working craft or trade shows brings a community of vendors together. Besides friendship, these people share knowledge on which shows to go to or avoid and which companies are the best to work for.

The RVing lifestyle offers many of its own communities. Check with the manufacturer of your RV to see if there is an owners club. Generally, owners of the RVs run these clubs, although in some cases the manufacturer runs the club.

Membership camping offers opportunities as well. Coast to Coast has a rally for their members every spring. RPI offers Mexican caravans every winter. When you belong to a home park system you will also find community between their parks. As you travel between their parks, don't be surprised when your neighbors move with you. Even traveling in the larger

Coast to Coast and RPI systems you are likely to find some of the same neighbors from park to park.

Good Sam is a camping organization for weekend campers as well as full-timers. When it comes to community with Good Sam they have over 2,000 chapters to select from. Chapters are regional, so you may decide you would like to join more than one.

Good Sam has implemented a program to make it easy for you to connect with the right chapter for you. If you call (800) 314-3510, and provide a zip or postal code, you will receive information on the local chapters, including any membership specifics (families, singles, women, etc.). Once you select a chapter, you may leave a message for the state or provincial director, who will then call you with more details.

FMCA (Family Motor Coach Association) is another large camping organization for owners of motorhomes. They sponsor a couple of the largest rallies every year, often with over 5,000 motorhomes in attendance. They also have subgroups for people with like interests.

Keep in mind that some large organizations, like Good Sam and FMCA, receive funding from the RV industry. The result *may* be a conflict between your needs and industry needs.

Ask other RVers about the communities they are part of. If this does not lead to the right community for you, create a community. RVers are a diverse group and you should have no problem finding others with similar community needs.

The Escapees Community

There is one community Paul and I would have great difficulty giving up. This is the community we find in the Escapees RV Club.

Escapee's mission is to provide a support network for RVers by fulfilling the RVers three basic needs that are represented by the acronym "S–K–P." S for Support, K for knowledge and P for parking. When said quickly, SKP sounds like Escapee. However, members often insert an "i" and refer to themselves as SKiPs.

The Escapees organization was founded by Joe & Kay Peterson on July 4, 1978. Joe and Kay hit the road at age 43 with children in tow. As they traveled, Joe found work at local unions in the construction industry. Kay would also put her nursing background to work.

With their full-timing experience it is no wonder Joe and Kay were able to create an organization that does an outstanding job of meeting full-timer's needs. But what they created is so much more than an organization, it is a road family. This is the only group of people I know of who show unconditional acceptance of you by offering a hug before introductions. (Don't worry if you are not a hugger. A hand extended in greeting will be respected.)

I cannot tell you how many stories I have heard of an Escapee coming to the rescue of another Escapee in a crisis. Many times these Escapees have never met before. What Chili Chuck said about Boomers is true of Escapees—We are all family. We will do things for each other that family members won't do.

Now, returning to the acronym "S–K–P," let's take a look at what the Escapees RV Club has to offer.

Support

The Escapees logo is a blue and white house in a red wagon. Many Escapees display this logo on their wheel estate and vehicles.

There are two types of subgroups in Escapees—Chapters and Birds of a Feather. Chapters are regional groups of people. You do not need to be from a region or live in a region to belong to a particular chapter. There is one chapter, known as the Mexican Connection, made up of people who like to travel in Mexico. Chapters often have rallies that anyone is welcome to participate in.

Birds of a Feather groups or BOFs are groups of people with like interests. BOFs often hold their own rallies and have a newsletter for their members. These groups interests range from ham radio to pet lovers to Christian fellowship to boondocking.

Boomers is one of these BOFs. The group brings together young full-timers with similar interests and concerns about life on the road. For a group with no officers and no rules Boomers is extremely successful in providing community. Many Boomers will tell you that the group has kept them on the road. When you join Escapees be sure to check out the Boomers BOF.

Other Escapee activities include breakfast, lunch and dinner gatherings across the country. You can find a list of when and where these gatherings are in the *Escapee* magazine.

While at an Escapee park you will find people gathering at four o'clock for a friendship hour. This is a great time for announcements, making new friends or learning how to complete a project.

Escapees also has services that make life on the road easier. One of these is a mailing service. Besides being reasonably priced, it offers flexibility that others don't, is very reliable and the staff provides outstanding service. Escapees also have a message service and calling card.

A unique service Escapees offers is the CARE program. CARE provides assisted living for full-timers who, for health reasons, are unable to travel but wish to continue living in their wheel estate.

Knowledge

This is where even old hats can reap benefits, but those preparing for a full-timing lifestyle will find their gold.

A bimonthly magazine called ***Escapees*** contains information about the club, the mechanics of RVs, legal considerations for the full-timer, wonderful places to visit, upcoming rallies, and various tips, just to mention a few topics.

There are Escapades twice a year. An Escapade is a five day seminar on RV living. But don't worry, if you get burned out on seminars you can attend craft classes, stroll through vendors row, meet with various BOF groups, win one of many door prizes and wrap the day up with one of several options in entertainment. Attending an Escapade is one of the best things you can do for yourself before hitting the road full-time. Yes, even if you have been camping all your life!

Joe and Kay Peterson share more knowledge in their books on the full-timing lifestyle.

Parking

We have met people on the road who believe Escapees is a membership park system. As you can see, Escapees is nothing of the sort. Some members do need a home base, however, so Escapees has created three different types of parks.

Some parks lease the lots, while others sell the lots. There is a waiting list for lots in most parks. Once your name is on the list it may only take months for a lot to become available, or it may take years.

All SKPs are welcome to camp at any of these parks. In addition to campground and boondocking sites, permanent sites are often added into the rental pool for visiting SKPs.

There are many other benefits to membership in Escapees. We became Escapees so we could receive a discount on trailer insurance. Little did we know Escapees would become so much more to us! Do yourself a favor and check out Escapees RV Club.

Whether you work to create a community before or after you hit the road, the options are endless. A few hours spent with full-timers will confirm this.

19

Working on the Road: How it is Done

Job Availability

Not everyone is independently wealthy or receives a big inheritance just in time to hit the road as a full-timer. This does not mean you must throw away your dreams. Jobs are abundant for full-timers.

Terry says, "If there is anything I have learned in the last two years on the road, it is that I don't need to worry about finding a job. There are plenty of jobs out there."

Walking away from job security is the hard part. Once you are on your own, you are likely to wonder why it took so long.

Janice and Gabby Lasko, who seek both an income and opportunities to snow ski, have been very successful with their job searches. Janice wrote an article for the February 1994 *Camperways* magazine about their diverse job experiences. The following is an abridged version of that article.

A benefit of working in this lifestyle is the network of people who are doing what we are and who share job possibilities. In a sense, one job has led to another in different parts of the country and sometimes with the same new friends.

One winter season we sold lift tickets at a ski resort in Oregon. One of the couples we met was doing the same thing and staying in the same RV park. We have remained in touch with this couple, have traveled with them and worked with them again selling pumpkins and Christmas trees in central California. By the way, the perks for the ticket selling job were numerous. In addition to salary, there was a company bus from town to the mountain (which gave our truck a much-needed rest that winter), free skiing and a locker at the base of the mountain to store our ski gear (which meant we had oodles of extra space in the rig that season). We were done selling lift tickets by 11:00 a.m. and were on the hill skiing by noon...following a discounted meal on the mountain.

Preparing the pumpkin and Christmas tree lots and subsequent six weeks of sales was physically demanding. However, that turned into a plus for us because the physical labor conditioned us for the slopes.

From the Christmas tree lot we went to Mammoth Lakes, California, where by mid-January we were working. Gabby went into show business—he worked the candy counter at the local theater—and one of his co-workers led him to a desk clerk job at one of the motels in town. Staying past the winter that year Gabby also worked in the maintenance department of this motel.

That season I was a nanny for a four-year-old and his sister, 13 months his junior. It was exciting to watch them grow and mature as winter turned to summer and eventually autumn. Their parents owned a restaurant in town and from time-to-time I'd fill in as a hostess. The drawback with this job was the growing attachment to the children. After eight months, it definitely was time to move on.

We had stayed in touch with a couple we met when we first began to travel via RV. This couple got us interested in working for a company that produces RV park guides with area maps. Although we didn't work for the company too long, we were rewarded with a very supportive home-office staff and the ability to remain on the move while we were working, in addition to complimentary campsites.

An added challenge to our job hunting is to leave our days free to ski and play. One season I did data entry for a catalog company filling Thanksgiving and Christmas orders. Willing to work the 4:00 p.m. to midnight shift meant time-and-a-half and sometimes double-time pay.

One interesting time found Gabby and I sharing the rig for a mere four hours a night. Gabby was the night shift bartender for a ski resort and didn't get home until midnight. I awoke at 4:00 a.m. to provide 50 radio stations with ski and weather conditions. When I was done at 9:00 a.m. I would pick up Gabby and we'd ski a few hours and start over. Again, we were provided a salary as well as free skiing.

I have worked behind the desk at an RV park checking in guests and booking future reservations, while Gabby did yard and pool work for the same park. For that work, we were provided a salary plus a free campsite. As fun as that was, it was difficult for us not to pick up and go every time someone started talking to us about their travel plans.

The jobs are out there almost for the taking. It's just a matter of attitude and willingness and honesty.

Pros and Cons of Working on the Road

There is a difference in how someone in the traditional lifestyle looks at a job and how a full-timer looks at a job. In the traditional lifestyle jobs are a security blanket. People often get caught up in the belief they must climb the corporate ladder to be someone.

Lives revolve around jobs and jobs revolve around possessions. There are house payments, car payments, utility bills and property taxes to pay. Some feel the loss of these possessions or the inability to buy new toys would be devastating. As a result, people work longer hours and do things they may not otherwise agree to, just so they can keep their job. Family, friends and your own well-being become secondary in the traditional lifestyle.

As a full-timer, family, friends and your well-being become primary. The cost of the lifestyle is less expensive, so jobs do not have the same control over your life. There are plenty of jobs just down the road and it is empowering to know you can hitch-up and leave when a job does not work out.

On a cross country vacation Sam and Jessica met Warren. Warren inspired them with his story about his security guard position at a Las Vegas casino. It seems one of the valets did not do his job right so Warren's boss told him to fire the guy.

Warren responded, "I'm not going to fire him! You fire him!" A response that totally shocked his boss, because nobody had dared question him.

The boss said, "What do you mean you won't fire him?!"

Warren replied, "Hey, I've got a full tank of gas. I can be out of here like that." His boss turned around, walked away and left him alone.

Warren knew it wasn't the end of the world if he had to go down the road and find another job. This knowledge gave him the empowerment and freedom necessary to do what he felt was right.

Sam and Jessica had the opportunity to apply this empowerment a few summers later. They were working for a houseboat rental company. Sam did maintenance and Jessica housekeeping. The owners made some promises regarding wages and a full hook-up site. When the owners tried to change the way Sam and Jessica were paid and did not complete the full hook-up site Sam and Jessica said good-bye and headed down the road.

Sam soon found himself working at Rocky Mountain National Park. Jessica quickly found two jobs in town, one at Safeway and the other as a tour guide at the Stanley Hotel. Jessica says, "We arrived in Estes Park and anybody could have walked downtown and had a job in five minutes. In June every shop had a help wanted sign out."

In addition to income, sophisticated full-timers look for benefits or perks a job may offer. These benefits may be nothing more than being in an area you wish to visit; a full hook-up site; or free entrance to otherwise expensive attractions.

Janice and Gabby wanted to ski, so they looked for jobs that would reduce or remove the cost of lift tickets, while providing an income. When they lived in the traditional lifestyle they could only ski on weekends and paid big bucks to do so.

Since full-timers seldom sit in one place for long, management jobs are not generally an option. There are advantages to this, however, as management jobs come with responsibility and generally the pay is not worth the resulting headaches.

If you work in five states one year you will have the joy of filling out tax returns for five states, unless they happen to be no income tax states. Before selecting the states you plan to work in, you may want to determine their income tax rate. Which one will take the least amount of your hard earned money?

Transition into Working on the Road

There is a lot to consider before you even start your job search. What do you need and desire from a job? What types of jobs are you willing to take? Will you be flexible enough to grab a job opportunity at the most unexpected time? Will you work for yourself or others? Are there jobs available? Terry tells how she and her husband's experiences have touched on all of these.

We have had no problem getting jobs, especially in tourist towns. It was a major adjustment for me to become an employee after so many years of being my own boss. A lot of tourist related jobs tend to pay poorly and have inept, young supervisors. It was a challenge.

After a year we have decided, for us, working with small mom and pop organizations is more suited to our personality. We especially like the jobs with limited or no supervision.

We began our sojourn working for a concessionaire at a national park. Terrible pay, long hours, poor supervision and low employee morale. It is very easy to get these jobs, however.

Next we spent five weeks visiting family in Denver and registered at a temporary agency. If you don't mind taking the tests and don't mind office work, this is an easy way to gain employment and the pay is decent. The better your office and computer skills the better the pay.

We enjoyed working a Christmas tree lot in Missouri, because we ran it as our own business, so it suited our personality. The drawback was the cold, which we were not prepared for. We also had to be there all the time.

We wandered into a job at a construction site on BLM land in New Mexico. It is important to be flexible and open to opportunities, no matter how bizarre they may seem. We built a water break of rock cages on this job. It was hard labor, great pay and a good experience.

When we spent some time in Sedona, Arizona, I looked at the want ads. The first day in town I was hired by a Bed and Breakfast as a housekeeper. Later I assisted with innkeeper duties and even ran the inn when the owners were called out of town. The pay was decent, the experience good and the people great. At the same time the newspaper led Joe to a job in the front office of a Jeep place.

*Another job we had was at a resort ranch in Colorado.
We had read an ad in **Workamper News** and applied for
the job the previous year. They kept our letter on file and
called us a year later. We negotiated a better salary than
initially offered and received full hook-ups. Even with
the increase in salary the salary was not great, which is
typical of the workamper positions. However, the trade
off was that the place was beautiful, a place we had
wanted to spend some time exploring via camping,
backpacking and mountain biking.*

*We have learned that good employees are hard to find
and if you are honest, friendly, willing and have some
intelligence you will have no trouble finding employment.*

Now it is your turn to figure out what your needs and
expectations are. Let's take one step at a time.

Determining Why You Will Work

The first step to finding jobs on the road is determining why
you plan to work. Some reasons might be:

   ✫   Put food on the table and pay the bills
   ✫   Supplement an income
   ✫   Pay for extra activities or possessions
   ✫   Buy a new RV or vehicle
   ✫   Invest for retirement
   ✫   For perks that come with jobs
   ✫   Obtain a place to stay in an area you want to visit
   ✫   Pass the time

Make a list of your reasons. They will help you narrow your
job search. If a job will be your only source of income, you
will be looking for higher paying jobs and may have to work

most of the year. If you are supplementing an income short term jobs should meet your needs.

If you plan to secure your financial future with an IRA or Roth you will have to work. Only earned income may be placed in these retirement accounts.

At some point your RV and vehicle will need replacing. Working a little each year could help save for this inevitable outcome. If you are just looking to pass the time, a job with perks or a camping spot in an area you want to visit should meet your needs.

All of these considerations factor into the type of job you will be looking for.

How Much Do You Need To Make

If your goal is to put food on the table and pay your bills your expectations are straight forward. Look at the budget you developed in chapter two to determine your expenses. Be sure your budget allows for any taxes that you will have to pay. You will probably want to make more than your budget states so you do not need to live from paycheck to paycheck.

Obviously, the more you make the less you have to work. To determine a target wage divide the income you must have by the number of hours you would like to work per year. If you know what a job pays you can divide it into your necessary income to determine how many hours you must work per year. Can you work this many hours and still enjoy the lifestyle?

What can you do if a job you would like does not pay enough? Pull your budget out and study your expenses. Is there an expense that you may be able to get the employer to cover?

Suppose you are offered a job as clerk at a small lumber yard and the pay is low. The pay is not enough for you to accept the job, as campgrounds are expensive in the area. If you could cover the cost of your camping the pay would be acceptable to you.

Chances are the owner of the lumber yard is not familiar with your lifestyle. He probably is not aware of the mutual opportunities that exist. Your solution may be to park at the lumber yard. Additional benefits may include access to power, water and phone. You can sell this to the lumber yard owner by explaining your presence would discourage theft. This solution solves your problem and offers the employer a valuable service.

Valuing Benefits and Perks

When there is more than a salary offered with a job you need to determine what those additional benefits are worth. Let's assume you are offered a property sitting job. The pay is $10 a day and a full hook-up site. What is that worth to you?

Where would you stay if you were not property sitting? We will assume you would be staying in this area with or without the property sitting job. Is there free camping in the area? Or would you be paying $20 a night? If you are paying out $20 per night and not receiving the $10 per day you are actually in the hole $30 a day.

Let's say you were going to be in the area for a month and you want a phone. Assume the charges for the phone are $50 for connection and $20 per month for service. If the phone is part of the property sitting deal you save $70 that month. On the other hand, if you were not planning to have a phone you have saved nothing.

What if the property-sitting job includes caring for animals at a certain time of day? Will this keep you from getting a second job you would otherwise get? If so, look at your bottom line for the property-sitting job versus the bottom line for the other job and staying at the campground. Maybe you could hire someone to take care of the animals, so you could take the second job. Or maybe you can find a second job that does not conflict with the property-sitting job.

In the case of house-sitting positions, it is not unusual for the homeowner to feel they are offering you a great deal. For example, maybe they can rent their house for $500, but they are letting you stay for the cost of utilities. Another option may be to camp free, with no utility costs, someplace else. The bottom line—you end up paying for the privilege of being tied down.

We worked for perks at Disney World two winters. Previous winters we had boondocked for next to nothing in the southwestern deserts. The winters at Disney World found us paying for camping, which ate half of our wages. Besides free entrance at the large parks, Disney gives employees discounts on products, meals and smaller attractions. The discounts are good, so of course we had to take advantage of them. These were expenses we would not have had otherwise. While I did not track our expenses against what we made, I believe we probably broke even. It was not a money making venture for us. However, others do make money at Disney World by working more and longer hours, moving between membership campgrounds and not taking advantage of all the perks.

Keep in mind, Uncle Sam may consider some of these benefits taxable. For example, if parking at the job site is required as a condition of employment the IRS will consider this "excludable income." Otherwise they will consider the parking space taxable income and the value is determined by the going rate in the region. One more thing to factor into the job equation.

As you can see there are many ways to look at the value of a job with benefits or perks. The value will be different for different people. How you manage benefits and perks can make a big difference. To maximize your bottom line take time to determine the value and tax impact of each situation.

Determining Your Job Expectations

Now that you know why you are working you should determine your job expectations. For example:

* ★ How do you feel about working for others?
* ★ Do you prefer to work alone or with others?
* ★ Do you prefer physical labor or a desk job?
* ★ Can you stand on your feet for long periods of time?
* ★ Do you want to be indoors or outdoors?
* ★ Do you want people contact?
* ★ Will you do potties?
* ★ Do you have enough motivation and self discipline to start your own business?
* ★ What don't you want to do?
* ★ Is there something you have always wanted to try?
* ★ How important are perks and benefits?
* ★ What specific perks and benefits do you want?

Write down five or six expectations that are important to you in selecting a job. These expectations will help you narrow your search. If you have been too specific you may have trouble finding a job. If this is the case, prioritize your expectations and work with only the top two or three. If, on the other hand, you do not feel your job search has enough focus, add a few more expectations.

Where You Work

This one can be scary for us nomads. We all recognize if we work in a state with state income tax that we must file and pay taxes in that state. The problem comes when a state expects us to become a resident if we take a temporary job in that state.

Most, if not all states have residency requirements that tie to how long you are in the state and length of employment in the state. I have only heard of two people who came face to face with these laws. In both cases, they had to get a vehicle license plate in the state where they were working.

If you plan to take a job driving a company vehicle, you may need a state driver's license, a consideration for the type of job you seek.

It is not practical to change your residency every time you take a short term job. And if you change your driver's license and license plate, while maintaining your residency in another state, you are likely to run into problems down the road.

We have been stopped twice in six years. Once in the middle of New Mexico, where they were stopping everyone. That time they checked our truck and trailer plates against Paul's driver's license to confirm they were all from the same state. Another time a policeman in Vancouver, Washington had seen our South Dakota plates two days in a row so he stopped us to ask questions about our residency.

While most states do not seem to be enforcing their laws, some do have large fines on the books. One day they may decide to enforce their laws and you could be the unfortunate one they start with.

It is wise to be aware of state residency laws and factor them into your job selection process. These laws may help you decide which states present you with the least risk. Be sure to talk with other RVers to learn about which states are enforcing their residency laws. You can rest assured working RVers will quickly spread the word if it is risky to work in a particular state. They will also join forces to see if they can get an exception to the rule for RVers.

You may want to have a contingency plan in case a state does approach you about residency. In our case, if a state approaches us we will hitch-up and leave the state. This, however, may not resolve issues such as taxes the state feels we owe them.

Other Things to Consider

Keep in mind what type of clothing and tools may be necessary for your preferred jobs. Work through a temporary service is likely to require that you carry several days worth of business clothes. Do you have space for this? Work, as an auto mechanic requires having tools along. Would you carry these tools anyway? How much weight do they add and is there sufficient storage for them?

The next chapter will look at how you can find a job.

20

Working on the Road: Obtaining a Job

The only thing left to decide before you start your job search is whether you will work for yourself or someone else.

Working for Others

There are all sorts of jobs out there for minimum wage or slightly more. Generally these jobs go to people with only a little bit of life experience, so when a more mature, reliable person comes along an employer will jump at the opportunity to hire them. There is also more turnover in minimum wage jobs, so your lifestyle and desire to work for a short time will not be a big problem for these employers.

Finding a job that pays more than minimum wage will be a little more challenging, but not impossible.

Is your profession one you can pack up and take with you? Often nurses and other medical personnel can find jobs for six weeks to three months at a time. Teachers may be able to fill in as substitute teachers in some communities for short periods. Tax accountants should have no trouble finding work the first four months of the year.

Second and third shift positions may offer higher wages. Jobs involving physical labor often pay better. The construction industry normally pays well and is used to high turnover. You may need to belong to a union, however.

Find out how and when overtime pay is given for a job. When we worked for Disney World we worked two 10 hour shifts a week. Overtime was paid after eight hours. Our neighbors, who worked six to eight hour shifts, three or four days a week, made less than us in the same length of time. If you work fewer days, but longer shifts you may be financially ahead!

It is important to have a big picture of your needs before applying for a job. Employers may not be aware of benefits they can offer to make up for low pay. Don't be shy, suggest benefits that could help you. This may determine whether you take a job. The worst the employer can say is "no."

Keep your ears open for job opportunities. Often jobs will come by word of mouth from other RVers. Other times a job may come along when you are not looking for one.

Sam and Jessica called Biker Chuck to let him know about a job on Lake Powell one summer. As a result of that call, "I spent three and a half months there working on tour boats," Biker Chuck says.

Gene and Kathy came across a job selling Christmas trees while visiting with other campers in a campground.

Jerry was enjoying western Colorado when he stopped in the local BLM office for information. He wasn't looking for a job, yet he left the BLM office as a campground host. The BLM was desperate for a campground host. Since Jerry didn't want a job he was in a great position to negotiate not being responsible for a couple of the tasks—cleaning outhouses and collecting money.

Look around you. What jobs do you see? Are any of interest to you? Could they fit into your new lifestyle? What changes could you make so that they would fit into your lifestyle?

Working for Yourself

If you are a self-starter, enjoy being in control and have entrepreneurial desires you may want to create your own job.

One couple sells solar panels and solar ovens from their RV as they travel across the country and in Mexico. Another sells computers and cellular phones.

Gene had a remodeling business before he hit the road. For a while, after he was on the road, he would return each summer to remodeling jobs. One of the things he does now is windshield repair. He likes windshield repair because it does not require much equipment and is easy to take along.

Another couple liked the idea of creating campground maps, but they did not want to work for the companies who normally provide these maps. Instead they invested in software for their computer. Then they signed up five or six campgrounds in areas they wanted to visit. Now every winter they visit these parks; sell advertising; design campground maps and brochures; and work with a printer to produce the product. In a matter of a few weeks they make about $30,000 while staying warm during the winter. Their business has grown to the point they now hire help.

If you plan to have your own business, *Finding Your Perfect Work: The New Career Guide to Making a Living, Creating a Life,* by Paul and Sarah Edward's can help you determine what your business should be. The Edward's show you how to take charge of your life, rather than letting a job run it. This book helps you match your interests to the lifestyle you wish to lead and determine how to put them to work for you. It uses actual stories, profiles, work sheets, pertinent facts, inspirational thoughts, illustrated key concepts and ideas to make generating creative work opportunities exciting.

Before you start a business of your own you will want to investigate requirements businesses face, such as: social security issues, income tax and business deductions, sales tax and tax numbers, licenses, incorporation, liabilities, handling inventory, advertising and record keeping. Many of these things will vary from state to state, so be prepared to investigate them in all the states where you plan to work. The individual states, Small Business Administration, library and a good accountant can all help you understand these requirements.

If you plan to start a business consider doing so before you hit the road. This way you can use your weekends, evenings and vacations to test the market and fine tune operations before you give up your traditional job.

Finding Jobs

While Christmas will generate the most holiday related jobs, Halloween, Fourth of July and spring break also generate jobs. Then there is tourist season. How about working at an amusement park, ski slope or national park? Tourist season also generates seasonal jobs in businesses like motels and stores.

Good old Uncle Sam is always going to generate jobs when tax season rolls around. Temporary service companies can help you find jobs any time of the year. Watch the local newspapers for job fairs. Terry and Joe attended one of these in the Jackson Hole, Wyoming, area and ended up with a job near Glenwood Springs, Colorado.

When you first arrive in town, stroll down the streets of the business district. Often employers will advertise for help in their windows or on their signs out front. Take time out for a cup of coffee in the local café. Visit with the locals and see what leads they may have for you. Check the local newspaper for opportunities. Stop by the Chamber of Commerce to see if any of their members are hiring.

Is there a product that impresses you that you would like to promote as you travel? Contact the manufacturer and discuss your promotional ideas with them. Walk through some trade shows looking for products you would like to sell. Ask the people at that booth what the job involves and how you could apply for the job.

Keep your eyes open, make people aware you are looking for a job and remain flexible. It is surprising how easy jobs are to come by!

Applying Before or After You Arrive

Should you find a job before or after you arrive in a community? If you have a specific job in mind, apply in advance. Otherwise you should consider two things:

☆   Are there plenty of jobs you desire in the community?

☆   Are the type of jobs you want going to be taken by the time you arrive?

If the jobs are likely to be taken, you will want to get busy and apply for them before you arrive. First you must find the jobs to apply for. Some resources that may help you find these jobs include:

☆   *Workamper News*
☆   *Workers On Wheels*
☆   *The Caretaker Gazette*
☆   Ads in regional newspapers
☆   Ads in the back of RV magazines
☆   Networking with other RVers
☆   The Internet
☆   Job Fairs

Once you find an attractive position, send a cover letter and resume, expressing your interest. Many employers will check your references. You should also check them out. Call the Better Business Bureau and Chamber of Commerce in their area and ask about their business. Better yet, look for RVers who have visited the area and ask if they have had contact with the business. What are their opinions?

Before accepting a position you may want to ask for the details in writing. This documentation should include your responsibilities; the hours you are to work; the wages and any benefits or perks. If the employer does not provide this information in writing, you can send them a letter stating your understanding of the agreement and ask for confirmation. This documentation may come in handy if the job is different than promised or if you are suddenly reporting to someone different.

When you apply for a job before arriving in town, it is critical that the prospective employer be able to reach you quickly and easily. It may cost you the job otherwise. Be sure to review the different methods of communication in the *Services for Full-timers* chapter.

Possible Jobs

The next page has a short list of possible jobs to give you an idea of what is out there. Make your own list and add input from other full-timers.

Resources

It is not possible in this book to cover getting a job on the road in the detail it deserves. If you will be working on the road gather as much information as you can. See the *Resource Directory* for some great starting places.

Seasonal Positions

Christmas Tree Sales
Package wrapping
Sales clerk
Fireworks Stand
Pumpkin Lots
UPS holiday delivery
Post Office—holidays

Positions With Perks

Campground Hosting
Disney World
Amusement Parks
Any job—Branson, Missouri

Self Employment

Park Maps
Windshield Repair
Solar panels
Solar ovens
Reunion Planning
Rally Organizing
Newsletter Publication
Freelance Writing
Freelance Photography
Cleaning Products
RV Washing
RV Repairs
RV Remodeling
RV Energy Audits
Consulting
Sell computers
Sell cellular phones
Computer services
Entertainment

Volunteer Positions

Habitat for Humanity
Laborers for Christ

Positions for Money

Temporary Service
National Parks
Forest Service
RV Repair
Waiter/Waitress
Sales Rep
Sales Clerk
Caravan Leader
Caravan Tailgunner
Tour guide
Mechanic
Construction
Gas pipeline leak check
Concessionaires
Harvesting

Positions in a Profession

Nursing
Teaching
Computer Consultation
Publications
Photography
Massage Therapy
Consulting
Barber
Beautician

Positions with Parking

Campgrounds
> Activities
> Check-in
> Maintenance
Property sitting
> House
> Ranch
> Construction Site
> Girl Scout Camp
Publication of Park Maps
Campground Rating

21

Work or Play:
A Mouse Adventure

Have you ever dreamed of playing and being paid for it? You probably thought it would be nothing more than a dream, but a certain Mouse says otherwise! He is looking for people who like to visit with his guests and put a little pixie dust in their life. And who could possibly be better qualified than full-time RVers for this task?

When we were in Florida the winter of 1994/95 we met several RVers who were working for Disney World. They got us excited about working for the Mouse, but time did not allow for us to do it that winter. The next winter we met Boomers in Arizona who had just finished three months at Disney World. These Boomers spoke so highly of the experience that they motivated many Boomers to try working for the Mouse. By the winter of 1998/99 there were at least 15 Boomer couples working at Disney World and several hundred other RVers as well. Most of the Boomer couples left with plans to return the following year. After all, how often do you have a chance to play and be paid for it!

Disney World employs between 51,000 and 57,000 people, depending on the tourist season. They have recently become

268 Take Back Your Life!

serious about hiring RVers to fill some of those positions. As a large employer Disney World offers many categories of employment. Some of the job categories include:

- ★ food & beverage
- ★ housekeeping
- ★ merchandising
- ★ custodial
- ★ life guard
- ★ transportation
- ★ attractions
- ★ culinary
- ★ office, technical, reservations

First some terminology. Employees are "Cast Members" and Disney World provides "costumes," not uniforms, for cast members to wear.

There are three levels of employment—full-time, part-time and seasonal. Full-time positions include paid benefits, but are difficult to obtain in some areas.

Part-time positions, referred to as Casual Regular (CR) positions, do not offer paid benefits. CRs must be fully available two days a week in most locations. They also must not exceed 24 hours of work a week, for more than half the weeks of the year.

Seasonal positions, referred to as Casual Temporary (CT) positions, are available during peak tourist season. These positions also do not offer paid benefits. These positions may last from a few days to a few months.

The starting wage for most positions in 1999 was $6.35/hour. Full-time cast members work either a four day work week, with nine to ten hour days, or a five day work week with six to eight hour days. Full-time positions do not guarantee a 40 hour work week. Full-time cast members receive overtime when they exceed their maximum hours in a day. They also receive overtime when they exceed their maximum days in a week, even if they have worked less than 40 hours. CR and CT positions receive time and a half when they exceed eight hours in a shift. Full-time cast members receive paid holiday benefits. Holiday pay is the same as any other day for CR and CT cast members.

RVers enjoy working for the Mouse because he provides great perks. Cast members are able to enter Magic Kingdom, Epcot, Disney MGM and Animal Kingdom with their IDs. The IDs also make you eligible for discounts on and off property.

If you work for the Mouse your kids, grandkids and even parents will want to visit. Not to worry. After 90 days of employment, CRs and full-time cast members receive a main gate pass, which allows them to take a limited number of guests into the parks a limited number of times per year. In 1999 the main gate pass allowed pass holders to bring up to 3 guests into the parks on 12 separate occasions.

Cast members hired before the end of October normally receive a Christmas package that includes significant discounts in stores and restaurants on Disney property, plus passes to bring three guests into the park.

Throughout the year there are specials for cast members, including discounts or free entrance to the water parks and other Disney attractions.

The hiring process is easy, but unique. Before calling for an interview, consider whether you are able to stand on concrete for shifts that may last as long as 10 hours. Do you want to work directly with guests? Are you willing to handle money? What type of position would you like and what are you good at? To schedule an interview call (407) 828-1000.

Disney World welcomes RVers as cast members, so let them know you are an RVer. If you have only one vehicle and need to work the same hours as your spouse, communicate this up-front. Express a desire for your interviews to be together. This will make the process easier for you and the interviewer. While Disney does not promise they can schedule you the same shifts, they will make every effort to do so.

The in person interview process is low key. You start by filling out an application and watching a movie. Some positions require you to take a short math test as well. Next you meet with an interviewer to discuss available positions. Be sure to take a photo ID and the necessary paperwork, such as a birth certificate or social security card, to prove you are a citizen of the United States. If all goes well, you will visit a nurse, watch another movie and complete more paperwork. This entire process can take up to five hours.

Once the hiring process is complete you will receive a schedule to attend Traditions, your first training class. Traditions lasts one to two days and provides you with background on the Disney Corporation. Next you will attend a training day for the park or resort area you will be working at. The final training is in your specific area. This training may take as little as a few hours or last as long as a month, depending on the position.

If you have whiskers, or a pierced tongue or nose, plan on changing your image. Disney has strict dress codes. Women may wear one ring per hand and only one small earring per ear. Men may not have beards and their haircut is to be above their ears. Body piercing and tattoos must not be visible when in costume. While Disney will provide the costume, for most positions you will need to provide footwear—shoes and socks or hose—that go with the costume.

When you are ready for a fun change of pace, head for Florida. Mickey Mouse is anxiously awaiting your arrival!

22

Wanderlust Singles

One of the biggest surprises I found when we started full-timing was the number of nomads who were single women. These women could have been my mother and some even my grandmother. Still observing from within society's parameters, my observation was typical—didn't these women have fears?

We have met a few senior men who travel alone, but not as many. I cannot say whether this is due to men dying earlier, fewer men having gypsy blood or the women having a dream they could not fulfill until they were on their own. Whatever the reason, the number of senior women on the road by themselves is amazing!

When we hooked up with the Boomers we found young single men on the road. The number of single men and women in the Boomers is fairly equal. However, more single men than women attend Boomer gatherings.

Being single actually has less impact on a person making the decision to become a full-timer than one might expect. Concern, especially for women, about security is one consideration. But then, how many couples have the same concern and even travel with a gun as a result? Some singles worry about loneliness on the road. Couples also get lonely. While the issues for couples and singles are not that different, there are some we will take a closer look at.

Selecting an RV

Being single will play a role in selecting your RV. You must be able to maneuver and park your RV without assistance. This often results in singles owning motorhomes, although I have seen some individuals who can park trailers and fifth-wheels without assistance.

Often singles choose to travel in a motorhome from a security standpoint. You never need to leave a motorhome when you park it for the night in an unknown area. If you find yourself in a bad situation you can just drive away.

Security

There are other security issues and they are not just issues for women. Biker Chuck enjoys boondocking out in the wilderness. He says, "I think a little bit about security because if I were to get sick or if something catastrophic was to happen I don't have somebody immediately available to help." To address this concern he keeps a Vial of Life in his refrigerator and truck. Besides medical information it contains personal information he feels is important if he dies.

The following is an excerpt from *On the Road Alone* by DeAnna Satre that was first published in *RVing Women*, July/August 1996.

One of the questions people frequently ask me about my traveling life is, "Are you scared?" It's a tough one to answer. I'm not scared in the sense that it is incapacitating or prevents me from camping where I want to camp, but I am edgy sometimes. It's disconcerting to be camped off somewhere deep in the boonies where you haven't seen anyone all day and then to hear a vehicle approaching after dark. But I count that edginess as an asset. It leads me to take precautions and assure myself that I have done everything I can to ensure my safety.

I won't even talk about guns because I don't own one and don't want to. But many women do have them and know how to use them. I do keep a pepper spray ready to hand, and once I stuck it in my pocket before stepping out of my rig to engage an angry redneck on BLM land. But he was all bluster and indirect threat and we arrived at agreement over our dispute. With the pepper spray as my only "weapon," I rely on common sense and a few rules for my protection. I don't stay in a place that doesn't "feel" right, even if I really want to. After a while you learn to sense places that are misused and might lead to trouble. In Mississippi in the first months of my travels I picked a site early in the day in a deserted campground in a national forest. I was really needing a quiet place to work and rest from travel stress, so I ignored the signs that began appearing in the afternoon. I was camped in a cul-de-sac at the end of the campground and off and on all afternoon pick-ups would drive in, circle around, and leave. I felt a little like a lone pioneer circled by vaguely threatening Indians. But I stayed put. That night two trucks arrived together, swept past me, and stopped nearby, and several men got out and began building a campfire. I was afraid and I tore out of there, leaving my doormat behind. My fear was probably out of proportion, but it was appropriate to leave. They were probably partiers, and it is unpredictable what might happen after a few hours of drinking. Now I pay attention to the signs earlier and find a different place if the one I've chosen doesn't feel right.

It is helpful to create some rules for yourself and abide by them no matter how unnecessary they may seem at the moment. One of mine is to *always* lock my doors when I leave my vehicle, even when I am just gassing up (especially then—bad people have been known to creep into cars when the driver goes in to pay for gas).

I think the most useful thing I'm learning that helps to put fear to rest is to look people in the eye and greet them, or wave to a passers by. If I've looked at someone directly, he or she becomes a person, not an anonymous and frightening other. And I'm in a better position to judge whether this person is a threat. At the same time, by engaging the direct attention of the other person, I've made myself visible as an individual, no longer a stranger. This helps, too, to relieve the sense of isolation that solo travel can engender.

Not all safety relates to threat from others. There is potential danger when hiking alone far from other people. My basic rule here is to watch the step I'm taking, not be anticipating the next step. This helps ensure that the ground I step on is firm, the rock won't slide, there are no snakes underfoot. I did encounter a rattlesnake on BLM land in Wyoming about ten feet from my motorhome. It was a little fellow, probably a prairie rattler, not a diamondback, and it was as eager to get away from me as I was to avoid it—I reacted by throwing up my hands as to a thief; it reacted like a snake and hurried away—but it reminded me of my rule to watch where I put my feet.

The fact is, after three years of travel, I have never really been threatened or in danger. With a little common sense, it's a safe world out there. I'm convinced I'm as safe as I would be in any other lifestyle.

Safety Tips

Regardless of whether a person is single or not the following safety tips are worthwhile:

  ☆　Always keep your RV and vehicle in good mechanical condition with the gas tank at least half full.

  ☆　Put a lock on your screen door and keep it locked when in isolated areas.

★ Be aware of people around you.

★ Keep family and friends informed of your travel plans. Use an itinerary or message service to do this.

★ Consider a cell phone for emergencies.

★ Amateur radio may be a good option for emergency communications. It gives you greater range and security than a CB radio.

★ When asking for help on a CB do so on Channel nine—the emergency channel—rather than the truckers channel, which everyone, including the bad guy, monitors.

★ If threatened, blow your horn. Bad guys don't like noise.

★ At a red light be alert to what is going on around you. Leave enough space so you can pull around if necessary.

★ Ask what areas to avoid when in a new town.

★ If you notice someone suspicious near your RV or vehicle walk in a different direction to seek help.

★ Beware of people in civilian clothes driving unmarked cars who show you what appears to be a police badge. Don't roll down your window or get out. Instead, call the police on your cell phone and ask that a marked police car be sent.

★ When boondocking, look for other RVs and park nearby.

★ Don't tell anyone that you are traveling alone.

★ When checking in at campgrounds imply there are two of you.

★ When alone in your rig talk to the "other" person in the rig as you go out the door to make it appear you are not alone.

★ Wave to the "other" person in the rig to make it appear someone is with you.

★ For women—place a man's hat on the dash, a large pair of shoes or boots next to the steps, and/or a large dog dish next to the steps (even if you don't have a dog).

★ Carry a personal alarm.

★ Lock your vehicle when you leave it, including at the service station.

★ Before placing decals on your RV or vehicle consider whether or not it advertises that you travel alone.

★ Keep an extra set of keys in a realtor's lock box attached to your propane tank or some other part of your RV.

★ Be creative when selecting your weapon. After dark, a raised shade followed by a flash from a camera will startle and scare off an intruder.

★ **Listen to your intuition**—be prepared to leave and leave anything you put outside behind.

★ Common sense and walking with confidence are two of your best tools for protecting yourself.

Safe Camping Spots

When you listen to your intuition and use your common sense you can safely camp many places. If you don't use these skills you will not be safe even in a heavily guarded campground. For that matter you will not be safe in the traditional lifestyle.

Many of us leave large cities with high crime rates to find ourselves traveling in small communities with lower crime rates. Just placing yourself in an RVing community reduces your risk. RVers are some of the most honest people you will find in today's society. We have seen chairs and coolers holding a camping site for days on end without being stolen. You can count on RVers to come running to help if anything looks out of place.

This does not mean, however, that when you are in a campground you can let your guard down. I have heard stories of bikes being stolen, cars being broken into and so on in campgrounds. I have yet to hear similar stories about people boondocking. However, this does not mean you are not at risk when boondocking.

One person shared a story at an Escapade. They were staying in a campground and a knock at the door woke them from a sound sleep. Instead of asking the typical, "Who is it?" they may have saved their life by calling out, "What do you want?" This led to the intruder, claiming he was the manager, to say their RV had a flat tire. They thanked him and said they would take care of it in the morning, never opening the door. The intruder then went down the way and held some other campers up at gun point.

I was co-hosting a Boomer Christmas gathering in southern Arizona when one of our group responded to a knock at his door. Instead of finding out who was at the door the Boomer opened the door, believing it was one of the other Boomers camped near by. Instead it was a Mexican alien looking for food. After quizzing the alien about his lack of food and money, he was sent on his way with some food.

This Boomer was fortunate. It could have been someone with a gun in his hand who knocked on his door. Even being camped close to friends does not guarantee your security.

Where you camp makes little difference, but how you respond to a situation could make all the difference in the world.

Avoiding Loneliness

As we heard from Coby in a previous chapter, community is a big concern for some people. Traveling without a companion may make this an even bigger concern for singles. There are several groups singles can join if they would like to become involved in an RVing singles community. Here are a few of those groups:

Loners Of America

LOA was founded in September 1987 as a not for profit singles RV club. In 1999 LOA had over 500 members. Members consider the club one big happy family that enjoys camping and caravanning. LOA does have one strictly enforced by-law, "Members of the opposite sex may not occupy the same rig, unless blood related, at a LOA function."

Loners On Wheels

In 1997 Loners On Wheels had approximately 4,000 members. They do require their members be *legally* single and members of the opposite sex are not allowed to share the same camping unit at club events. The average age of their members is 65, although they do have some members in their late thirties.

The club has chapters across the United States. The chapters have three to four day camp-outs once a month during the appropriate season for their area. They also have scheduled happy hours and dinners out. The national newsletter lists the activities so members outside the chapter may participate when in the area. Chapters plan rallies and list them in the national newsletter. There is generally a fee to attend rallies. Individual members plan caravans, but they are not official club functions. Loners on Wheels also offers their members a mail forwarding service.

Wandering Individual's Network

Wandering Individuals' Network, Inc. or WIN, considered a club by their members, is actually a corporation providing a clearinghouse of information. In 1997 WIN had 700 members. The average age of their members was 61, with the age range being between 33 and 70. To join WIN you must be under 70 at the time you join, but once you are in you can stay as long as you like.

Currently WIN operates on volunteer help, but expects to be able to afford paid help when they reach 1,000 active members.

The corporation sponsors no events. However, the members volunteer to host parties—called gatherings—which, are printed in the newsletter. A low gathering fee exists to prevent the volunteer host from being out of pocket for the gathering.

Participation in caravans is free, with all travel and food costs being picked up by each individual. Circuits—caravans lasting five to seven months—allow people to drift in and out of the circuit. Members must be active in the group and not just using the group as a "safe place to park." While a person could live within the WIN system, there is no guarantee they will not have to travel alone.

WIN's membership is almost a 50:50 ratio of male to female. They are a social group that has no business meetings and offers many activities. WIN's target is the young single RVer. The size, age and price of your RV is not an issue—no one is trying to impress anyone. WIN members do consider each other family and a hugging tradition exists.

RVing Women

RVing Women or RVW is a support network for women, providing support and information on RVing. It is not necessary to own an RV, but one must be a woman to become a member. Married women are invited to join, but their husbands are not welcome at RVW functions. In 1999 RVW had 4,000 members with an average age in the mid fifties and an age range from the twenties to the eighties.

RVW has a paid staff of two. Volunteer members work closely with the staff to plan and direct rallies. The staff plans events and caravans with input from members. *RVing Women* magazine (which even Paul was impressed with) lists rallies, events and caravans at least six months in advance. Rallies and events happen from coast to coast throughout the year. Caravans may go anywhere from Alaska to Mexico.

Members may attend mechanical and other RVing classes that teach members how to survive the RVing lifestyle. Once a year there is a five day national convention offering seminars, classes, displays, exhibits, entertainment and fun with other RVing women.

Another resolution to loneliness might be to find a traveling companion, not necessarily a spouse, to travel with. This is what Pat and Shelia did.

Shelia was traveling part time, but often found she would invite someone to join her on her trips to overcome loneliness.

Pat, who had never been on her own before, found traveling full-time gave her independence and freedom. She also found she enjoys being alone with herself. When she was lonely she would also invite someone to travel with her.

Pat wasn't interested in marriage and wasn't looking for a traveling companion when she and Shelia met at an RVing Women Rally. They hit it off with similar pasts, interests and values and in the next year and a half became close friends. Eventually they decided to try sharing the same RV.

They parked the smaller motorhome and moved into the larger motorhome. After a year they decided they enjoyed traveling together and that it was time to upgrade their RV, so they sold the small motorhome and traded the large motorhome for a new motorhome. They have now been traveling full-time together for four years and have moved up to a bus conversion.

Solo's

Solo's is an Escapee Bird of a Feather group. They have a bimonthly newsletter and are very organized. Rallies and cruises are just some of the organized activities for Solo members. You must be an Escapee to belong to this group.

Finding Companionship in Unique Ways

Jerry, an only child, enjoys being by himself. When he needs a people fix he looks for his Boomer friends, not a single's group. Even though most Boomers are married he feels accepted among these friends who have similar interests and values. He also enjoys a good time without the pressure of deciding if he would like to spend more time with a particular woman, since they are mostly spoken for.

Jerry would like someone special in his life to share the wonders of full-timing with. He has met some nice women as a result of helping a fellow camper with a generator problem. The camper offered to pay him, but he refused. Jerry felt he was just helping his neighbor.

The camper with the generator problem wanted to do something for Jerry. When he learned Jerry was looking for that special someone he knew what he could do. It seems the generator owner is the publisher of a single's resource newsletter. He offered to run an ad for Jerry. As a result Jerry has corresponded with women across the United States. If it seems the relationship might have potential he meets them in person. As a full-timer Jerry can go and stay wherever the right relationship takes him.

Other Tidbits

Traveling alone will wear you out quicker than traveling with a companion. To ease the impact, plan your route before departing. Write down the route or highlight a map, noting fuel and rest stops, and post these directions on your dash. If you have a computer there are many good map programs that will draw you a map for each journey.

Be sure to keep track of where you are; which towns you are between and how far it is to the nearest town. Also keep track of the mile markers and watch for signs indicating police, hospital, clinic, service station, chamber of commerce and other places you can obtain assistance. This will help pass the time and get you help quicker if you should have problems.

If you are planning to work on the road be sure to know whether the positions you plan to consider require couples. Jobs like campground hosting and selling Christmas trees often require couples. If you want the job you may need to find a partner to share the job.

Not mechanically inclined? In a community where you plan to spend time every year find a mechanic you trust. Let them know you will return to them when you are in the area, but ask if they are willing to be a consultant if you have problems in another community. This way you can discuss repairs with someone you trust before you have the work done.

Everyone does things differently. There is no right way. Do what works for you. Be aware and knowledgeable. You and you alone are in charge of your life.

Finally, if you would like to be a full-timer, but are not secure in taking that first big step, consider joining one of the singles groups. Spend some time with these people and learn all you can. If the first group doesn't meet your needs try another group. Not everyone fits into any one group. You might even consider buying a small, inexpensive RV, just to spend some time testing the waters. If you decide the lifestyle is not for you, you will not be out much money. If, on the other hand, you love the lifestyle, you will have a better idea of what your needs are for that perfect wheel estate.

23

Gypsy Kids:
Little Tikes and
Homeschooling

Have you been dreaming about full-timing, only to have the dream burst when your kids come running through the house? Obviously you will have to shelf that dream until they are on their own. Or will you? In the next two chapters you will hear how three families have taken to the road. We will also look at some concerns that come up when you plan to travel with kids—concerns like homeschooling, socialization and finding the right wheel estate. Finally check the resources in the **Resource Directory** for help in starting on your journey.

As you consider traveling full-time with your kids many questions will come to mind. Some of these questions may be:

★   How will your children adapt to the full-timing lifestyle?
★   Can you all survive in a small house on wheels?
★   Where does a baby fit in the picture?
★   What are your child's social skills now?
★   How will their social skills develop on the road?

☆   Will an only child's social development be hindered with mostly adult socialization (no sibling interaction) or will it be enhanced—making the child a very successful adult when he grows up?

☆   Will homeschooling provide a good education for your children?

☆   Should you try homeschooling before hitting the road?

☆   What are the homeschooling requirements in the state that will be your domicile?

☆   Can you live with these requirements or should you consider domicile in another state?

The answers to these questions will be different for each family. However, we can take a closer look at some of the issues and see how three families have overcome them.

Babies and Little Tikes

Yikes, where does the baby go! Traveling with babies and preschoolers presents a whole new challenge. The following are a few tips Shelley Zoellick shares in her **Families on the Road** newsletter and web page.

Where will the crib, dresser, changing table and rocker go? Well, you can stop worrying as a baby does not need all of that "stuff." A collapsible travel bed works as well as a crib. There is even a travel bed that makes into a changing table. When the baby outgrows the travel bed they can sleep on a couch or a bed if you have a second bedroom.

You won't have a dresser and the baby doesn't need one either. Just be sure the RV has plenty of storage space. As for a changing table, your bed or the kitchen table will work just fine.

Since you will be on the go a good stroller is important. It should collapse easily to fit into a storage compartment. Make sure you can remove the cover for cleaning. Combination items such as stroller/baby carrier/infant car seat come in handy when you are short on space. If you plan to do any hiking a backpack may also be useful.

Need some peace of mind? A swing may be just the thing. They are portable and can be stored out of the way.

It can be a challenge to keep the upholstery and window coverings clean when little ones have food in their hands. A high chair that is easy to clean and folds up to store under the table would be a good investment. Set the high chair at the end of the table to keep those messy little hands and spills away from the upholstery and window coverings. Possibly a better choice than a high chair is an inexpensive baby seat that clamps to the end of any table. They are light weight, take up little space and can even be used at a picnic table. Before buying one of these, check the underside of your dining table for cross members that may prevent their use.

Don't forget to childproof an RV just like a house or apartment. You can start with electric outlet covers and childproof cabinet latches.

Kids do not need many toys. Shop for small ones that take up little space. Set some aside so you can rotate them when a child grows tired of his toys. This saves the expense of buying new ones to clutter the RV.

RVs may not have a room where you can put the baby down and close the door. This means it could be hard to watch TV or visit with friends in the evening. Changing the baby's sleep schedule to match your schedule may be a solution.

Visit with your pediatrician or family doctor about your new lifestyle. Ask if you can contact them with any concerns you may have while you are traveling. This may save you a trip to an unknown doctor. If you must see a doctor on the road, you will have the doctor from your previous lifestyle to call for a second opinion.

Summers on the Road

Shelia and Dan travel during the summer with their young children. They cannot go full-time yet because they need the health insurance coverage from Dan's teaching job.

Their first summer on the road Dan and Shelia had only two children, one four and the other almost two. Their third child was on the way.

Shelia and Dan selected their RV based on price and the fact it had a real tub, a necessity with small children. The sleeping accommodations were not ideal. Dan slept on the pull down bed over the driver and passenger seat, as the girls were too young to sleep there. Shelia and the two girls slept on the pull out couch, which worked fine since the girls were small. With the arrival of the third child they plan to use the dinette as a bed also.

Shelia says, "There is really no time alone, but that is just like being at home with young kids, no time alone." She recommends, "Before buying an RV parents should consider whether there is a permanent bed built in or if the bed must be "set up" each night. This is especially something to look for if you have small children who need naps."

With limited storage space, a box of toys is kept in the RV while the trikes, stroller and wagon go in the towed vehicle.

Dan and Shelia combine traveling for pleasure and visiting relatives, with business—a mobile on-site detailing business. When business is good they stay a while, otherwise they move on.

While the kids are too young for school they do keep a children's atlas handy and use it to find the states they visit. They also look to see where license plates in the campground are from.

Shelia says they find more kids in state parks than other types of campgrounds. "Young kids seem to make friends so easily," she says, "and they did not seem to mind that they were just a day or two in a place. Of course, maybe it was because the goal was to get to grandma's and grandpa's house."

With limited space, especially with kids, the walls can start to close in on you. An outing should help to relieve that tension. Visit a mall, library, museum or just take a walk and see if your spirits don't get a lift. Shelia recommends, "Stop at places kids will find interesting and take along a bike for them."

Full-timing with an Only Child

Jeff and Susan have always had some gypsy blood in them. When they were first married they spent ten months touring Europe, staying half the time in a tent and the rest of the time in hotels. After working a few years to build up their finances, they were ready to hit the road again. This time they customized a van and traveled for 18 months in North America. Again they returned to work and started to save for early retirement, never realizing how early retirement would come for them.

Samantha came along when Susan was 40. By this time both Susan and Jeff were well established as a childless couple and neither of their jobs would accommodate a child. When Susan looked within herself she realized she wanted to enjoy her child as much as she could, yet she did not want to stay at home. It was with this realization that she proposed to Jeff that they return to the gypsy lifestyle of previous years.

Jeff and Susan told their families they planned to travel full-time with Samantha. The families' response was concern for Samantha's well being. Then Jeff's brother, a psychologist who never travels the way they do, thought about it and gave his blessing. He thought it was significant that they were taking Samantha's environment with them. This would give Samantha a sense of security that military kids do not receive. Yet it is perfectly okay with society to shuffle military kids from one environment to the next.

With three-month-old Samantha they loaded into their van and took off. It didn't take long for them to realize that they needed more room for Samantha's "stuff," so they bought a travel trailer to pull behind their van. This was back in 1989. They continue to travel full-time today, only their wheel estate is now a motorhome.

"This lifestyle has been so indulgent," Susan says, "because Jeff and I have been there every step of the way watching Samantha grow."

"When we started out," Jeff says, "we thought we would be on the road one year minimum, five years maximum, then we would put her in school. In our second year on the road we met several Escapees who were retired teachers and administrators from public schools. They uniformly recommended we consider homeschooling rather than putting Samantha in public schools and reminded us to not overlook the quality of education she would get from traveling."

Homeschooling programs were not the only thing to consider. A concern with the homeschooling concept, regardless of whether a family is traveling or not, is the child's socialization. Jeff looked back to his school days and realized, as an adult he doesn't have any friends who were also childhood friends. He has stayed in touch with one high school and one college friend, but that is it. "So, I figure," Jeff says, "it is not as important as a lot of people think, as long as she learns how to interact with people. It doesn't matter what the ages are. Actually she is probably learning better interaction skills by interacting with adults than she would with her peers."

Jeff and Susan also had a concern with how surroundings affect a person's behavior. For example, a nursing home may cause a person to give up. While in their own environment the same person would thrive, knowing they had value in society. Schools also cause institutionalized behavior. Kids associate only with kids their age and may even pick on younger kids. Grades have the potential to impact on a child's position in society later in life. Kids are picked on for their physical appearance, destroying self-esteem.

Homeschooling, on the other hand, brings back the idea of one room schools from days gone by. Homeschooled kids learn at their own pace. Their learning abilities do not affect their social position. They interact well with kids of any age, adjusting their activities accordingly.

Homeschooling lessons also allow a child to stretch their creativity and make learning more interesting. For example, Samantha likes to make games out of her lessons, which increases what she learns from the lesson. When she reads a story she enjoys changing names and even the sex of the characters in the story, which she could not do if she did not already understand the lesson.

Jeff and Susan did their research on homeschooling programs and decided to use the Calvert system. They are happy with the program and continue to use it today.

As Jeff, Susan and Samantha travel, they go on field trips to museums and other interesting places. These field trips are a great learning experience for all three of them. In the future they would like to follow some historical routes, like the Oregon Trail or Laura Ingell's travels.

Jeff and Susan realize they must keep the door open to the traditional lifestyle and public schools. Each year they re-evaluate the situation before ordering the homeschooling program for the next grade. So far Samantha does not have a desire or need to attend public school.

The Value of Homeschooling

Let's take a closer look at homeschooling. It is legal in all 50 states and Canadian provinces. Each state and province has their own regulations, however. These regulations may require as little as notifying the school district and having the child tested. Or they may be as complex as meeting the requirements of becoming a private school.

Homeschooling in the United States costs an average of $546 a year per child while the average public school cost, excluding capital expenses, is $5,325 per child. It takes only a couple of hours of homeschooling to teach what it takes public schools six hours to teach. With all this in mind, you would expect the best education to come from public schools, but that is not the case. Homeschool students score, on average, between the 80th and 87th percentile in every subject on standardized achievement tests. Public school students score in the 50th percentile.

The benefits of homeschooling do not end here. The additional time parents spend with their children helps them develop solid character and moral values. These values help children withstand negative peer pressure.

Homeschooling also forces a child to think for themself. As a result the child grows up to be an independent thinker, rather than an imitator of thoughts.

Socialization and Homeschooling

One of the biggest concerns expressed about homeschooling is how a child will learn to socialize. For some reason society seems to think the only way a child learns to socialize is by interacting with people their own age. As adults we socialize with the youngest and oldest members of society and everyone in between. Why shouldn't a child learn socialization skills through the same broad range of people?

What do children teach other children about socializing? Often they teach judgment and discrimination. Does a child have the right brand name clothes? How do they do in school? Are they on the football team or a cheerleader? Do they look different? All of this can have an adverse affect on how a child perceives themselves the rest of their life.

Children need the guidance of adults who have successfully dealt with similar issues in their lives. This allows them to learn how to effectively socialize and maintain high self-esteem.

In the full-timing lifestyle, children meet people from all walks of life. This exposure to people goes beyond socialization. Often, full-timing children are adopted by other RVers, who teach them hobbies, play cards with them and raise their self-esteem. The memories and impressions from these relationships will live on in a child throughout their life.

What parent doesn't dream of their child being independent and achieving their dreams? Something all full-timers have in common is independence and the ability to achieve dreams. What better role models could a child have for these traits?

Samantha Enjoys Socializing

Regardless of the environment, some kids are naturals when it comes to interacting, while others will struggle to develop this skill. In one campground Samantha met an eight year old who knew how to work the campground. He would round up all the kids in the campground and they would play at his RV. He did the same thing at the next campground where Samantha saw him again. "You couldn't have a better role model for her to learn how to do it," Susan says. "The kids that are going to be successful are the ones that are going to be able to make friends and have fun together."

Susan says, "Samantha makes friends easily and finds she is very popular. She considers our adult friends to be her friends as well and she even has her own time with them. We have been astounded at the number of people who have spent time with her."

Jeff shares a story on how these friendships develop.

We were at an Escapee park and Susan was sick so Samantha and I went to Happy Hour by ourselves. When it came our turn to tell a little bit about ourselves I introduced Samantha and just on a whim I told how she loves animals. I then asked for a show of hands of how many had dogs or cats that Samantha could come and pet. Instantly about 25 hands went up. I promised we would make the rounds if people would let us know where their sites were.

I wasn't that serious about meeting all the pets and figured walking around we would occasionally run into some of these people. I just wanted to make it known that Samantha loves pets so when she was out in the park and met someone she could also meet their pet.

By the time we had been there a week I started to get complaints because I had not brought Samantha to meet their pet. Samantha would go out on her tricycle and I would follow her on the rounds, which took several hours. People would greet her by name and she would wave at them. If they had a pet she would pull in and stop.

When it came time for us to leave we had to make the rounds one last time to say good-bye to all of Samantha's friends.

To develop Samantha's group interaction skills Susan and Jeff enroll her in children's programs—such as a winter camp in California or tap and dance classes—when they are in one place long enough. She socializes quite well with small groups of kids, but is uncomfortable with large groups of kids. But then how many kids in the traditional lifestyle face the same discomfort with large groups?

"It is funny," Susan says, "because she talks the talk and does all this stuff other kids do, even though she doesn't interact with other kids in the traditional sense."

Susan's sister has a daughter two years older than Samantha. "I have to tell you," Susan says, "it is weird because I can't say that there is that much difference between these children. My sister has raised a child in one location and has quite a different lifestyle, yet the girls are really very similar."

Homeschooling and Full-timing

One homeschooling parent says, "Homeschooling is always a commitment—when you're "on the road" it's an even more demanding commitment, but definitely worth the effort!"

Full-timing greatly expands the child's classroom. Children learn history by visiting historical sites and science by visiting national parks and dinosaur digs. Keeping a journal and writing stories about actual adventures teaches English. Exposure to culturally rich communities teaches children how others live.

If you are uncertain about how you and your children will adjust to homeschooling, try it before you hit the road. A phased transition into full-timing can make the adjustment easier for the entire family.

Do You Have What it Takes?

By now you are beginning to see the advantages of homeschooling your children. But what about you? Do you have what it takes to successfully homeschool your children? Parents are the first teachers children have. You teach your children to tie their shoes; say their ABC's; extend common courtesies; and many other things. You may not be certified to teach your children, but you are certainly qualified.

If you can answer yes to the following questions you probably have what it takes to homeschool your children.

- ☆ Are you willing and able to spend a lot of time with your children?
- ☆ Are your children people you like and respect as individuals?
- ☆ Do you enjoy your children's company?
- ☆ Is learning something you enjoy?

At this point you may want to do your own research on homeschooling. See the ***Resource Directory*** for a list of places to start your research.

Once you feel comfortable with the idea of homeschooling your children there are three steps you will take to get started.

* ★ Determine the homeschooling laws for your state of domicile. Do you need to change your domicile state?
* ★ Evaluate the different teaching methods and determine which will work best for you and your children.
* ★ Find the curriculum, books and other tools.

Two of your best resources will be families who are already homeschooling and homeschooling organizations in your area. These families and organizations should be able to answer your questions and get you off to a fast start. The school district and churches in your area may be able to put you in touch with these people.

24

Gypsy Kids:
A Large Family
and Selecting a Home

I learned about the following family at the spring Escapade in 1997 and was on my way to meet them when they pulled out. Disappointed, I sent them a letter asking about life on the road. After exchanging a couple of voice messages, learning the children were actually young adults and sending on some additional questions for the "kids" I received this story.

Full-timing with Four Kids

Children's Ages:

	June 1997	June 1990 when they started traveling
Deanna	19	Age 12
Matthew	17	Age 10
Jason	15	Age 8
Carissa	12	Age 5

First we hear from Joyce (the mother) who shares the story of their life on the road.

>   *The first year Steve [a teacher] took a leave of absence (no pay) with the promise of a contract offer again in the 1991-92 school year. This way we were free to travel and work along the way. We didn't have any payments to make.*
>
>   *We had converted a 35 foot school bus. It had four bunks in the back room, a couch midway that made into a full bed, two very small closets, lots of under bed boxes, a porta potti in the bathroom along with a sink and a 32-inch square shower. It was three years before we installed a black water holding tank and real toilet. The bus also had an apartment size stove in the kitchen area across from the bathroom, a small semi-automatic washer, a water heater, a furnace, a small couch up front and two sets of coach seats facing each other with a table between. An RV made for us by us!*
>
>   *We sold most of our household items, and stored a few others. We had been renting a house in Vermont, which we gave up. Our two older children were already on their own.*
>
>   *We had been homeschooling in Vermont for two years and decided that we could see some of the places we studied about while keeping up with the homeschooling. We had Steve's summer pay, plus $1,000 in the bank, which we saved to rent a place when we returned the next summer. We towed a small Datsun station wagon. Our original plan was to be gone for just a year.*
>
>   *As we traveled we did not eat out or pay money for tourist attractions—we just went to see the country. We stopped in Shipshewana, Indiana, for a week or so the first summer and met some friends there. We also got to know some Amish families. It was there that we met a fiddler who inspired our family into music. He was*

making his living playing the fiddle in flea markets and selling tapes and other miscellaneous items. His home on wheels was a very humble rig.

In Elkhart, Indiana, we spent some of our money on a new gas/electric refrigerator. Up to then we used a small 110-volt fridge and found it very inconvenient to buy ice while traveling and not plugged in.

Steve did not work till we were in Washington that September. He got a temporary job at an RV repair shop in Kent. He also worked at a fish fry booth at the Puyallup Fair for a couple weeks. We found that temporary jobs were available for minimum wage up to seven dollars an hour or so—no benefits, but enough to support our lifestyle.

We do not have health insurance and do realize that if we need emergency care, we'd have to pay the bill. We trust the Lord as our "Caretaker" and provider of health and ability to find work as needed. We know that this is not the way most people travel, but for seven years we have traveled this way. Our needs have all been met, as well as many of our wants!

This has been a big difference from living in a traditional home with all the home expenses! We shop yard sales and thrift stores for bargains. At first we could only carry bare essentials for clothing. Since we have started entertaining, our needs and essentials have changed, along with the size of our bus!

Now when we need something, we know about thrift stores, specialty stores and Wal-Marts all over the country. Since we do travel through the same places often, we wait to shop where we know that we can find what we need. Wal-Mart is also a favorite overnight spot, but we always ask permission and are given it.

Back to homeschooling. We have used various curriculums, but have settled on a mix of textbooks and some old secular workbooks that an Amish printer has kept in print. We do homeschool with Vermont state knowledge—that is our official state of domicile at this point—but we are free to use any curriculum that we choose.

We decided to homeschool while we lived in Vermont because we wanted to be in control of what our children were taught.

We know other families in different states that homeschool and we see them each year on trips north, south, east and west. Our children exchange ideas, friendship and letters with these other homeschoolers. They also have friends who go to the public schools in different areas where we spend time. These friends are involved with music in some way, so that is a common bond now.

Matthew and Deanna both took their GED test in Arizona and now have a General Equivalency Diploma.

Now, to the socializing aspect. Since we have been traveling our children have developed friendships with many people—young and old—along the way. Yes, they do have friends their own ages, but also have 60 and 70 year old friends as well as others at ages between. I feel that this has been a real important part of their education. They have learned many things from these older people which "traditional home" children do not get the opportunity to do. Our family has many diverse interests because of the encouragement of the adults along the way.

Deanna is a good seamstress, a good cook, as well as a good musician and song writer and some "Gramma or Grampa" along the way is always showing interest in her newest creation.

Matthew has learned the trade of hat making—Western style hats—and has made over 35 custom style and fit cowboy/Western hats in the last year. Matthew also has learned to repair all the fiddles that we have acquired, also the bass and is willing to do minor repairs on other instruments. He is our own in house Luthier!

Jason mows lawns and does odd jobs for people that we are around. He repairs bicycles, has learned to make hats also, teaches others to play the bass and is learning how to fly model airplanes after having made two with guidance from several retired friends he has met along the way.

Carissa has learned to knit and crochet from retired friends and has made baby afghans and dishcloths too. She also learned to sew with the help and guidance of a good friend who is retired. Carissa also has taught others to make dishcloths, even a mother of one of her good homeschooling friends.

Well—all this said—I think that any family wanting to travel shouldn't get hung up on providing socialization with other young people. If it happens, fine, but friendship with all ages is a real life situation and has not hurt our family. Maybe young people could benefit from a mix of socialization—peer pressure is not a problem then.

Since we have been in a bus for seven years, our children have been involved with the upkeep and repairs, just like in a traditional home. They just don't have their own lawns to mow. Windows need to be kept clean so that we can see the country; roof vents need to be repaired or replaced; the van has to be hooked up regularly and lights checked, etc., etc.!

We converted our school bus with the idea of using it for summer vacations. After one year of travel and returning to Vermont—to a traditional home and job—I think we were all ready to be back on the road! Especially after we found we could survive. We all had worked striping small parking lots; Steve worked at RV repair; we worked in a flea market; Steve worked in a cactus nursery—all this in the first year.

By November 1991 of the "return" year, Steve was disgusted with the public school scene and was ready to leave—so he got released from his contract and in January 1992 we packed the bus once again (at 22 degrees below zero). We headed south with four inches of snow and ice on the roof of the bus! Since then we have been on the road following the sun.

One thing we have found is that some areas and some states do not welcome school buses—even neat ones—or families with children into RV or mobile home parks. We don't like to be in the typical family parks for the same reasons that adult parks exist! Since we homeschool, our family has learned to keep busy reading, hiking, sewing, etc. and does not spend every waking hour playing. It is hard for other children to understand this concept and they want the children out playing all the time. Now that the children are teenagers they all seem to have some project or other to work on to keep them so busy even I can't always get their attention! We have taught our children to respect other people's property and privacy, so they have learned to live in their own area. Don't get me wrong—they love a good ball game, or ice skating or bowling, or hiking—we just do these things with other families or with other adults who have the same interests.

When we were in Washington, the first fall, we stayed in the bus on the edge of a friend's driveway. Steve's temporary work was a long drive—40 miles—so we needed to be closer. Campgrounds were not near enough or they cost too much—base rate plus so much for each extra person over two people. We consulted our FMCA directory and found a woman who offered us a corner of her very private yard way out in the country for as long as we wanted to stay. She became a good friend. We stayed six weeks till the rain and dampness drove us to Arizona and a dry climate.

We have certainly found that our family has been shown the utmost hospitality and we certainly have appreciated, but not expected it. In many cases we have been surprised by the cordiality of total strangers—soon to be friends!

One great complaint that I see as a problem to RV traveling from campground to campground: originally camping was a cheap way for families to vacation and travel. Now if a family can afford an RV or has converted a bus, campground rates have gotten so high that it is almost impossible for any but the most well off to travel to them. Most rates are for only two people and many in snowbird areas prohibit children, except for a short visit.

In Arizona we had most parks turn us away, even though they offer monthly rates. We made a lot of retired friends when people got to know our children at music jams. In one small park (11 sites) we were invited by a vote of those in the park to stay in their park. It has been our winter home for four years now.

Since our first year traveling and meeting musicians along the way our children have picked up instruments to learn. The fiddle and mandolin were the first instruments acquired in our first Arizona winter. In June Matt picked up the fiddle and tried to play it and he could. He didn't know many songs but certainly had "the touch." He has since become a wonderful fiddle player—recognized by many as a champion.

Deanna had played piano when we left in June 1990 but when Matt picked up the fiddle she played an accordion that we found at a yard sale for five dollars. She then tried the mandolin and really mastered it. She now plays just about any instrument she picks up.

Carissa and Jason learned to play a harmonica first, then both went on to the fiddle. Carissa also plays a little accordion and Jason has become an awesome bass player. All this has happened since we have been full-time on the road!

The winter of 1993-94 marked the time we decided to have Steve play guitar (which he had learned as a child) with the children for an income source. By then many people were really enjoying and encouraging our family's musical talents!

At first the instruments gave the children something to stay busy with. We have no TV. Now they are excellent musicians because of the many others who have played with them and encouraged them along the way. They have developed a talent that we did not know existed!

Since 1993 we have been entertaining and find great pleasure in the enjoyment others receive from our music.

We now have a 40 foot converted GMC bus, which we converted as a family in the summer/fall of 1995. The boys know as much about our bus as Steve does—they help him with mechanic work. They also did a lot of the inside conversion—working day and night for weeks, as we all did. It is truly our bus!

We made an open living/kitchen/dining area; put in a side aisle with two separate bedrooms—one for boys and one for girls; a bathroom split into three parts—a hall sink, a shower room and a toilet room (each just big enough); a washer in the kitchen and loads of storage in three big bays—which even contain a dryer.

We carry four bicycles and many, many instruments. We now tow a Ford van as we needed something bigger to carry us and our equipment to shows.

We winter in Arizona, then travel during the summers to visit our oldest son and daughter and our parents. We do some shows in the summer, but our busiest time is in the winter at the many festivals and shows in RV parks in Arizona.

Our bus is so comfortable to travel in and it is nice to know that we have everything with us as we travel and that we can stay in our own home anywhere! We have made many good friends along the way and have had so many wonderful experiences that I think it has been a good way of life for our children.

Deanna compiled the following responses from Matthew, Jason, Carissa and herself to questions I sent them.

What things do you like about traveling full-time?

We get to meet a lot of interesting people, besides visiting friends and family everywhere. Plus we've been places that most kids only get to read about. We know lots of adults who have never been out of their home state!

What things do you not like about traveling full-time?

We've been in nearly every National Park and the ranger talks bore us to tears!

If you could choose to live in one place or to continue to travel, which would you choose and why?

Jason would choose to live in one place. A 40 foot bus does not give him much room to spread out for hobbies, etc.

Carissa would choose to live in one place. She likes horses and would like to own one of her own.

Matt would choose one place also. He has a hat making business that he's starting up and that takes more room than we have.

I'm looking forward to settling down. It's been fun being on the road for seven years, but it's not something I want to do forever. Obviously, the fact that I'm getting married in June of 1998 has some bearing on this!

Basically we're all getting older and developing different interests and independence. However, our seven years on the road have been educational and are not something any of us would change if we could. For now, because of our band, we have good reason to stay on the road.

Do you have friends your own age? How do you make these friendships and stay in touch?

Yes, we have many friends our own ages. We meet a lot of fellow homeschoolers as we travel, plus we meet lots of kids at music festivals and fiddle contests who share similar interests (that's how I met my fiancé!).

We stay in touch with letters—piles of them—and occasional phone calls to special friends. We usually get to visit about once a year, depending on where they live.

What do you do in your free time?

Jason flies and builds (flies and rebuilds☺) remote control planes. He has three—the biggest one has a 63 inch wing span. We carry all three with us (you can see why he'd like more space!) He is usually able to find an RC airport in the area wherever we are and a helpful person willing to help him out, as he is still a beginning flier.

Matt spends his time either making hats, repairing some of our instruments (or someone else's), or reading—a hobby we all enjoy. We usually try to get library cards or borrow someone else's when we're in one place for a while.

Carissa spends her free time—when school is over—knitting or crocheting, listening to music and walking anyone's dog she can get a hold of!

I like to sew, when I have the space. I make a lot of the clothes we wear on stage. I also like to bake and cook—someone has to!

What do you like and dislike about how you go to school when you travel?

We have always homeschooled, even before we traveled, so that hasn't been an adjustment for us. We all are in favor of homeschooling because we can basically make our own schedule. There is a certain amount of work to be done in a year so we can take it as slowly or as quickly as we want to. And there's no homework! ☺

Dating and getting together with friends is a big thing for teens. How do you accomplish this when you don't stay long in one place?

As for our "socialization" as teenagers, I guess because it's always been this way for us we don't consider it a big deal. We get together with friends when we can and probably appreciate it a lot more than if it was a regular occurrence.

What do you do when you just need some space and need time to be by yourself?

Privacy is hard to find in a 40 foot rig! We usually go outside—on walks or whatever. We girls share a room and so do the two boys. Both bedrooms have doors, so it's usually possible to get the room to yourself for some part of the day anyway.

This family and those from the last chapter make it sound easy to pack up your kids and hit the road. It isn't always easy, however. Jeff and Susan met one couple who tried to raise their three kids on the road but, the kids were not happy in the lifestyle. When they reached high school age they sought stability in the traditional lifestyle by moving in with friends and relatives.

I read about another couple who hit the road with three teenagers. Two adjusted quite well, while the third did not. In the end the unhappy teenager lived with friends until he graduated from high school. While this worked for this family it certainly would not work for all families.

There is one significant thing the three families you read about have in common—the father's careers. Dan, in the first story, is a school teacher; Jeff, in the second story, was a juvenile probation officer before hitting the road; and Steve, in the last story, was also a school teacher. Isn't it interesting that with these backgrounds they all believe the lifestyle is good for their kids!

Selecting the Wheel Estate

There is one final thing you must do before you can take your family on the road. You must find a wheel estate that meets your needs.

Shopping for a wheel estate can be challenging when you have kids. You may want to start by making a list of each individual's priorities. Joyce, Steve and their four kids showed us how you can hit the road with very little and still survive. By the time they converted their second RV they knew privacy was important to them, so they built three bedrooms.

Samantha sleeps on the couch in their RV, which means putting her bedding away every day. However, the bedroom in their wheel estate has a door. This gives Jeff, Susan and Samantha a place to be by themselves for a while.

What activities do different family members have? Homeschooling requires a work space for assignments. Will you need space for a computer as well?

Shelia felt a bathtub was important with small children. Is it important for you? How many people need to sit down for a meal? With kids you probably do not want them juggling their plates on their lap.

What will each person bring along? What space do you need for hobbies? Remember Jason needed storage space for his RC airplanes and Matt needed space to make his western hats. How will the space requirements change, as the kids grow?

Make a list of each person's priorities now and what they may be in the future. Then write out a description of the perfect wheel estate for your family. Take this description with you when you go shopping.

If you cannot find an RV that comes close to the description of your perfect wheel estate it is time to step back and re-evaluate things as a family. Remember, if one family member's needs are not met the entire family will be unhappy.

If the shopping gets tough start looking at what it would take to remodel an RV to meet your needs. After all, most RVs are not built for a family to travel in full-time. If you can afford it you might want to look into custom or semi custom RVs. Some manufacturers will modify an RV to meet your needs. Then there are a few manufacturers who will build the RV completely to your specifications.

Moving In

It will take a while to get a family settled into a wheel estate. Go for several camping trips before permanently moving in, just to start growing accustom to your new home. On each camping trip make a list of things each person misses and feels they need to take along. If there is something you do not use, seriously consider giving it up.

One family had a great way of settling into their wheel estate. If time allows it may work well for you too. The family moved into their RV, but stayed parked in their driveway. This way they could exchange things in the trailer for what was in the house until they had just what they wanted to take along. Once they had what they needed they moved to a campground and auctioned everything in the house.

This and That

Not all campgrounds welcome children. Do your homework and know the regions where you are likely to experience this. Places where seniors go to winter will be at the top of the list. As Joyce shared however, they were still able to find a park in Arizona that would take them for the winter. This was because Joyce and Steve's kids knew campground etiquette. Instead of being pests they were young people the residents of that park wanted to spend time with.

As you travel you will find opportunities for the entire family to socialize at friends, relatives, campgrounds, churches, volunteer projects and YMCAs or YWCAs. For young children check the libraries for story hours. If you plan to be in an area for a while you can do what Jeff and Susan do with Samantha and enroll the children in camp or special classes. A couple of the resources in the **Resource Directory** offer directories of homeschoolers who welcome traveling homeschoolers. The opportunities are there. You just have to stretch your imagination a little to find them.

If you would like to communicate with full-timers who are homeschooling join Escapees and their RVing with Kids BOF. Subscribe to the **Families on the Road** newsletter. Also checkout the **Families on the Road** web site at *http://www.familiesontheroad.com.* Checkout the forum, chat and e-mail list, where you can visit with families on the road!

Preparing to travel full-time with children will not be easy, but the rewards will be huge! The family will come together to deal with issues and grow together. You and the children will have fun while learning through exploring, investigating, identifying and discovery. Why not try a full-timing adventure?

25

Physically Challenged Nomads

Double the Challenge

Colleen and Ed have always enjoyed camping. They started out sleeping under the stars, graduated to a tent, then added cots. Eventually they moved up to a van and finally a full sized RV. The first three years of their marriage they saved all their money so they could spend a year traveling in the United States and Mexico. After 37 years of marriage, with their two kids off on their own, Colleen and Ed hit the road full-time.

It sounds like a fairly typical full-timing story, however, I have left out one small detail. Struck with polio as teenagers, Ed and Colleen have been in wheelchairs since then. When I say small detail I am not discrediting the impact being in a wheelchair has on a person's life. I am simply acknowledging that after being in wheelchairs for nearly 45 and 50 years, Colleen and Ed do not think of wheelchairs as the obstacles that able bodied people consider them to be. Sure, there are things that they have to rely on others to help them with—washing their travel trailer for example—but it does not hold them back from living life as full as any able bodied person, and sometimes fuller than many able bodied people.

When I asked Colleen what good things full-timing offers a person in a wheelchair she said:

Not having to find an accessible motel every night. Flying isn't all that easy either, what with long walkways, riding cherry picker type equipment to get in and out of the plane or being carried on the plane in a tiny chair which leaves you feeling like you will fall out on your head. And of course the bathrooms in airplanes are impossible, although they are working on that. Then, once you reach your destination, you have to rent a vehicle, often with special controls or a lift, which is expensive.

When you are traveling it is easier to have your own home, your own bed, your own bathroom and your own kitchen to go home to at night. Plus, it gives us the ability to go visit my brother in San Antonio and my mother, who is in a nursing home there. We can also easily go see our kids whenever we like.

I don't think we ever stop at night, get out and start setting-up before somebody walks over and says, 'Hey, can we lend you a hand?' We have had many good times and met some really wonderful people, which is probably the nicest part about the RVing lifestyle—the people you meet.

Equipment came to Colleen's mind when asked about problems with RVing in a wheelchair. "You have many systems on an RV and we just add to that by adding lifts and other equipment."

Colleen and Ed have had trouble with equipment.

Late one night I came home from a music jam in the campground. Ed had gone home earlier and was sound asleep. When I tried the lift it wouldn't come down, so I ended up spending the night in the van.

On another trip, we were driving our motorhome down the road and heard a horrendous explosion. We thought it might be the tires, but they seemed okay. Then all of a sudden there was another explosion. By this time we had pulled over and realized the noise had come from the door, which was old, warped and separating. Apparently some air got in where the door was separating and caused the explosions. Torn and jimmied the door would not open. We went on to the next town, looking for some help, found a AAA repair truck and the driver directed us to an RV repair facility. There we sat outside until someone came out and we could explain our problem. They provided a temporary fix until we could have the door replaced.

Today Colleen and Ed carry a cellular phone to call for help. If they were trapped in their RV they would not hesitate to use the exit window. Colleen and Ed also carry a copy of the **Travelin' Talk** directory, which lists people, often physically challenged themselves, in different communities throughout the world. Those listed in the directory are available to assist with planning a visit to their area and dealing with problems—such as a broken wheelchair or needing a doctor—when visiting their area.

Stroke of Luck?

I met Ted at a Spring Escapade. He is an outgoing person who does not intend to let life get him down. Ted shared his story with me while jumping at the opportunity to quiz me about those rowdy Boomers. He felt he was too old to join the Boomers, but I assured him his spirit was as strong as any other Boomer. After joining us for a couple of our gatherings that week he quickly signed up to be a Boomer.

Ted loved his job as district sales manager for Baldwin Piano and Organ Company and had no plans of ever retiring until June 30, 1990, when his world came crashing down around him. Ted had a stroke that day.

After several days in the hospital, and several months of rehabilitation, Ted returned home to his tri-level house and a marriage that had been in trouble for some time. It didn't take long for Ted to realize it wasn't going to work, so he decided to try a retirement home.

While the retirement home was agreeable, it was expensive and Ted dreamed about how much traveling he could do in his motorhome with that money. Just over a year after his stroke Ted took his motorhome to Louisiana to visit RV friends. That visit resulted in his decision to become a full-timer.

Before Ted could hit the road however, he had to come up with a permanent way of meeting his physical challenges on the road. Ted gets around with a three-wheel cart, which if he had to do again would be a four-wheel cart for additional stability. He has a Handi-lift, which he can operate himself, on the back of his motorhome to carry his cart. Ted's quad cane works fine to get him from the Handi-lift to the motorhome when he is ready to go. Strategically placed handles at the door of the RV and in the bathroom are also a big help.

"I can handle most things by myself, but I have learned to ask for help when I need it," Ted says. "I appreciate the willingness of people to help when asked. This includes young folks, especially teenagers."

Ted tells of one such incident. "I was pumping gas and I accidentally dropped the hose. My stroke makes it very difficult for me to bend over, so I was standing there trying to figure out how I was going to pick up the hose when the guy at the next pump walked over. He picked up the hose, handed it to me and said, 'You really screwed up that time, didn't you?' We just looked at each other and had a good laugh."

"Many times people don't know whether to help or not. I can see it in their faces." Ted recommends offering to help and leave the decision to the handicapped person.

My Life Will Not Be Paralyzed

In 1978 Robert was partially paralyzed from his waist down. He now uses forearm crutches to get around. In 1980 Robert returned to college for five years, hoping to start over. It wasn't long after graduation that he realized no one would hire him due to a fear of lawsuits. Next Robert spent some time fishing from his own boat until one day he decided to try full-timing.

"Retrofitting my rig didn't require a lot," Robert said. "I have a fifth-wheel, but I don't use the stairs. Instead I slide in on my fanny, transfer to the first step in the hallway, then transfer to the couch, from where I can use my crutches. It works for me."

Robert boondocks a lot with the help of solar panels, an inverter and a small generator mounted in the back of his pick-up. He had an electric cart but found keeping it charged, when boondocking, was a problem.

Robert shares the following wisdom. "First, considering full-timing as a lifestyle will make anyone anxious. A person can find all kinds of reasons not to go. Sometimes it requires literally forcing yourself out the door. I think most will be surprised and happy they did it."

"Second, not only are there adjustments to be made and things to be learned by handicap people, there is a lot for any new RVer to learn. The more you go, the more you learn and therefore the more confidence you gain. I know I have discovered ways of doing things that have helped me. They may not be right for someone else, but they do work."

"For instance, I keep a walker in my kitchen when I'm preparing meals—it's easier to cook and do the dishes. I also have a shower bench for bathing. The best thing about RVs is the walls are only a fingertip away when we need help steadying ourselves. Since my left leg has 95 percent use I had a left foot accelerator installed in my truck."

"Finally, you are going to have fun, health permitting. When the day arrives that you cannot do it anymore, you can move your home permanently into an RV park and you will have some beautiful memories to look back on!"

Obviously Colleen, Ed, Ted and Robert all have a real will to live life and get the most out of it. They don't see their challenges as a barricade to life, but as an opportunity to grow and experience more in life.

Support and Resources

Two support groups are actively trying to meet handicapped RVers needs. Escapees has a BOF (Birds of a Feather) Group for the physically challenged. The No Limits BOF works to provide support for both the physically challenged and their care givers.

The Handicapped Travel Club (HTC) is another group. Five disabled couples who received a great deal of therapy from travel and association with other disabled campers founded HTC in 1973. These couples decided to form the HTC to encourage other handicapped people to travel, meet and exchange ideas.

In 1997 HTC had 250 active members. To receive the most benefit from HTC, members should have an RV or be in the process of getting one. If you are unsure of how to obtain an RV with the necessary modifications, HTC will connect you with members in your area who can help you with the process. HTC also publishes a newsletter, schedules get togethers and has an annual national rally.

As full-timing is not for every able bodied person, it is also not for all disabled people. A handicapped full-timer must be outgoing, creative in overcoming obstacles, comfortable with asking for help and have a desire to travel. As a handicapped person, if you have the desire and personality for full-timing, then go for it! Don't let anyone tell you that you can't. Colleen, Ed, Ted, Robert and others are testimony that you can!

26

Well Traveled Pets

Tiffany

My human promised that I could tell my full-timing story. I am Tiffany, Stephanie and Paul's fur friend and head of the household. I am a purebred cock-a-poo-peek-a-poo-poo. As unique as that sounds, I look very similar to an apricot poodle with a long tail.

I was six when we hit the road. I had stayed in a motel once and had traveled only a few times to Paul and Stephanie's parents. They refer to me as their "Granddog."

When my humans sold our house we moved to The Ranch, Paul's sister's home. I had spent a great deal of time here over the previous year, playing with my human cousins, the kittens and staying out from underfoot of the draft horses. I felt right at home.

Three weeks later I was in for a shock when slowly I saw what my humans were up to. They loaded a U-Haul trailer and we piled into the truck for three days! At night we would stop at these different rooms with a bed and bathroom. Every time I had to go to the bathroom my yard was different. The only thing familiar, besides the two humans I was quickly becoming disgusted with, was my bed. Thank goodness they brought that along!

On the fourth day we pulled into a parking lot and they put me, along with their bags, into a miniature house on wheels. The house sat up high and I could just about look eye to eye with anyone who came to the door. I had had enough of these human games, so when a stranger, who they called a salesman, came to the door I nearly scared him to death with my barking. I didn't want anyone getting the idea that we should move on. It was time to settle down! Ha! Little did I know!

That day I went back and forth between the truck and what they called an office. At least the people in the office were nice and gave me cookie bones! When it got dark we piled back in the truck, but this time that little house on wheels was attached to the truck. My humans had moved boxes upon boxes into the house on wheels. After a short drive we parked and all climbed back into that funny little house. I wanted to spend some time exploring, but there was no way I could move around all the boxes! I found an out of the way corner and buried my head in misery! What was happening to my wonderfully peaceful existence?

For three weeks they unpacked boxes and moved things around. Then we started to get back into a routine, although for a change they were home all day everyday. We were also moving to a new yard every few days. I stayed close and when they started to connect the little house on wheels to the truck, I insisted on supervising. I still prefer to supervise from outside and insist on riding in the truck. The humans think I don't know the little house on wheels arrives where we go. Actually, I don't trust the little house on wheels when it goes bouncing down the road. I stay close to my humans for safety.

After two months on the road I realized my humans would not leave me or the little house on wheels behind and I decided to drag my toys out all over the house. Boy did they get excited about that! Of course the little house was not long enough to play a decent game of ball, so I settled for tugging on an old sock.

I now look forward to a new yard every few days. It makes life exciting. A few weeks into the trip we stopped on the Oregon coast. My humans took me out to run in this fine loose beige stuff. They call it sand and said the mountains of sand are dunes. I ran all over the mountains of beige stuff. It was so soft and loose I thought it was like that white stuff my humans now call a four letter word. I dove nose first into the beige stuff and boy was I in for a shock! It scratched and hurt, while the white stuff is just cold and turns to water. I haven't done that again!

Three months into the trip I really shocked my humans when I stretched out on some lush grass and did not get up to climb in the truck when it came time to move. I just did not want to leave this place I really enjoyed.

My favorite spot to camp is in the desert, where I run free, under my human's watchful eye. Something about coyotes in the area. When I am inside and my human's are outside I sing the coyote song to make them aware I want to be outside. There is so much to smell and investigate in the desert! My humans say I have become a regular little desert rat!

I have also discovered squirrels and chipmunks, something that did not exist in my previous life. I enjoy sneaking up on the squirrels, but can never get very close, even though I squat down and tiptoe toward them. Chipmunks were a new discovery three years into our travels. I got good at treeing them and sitting at the bottom of the tree waiting for them to come down. I just don't understand why neither the squirrels nor the chipmunks want to play with me!

I am not the only furry head of household that did not much like the idea of traveling at first. My friend Nutmeg O'Cat didn't like it much either.

Nutmeg O'Cat

My humans, Lin and Betty, would take off and be gone for a couple of days every few days. I enjoyed the peace and quiet of being home alone. Then one day they got it in their head to take me along! Oh drats!

They hauled me out to this box with furniture in it. I wandered around the box, checking things out when all of a sudden one of my humans took a seat by the big window and the other slammed the door and said, "Let's go!" With that the box roared to life and started to vibrate and bounce. Like any good cat, I like to check things out carefully and at my own pace, so you can imagine how frightened I was by the noise and bouncing. I am a California cat who knows the ins and outs of earthquakes, but this was worse! I started to yowl with horror and continued to yowl for 45 minutes. I was sure my humans would end my misery, but they put their earplugs in and continued to do their thing.

Finally it was obvious they would do nothing and I crawled under the couch, letting out a "yek" between the tears running down my face. Eventually they came down to check on me and I was vibrating like a back massager. When they finally parked that monster box I went into hiding for several days.

I slowly became more comfortable with the box and ventured out to explore. My favorite discovery was the big window where I could lie sunning myself and safely watch the dogs go by.

Then all of a sudden my humans did it again, they made that awful box roar to life and shake me to death. I started to yowl and after 20 minutes realized the humans did not care, so I curled up in a corner and alertly watched for the next disaster to occur. It never has occurred and today I look forward to watching different dogs, birds and squirrels out the window in my new yards. This thing my humans call full-timing isn't so bad after all!

There were some changes that needed to take place in our box house. My humans put my litter pan in the shower. I was okay with this but I guess they got tired of having to clean the shower each time before using it. Then they came up with a great idea. Our little box house has a basement and they cut a hole beside the steps coming into the house to allow me to use my litter pan in the basement. I get privacy and they get my litter pan out of their way. I have some smart humans, if I say so myself!

Skeeter

I was 10 when my humans, Fred and Peggy, decided to become full-timers. This was quite a shock for me as I was very independent. I had a doggie door, so could come and go to the yard as I pleased. All of a sudden I found myself in a dog house on wheels with no doggie door. I had to beg to go out and then I had to wear one of those awful ropes.

We had been on the road for a few months when we reached a beach in Nova Scotia. I was about to have the thrill of my life and teach those humans a thing or two about me. We went down to this beach to take a walk and they took that awful rope off. I didn't waste any time making up for my lost freedom as I charged up and down the beach. I must have run for an hour and a half! Finally I flopped down on the beach and my human's came over and said, "So you like to run! We never knew." They are good about getting me out to run more often now.

About four months into our trip my humans took me for a check-up. The Vet said my liver enzymes were up, which concerned my humans. They took me for a re-test later and everything was okay. My human's were not the only ones stressed over the lifestyle change, but with time I came to accept the new lifestyle and felt better. Full-timing offers me so much more. My life is no longer just the backyard. Now it is as big as my human's allow it to be and there are no limits!

A Human's View

As these pets share, it can be very unnerving for a pet to make the transition into the full-timing lifestyle. Be sure to consider the changes your pets will experience and look for ways to help them through their adjustment period.

When it comes time for the annual shots you will have no problem getting them from a local Vet, wherever you are. Some states require rabies shots annually while others only require them every three years. If you plan to go to Canada or Mexico you will need documentation that your pet has had the necessary shots. It is very important when returning to the United States that the shots are current or your pet may not be allowed to return.

We have found the cost of Vets vary a great deal from town to town. Small community Vets seem to be the least expensive. If time allows, shop around to get the best price.

Escapees has a Birds of a Feather (BOF) group for humans traveling with their fur friends. They even have a newsletter that shares information on meeting our fur friends needs on the road.

A Final Note From Tiffany

I love to meet new humans. Your hands were created to pet furry friends. I will be anxiously awaiting your arrival on the road. Look me up, as I intend to put your hands to good use!

Epilog

Freedom to take charge of your life, to experience life. *Footloose and fancy-free.* Meeting wonderful people and seeing beautiful sights. Experiencing things you never knew existed. This is what full-timing is all about.

Life is short. Will you live to experience your dreams? Many do not. Is this a risk you are willing to take? If full-timing is a dream of yours, you can start making it happen today. All it takes is a piece of paper, a pencil and a few minutes to make a list of what must be done to become a full-timer. Your list will be fairly complete if you incorporate the things you have just read.

Next, organize the list in the order you plan to tackle it. Be sure to leave space to add to the list and break the steps down further as your plan evolves. Place the list on the refrigerator or bathroom mirror. If this overwhelms you, put the list in a drawer and place only the one or two items you are focusing on this week on the refrigerator or bathroom mirror.

Had a bad day at work? Get the list out and see if there is something you can do right now to move you just a little closer to your goal. Maybe you can just find something to cut out of your budget to get you there a little quicker. Or surf the Internet to learn more about the lifestyle or wheel estates that are available. If time allows walk through a campground and find a full-timer to visit with.

Making a lifestyle change is not going to be easy, but it will be well worth the effort. The following is just one of the journeys we would have missed if we were not full-timers.

The summer of 1999 we traveled through the Canadian Maritimes. Our community, four other Boomer couples, came with us. The most magical moment of the summer for me was the day we disembarked the ferry in Port aux Basques, Newfoundland.

It was late afternoon as we headed north out of town to a campground a few miles down the road. The beautiful landscape was different from anything we had experienced to date. The grassy rolling foothills were littered with gray and white boulders. In the low spots were bogs where fish and frogs thrived. A little further north the mountains climbed steeply toward the sky on the right. To the left the ocean crashed on beaches.

Newfoundland is an island the size of California with a population less than Boston. People are spread far and wide. This means life is different than we know it in the United States. In many places there is no TV signal and no cable either. Communities entertain themselves. Music is one thing everyone is involved in. Most of the music is Celtic, using fiddles, accordions, hand drums and ugly sticks.

Ugly sticks are homemade from a stick with a boot or shoe attached to one end and a tin can to the other end. Bells may reside under the tin can which may sport a face. Beer bottle caps are attached with nails up and down the stick to add a jingle when the stick is pounded on the ground. A wash board like stick is rubbed against the ugly stick to add another texture to the music. Newfoundland music is as magical as the ugly stick is unique!

One night we gathered on a beach at dusk with many Newfie families to catch capelin, a fish slightly larger than a minnow. With nets in hand and waders on, everyone stood at the edge of the surf. Sharp eyes observed a dark spot coming in with the surf and nets went splashing into the ocean, coming up full of tiny fish. Capelin only come in for about a week each year. Some use these small fish to catch larger fish while others dry or smoke the fish to eat themselves.

We visited many fishing communities. Fishing is an important, but hurting industry in Newfoundland. The economy suffers as a result.

As we looked across bays the use of color in the homes stood out. Many shades of red, green, blue, turquoise and purple. Homes, with the exception of a few in St. Johns, are small. Some are little more than shacks. One very strange thing was the way the front door had no porch and was often a story above the ground. When we asked we were told this was the mother-in-laws door. With a chuckle we were then told no one wants people tracking into their good room, but insurance requires a second door on the house. I still am not sure of the real reason for this, but it was intriguing.

We learned new terms like "screech" (a strong shot of whisky), "from away" (that's us) and "nippers" (mosquitos).

We visited small communities with unique names, such as Twillingate, Happy Adventure, Witless Bay, Leading Tickles, Ferryland and Killigrew. We watched icebergs float in the ocean, appearing and disappearing overnight with the ocean currents.

Boggy ground meant trails must be boardwalks. At Kings Point we hiked a trail that was being upgraded, experiencing the muddy bogs where the boardwalk had yet to be installed. It gave us a real appreciation for what goes into building a trail.

We did not take our wheel estate to the trail head but when we discovered it was a great place to camp we notified two couples who were a week behind us. When they arrived with their wheel estates, rather than hiking the trail they were greeted by the entire town, including the mayor and tourism director, turned out to greet them. They enjoyed their visit, but missed out on the trail.

Campgrounds are few and far between in Newfoundland. The season is too short to break-even in this business. Gravel pit camping is the norm. Gravel pits are everywhere, having been left behind from road construction. One day we came home to one of these gravel pits to find two of the couples had caught up with us. What an amazing experience to be in the middle of nowhere in a foreign country and have friends show up. But that is the full-timing lifestyle.

We stayed in many gravel pits and in the process helped provide the local entertainment. RVs in Newfoundland are small trailers and class C motorhomes. So when we parked our big wheel estates with slide rooms in a gravel pit the entire community would hop in their cars and drive by slowly to have a look.

One weekend we headed for Killigrew where there was to be a Soiree, or festival. Wanting to be close to the Soiree we stopped at a store down the hill from the event and asked if we could stay in their parking lot. They said sure, they would notify the Soiree coordinators not to bother us when they used the parking lot as an overflow lot for the Soiree. That evening we traveled three communities over for some of the local events. When we mentioned that we were visiting from the States, they commented we must be the ones staying in the parking lot.

During our last day on Newfoundland we found ourselves caught off guard by a series of steep grades. We reached the top of a hill and stopped in the middle of the road to let the transmission cool off. There were no shoulders. As we sat waiting only three cars came from the opposite direction and each stopped to ask if we were okay. Continuing down into the next valley we heard a strange noise and had to stop just as we were starting up one of these steep grades. We were quickly surrounded by a couple and their children. He crawled under the truck with Paul to see if everything was all right.

That evening we were boondocked in a grocery store parking lot when there was a knock at our door. It was a gentleman asking if we had any questions he could answer.

Words cannot describe the magical experience Newfoundland has to offer with its beautiful scenery, intriguing music and wonderful people. This is only one of many wonderful and magical experiences we have had since hitting the road. If we were still in the traditional lifestyle we would never have considered going to Newfoundland. Time just would not allow it. And look what we would have missed!

You too can have experiences like these if you choose to turn this dream into reality! What are you waiting for?

Appendixes

Appendix A

Budget Comparison

	TODAY'S MONTHLY BUDGET	FULL-TIMING MONTHLY BUDGET
Groceries		
Eat Out		
Mortgage		
Property Taxes		
Home Owners Dues		
Utilities		
Home Maintenance		
Home Insurance		
Rent		
Renters Insurance		
Cable/Satellite TV		
Phone/Calling Card		
Work Related Expenses		
RV Loan		
Camping		
Propane, Electricity		
Membership Dues		
RV Maintenance		
RV Fuel		
RV Insurance		
RV Registration		
Entertainment		

Budget Comparison (Continued)

	TODAY'S MONTHLY BUDGET	FULL-TIMING MONTHLY BUDGET
Vehicle Loan		
Vehicle Insurance		
Vehicle Fuel		
Vehicle Maintenance		
Vehicle Registration		
Laundry		
Medical Insurance		
Dental Insurance		
Vision Insurance		
Other Medical Expenses		
Postage		
Mail Forwarding		
Clothing		
RV Supplies		
Daycare		
Home Schooling		
State Income Tax		
Federal Income Tax		
Miscellaneous		
Other:		
MONTHLY BUDGET		
ANNUAL BUDGET		

Appendix B

Weight Worksheets

Weight Ratings

	TOW VEHICLE	TRAILER	MOTOR-HOME	TOWED VEHICLE
GVWR				
GAWR				
Front				
Middle				
Rear				
GCWR				
GDW/UVW				

Fluid Capacities

FLUID	WEIGHT/GALLON	GALLONS	WEIGHT
WATER	8.34 lbs/gallon		
PROPANE	4.0 lbs/gallon		
DIESEL	7.1 lbs/gallon		
GAS	6.2 lbs/gallon		
TOTAL WEIGHT			

Ratings and Weights

	TOW VEHICLE RATING	TOW VEHICLE ONLY WEIGHT	VEHICLE & TRAILER WET WEIGHT	TRAILER RATING	TRAILER ONLY WEIGHT
GVWR					
Tow Vehicle AXLE					
Front					
Rear					
Trailer AXLE					
Front					
Middle					
Rear					
GCWR					
GDW/ UVW					
Gross Weight					
NCC					

Capacities

	MH OR TOW VEHICLE	HITCHED MH OR TOW VEHICLE	MH OR TOW VEHICLE & TOWED OR TRAILER	TOWED OR TRAILER
Payload Capacity (GVWR—Gross Weight)				
Axle Payload Capacity				
Front				
Middle				
Rear				
Total				
Combined Payload Capacity (GCWR —Combined Gross Weight)				

Appendix C

TO: (state) Department of Revenue [The proper state department varies by state. See *Selecting An RV Home Base: State Tax & Registration Information* for the appropriate department and address.]

SUBJECT: Residency Requirements

We are researching residency in your state and would appreciate your response to the following questions.

VEHICLE

The following questions pertain to a (year, make, model of vehicle. Also GVWR, and fuel type for pick-ups), that we plan to buy (or) that we bought in (month, year). We paid (percentage sales tax) sales tax to (state) when we bought it. The vehicle is used for recreational purposes.

1. What will the licensing fee be? _____
2. Will any sales tax be required when licensing the vehicle and if so what percentage? _____
3. If so, how is the sales tax calculated? _____
4. Are there any safety inspections required and if so with what frequency? _____
5. Is there a smog device requirement and if so what? _____
6. Is smog testing required and if so with what frequency? _____
7. Must smog or safety tests be completed before license renewal?
    _____
8. If required, but not for renewal, when must it be completed?
    _____
9. If I am out of state when my vehicle license renewal is due, will you forward the plates to me upon receipt of my renewal check?
    _____
10. If safety or smog tests are required for renewal and I am out of state when renewal is due, how do I get the tag for my vehicle?
    _____
11. What is the fee for title transfer? _____

RV

(For a motorhome ask the above questions. For a trailer ask the following questions.)The following questions pertain to a (year, length, brand, style trailer, model, gross dry weight and GVWR rating) which we plan to buy soon (or which we currently own and paid x% sales tax on).

1. What will the licensing fee be? _____
2. What sales tax, if any, will be due when licensing this trailer? _____
3. How is this sales tax calculated? _____
4. Are any safety inspections required, and if so with what frequency? _____
5. Are inspections required for license renewal? _____
6. If required, but not for renewal, when must they be completed? _____
7. If a safety test is required for renewal and I am out of state when license renewal is due, how do I get the tag for my RV? _____
8. What is the fee for title transfer? (ask only if you already own the RV) _____
9. Are there any regulations that allow you to tie the trailer license to the truck? If so, what are they? _____

Please indicate which of the following items are necessary to license the above vehicles:

	Pick-up/ Car	Trailer/ Motorhome
Drivers License	_____	_____
Street address	_____	_____
Post office box	_____	_____
Vehicle title	_____	_____
Insurance	_____	_____
Other _____	_____	_____
Other _____	_____	_____

What are the vehicle and RV insurance requirements in your state?

_____

RESIDENCY

1. What requirements must be met to become a resident of your state? _____

2. Is a post office box an acceptable domicile address? _____

3. Can a post office box address be used on a driver's license and vehicle registration? _____

4. Is a street address required to establish residency? _____

5. Is a driver's license required to establish residency? _____

6. Does registering a vehicle in your state establish residency?
    _____

7. Does obtaining voter registration in your state establish residency?
    _____

8. How soon after becoming a resident must I obtain vehicle license plates? _____

9. How soon after becoming a resident must I obtain a new driver's license? _____

Please return this survey in the enclosed self addressed stamped envelope. If you have literature on moving to your state, please include it. If we need additional information who may we contact?

Name _____

Title _____

Dept./Division _____

Address _____

_____

Phone _____

Thank You for Your Assistance!

   (Your name and address in case they misplace the SASE)

Appendix D

Contract Check List

Park can change anything at any time.	Yes	**No**
Requirements to terminate the membership are in the contract. List requirements:	**Yes**	No
Sales presentation items are in the contract. List specific items:	**Yes**	No
Multiple park privileges are in the contract. List specifics:	**Yes**	No
Length of visit, frequency with which you can return, time out before return. List specifics:	**Yes**	No
Annual Dues are in the contract. Annual Dues are Frozen at $_____ or Maximum annual increase of $_____ with dues starting at $_____ .	**Yes** **Yes** **Yes**	No No No
Contract allows for special assessments.	Yes	**No**
No charge for Coast to Coast and RPI letter of release.	**Yes**	No
Clauses you would like to write in.		

When completing the contract check list circle the responses that apply. The response in bold is the one you are looking for. If the items on this check list are not in the contract write them in.

Membership Park Investment Analysis

Initial Investment	$_____
Annual Home Park Dues	$_____
Nights per Year in Home Park	_____
Membership Dues	
Coast to Coast	$_____
RPI	$_____
Other	$_____
Other	$_____
Nights per Year in Host Park	_____

Use the following formula to determine the nightly costs.

$$\frac{\text{Int. Inv.} + (\text{Yrs. x Home Park Dues}) + (\text{Yrs. x Membership Dues})}{(\text{Yrs. x Home Park Nights}) + (\text{Yrs. x Host Park Nights})}$$

Resource Directory

Resource Directory Contents

The data in this Resource Directory was verified just before going to press. As resource directories go, it will become dated with time. Since I travel full-time and seldom have access to a computer for more than a half hour at a time your help in notifying me of changes and new resources is appreciated. Please e-mail any input to *stephanie@escapees.com.* Check for *Resource Directory* updates at *http://www.rvhometown.com.*

Books and Directories

Campground Directories
Trailer Life's RV Campground & Services Directory
Wheelers RV Resort & Campground Guide
Woodall's Campground Directory
The above directories are available at RV stores.

Campbooks, from AAA for their members
RV Park & Campground Directory, from Allstate Motor Club for their members.

Cooking
The Happy Camper's Cookbook: Eating Well is Portable, by Marilyn Abraham and Sandy MacGregor. Wonderful recipes that don't require a campfire. Available by calling (800) 253-2747 or at *http://www.amazon.com.*

Financial
Two Incomes and Still Broke by Linda Kelley

The Millionaire Next Door: The Surprising Secrets Of America's Wealth by Thomas J. Stanley, Ph.D. & William D. Danko, Ph.D. Discusses the traits of millionaires and how you can use these traits to improve your financial situation.

Your Money or Your Life by Joe Dominguez and Vicki Robin

Full-timing

Complete Guide to Full-time RVing: Life on the Open Road
by Bill and Jan Moeller. Presents a complete overview of the
full-timing lifestyle. Available in RV and book stores.

Encyclopedia for RVers II by Joe and Kay Peterson. This book is
broken into three parts. First a brief overview of: equipment and the
lifestyle, second RV lifestyle tips and finally over 100 pages of
addresses and phone numbers for the full-timer. Order from
RoVer's Publications, 100 Rainbow Drive, Livingston, TX 77351,
(888) 757-2582, *books@mail.escapees.com,*
http://www.escapees.com/website/knowledge/books.htm

**First We Quit Our Jobs: How One Work-Driven Couple Got on the
Road to a New Life** by Marilyn J. Abraham. This book tells about
how Marilyn and her husband took to the road in a motorhome while
they sorted through what they would do next in life. Available at
http://www.amazon.com or by calling (800) 253-2747.

Home is Where You Park It by Kay Peterson. This book shares
the ins and outs of the full-timing lifestyle. Order from RoVer's
Publications, 100 Rainbow Drive, Livingston, TX 77351,
(888) 757-2582, *books@mail.escapees.com,*
http://www.escapees.com/website/knowledge/books.htm

**Movin' On—Living and Traveling Full-time in a
Recreational Vehicle** by Ron and Barbara Hofmeister. Ron and
Barb share their adventures in and insights to the full-timing
lifestyle. This book gives great insight into everyday life as a
full-timer. Order from BookMasters at (800) 247-6553 or online
at *http://www.movinon.net.*

**Over the Next Hill: An Ethnography of RVing Seniors in North
America** by Dorothy Ayers Counts & David R. Counts. Dorothy
and David are anthropologists who studied the RV lifestyle by
experiencing it themselves. This book looks at the life-style in a way
no other book does. Over the Next Hill may be just the book you

need to help family and friends understand the life-style. Available from Broadview Press by calling (705) 743-8990.

Roads from the Ashes: An Odyssey in Real Life on the Virtual Frontier by Megan Edwards. When Megan and her husband, Mark, lost their home in a wildfire outside Pasadena, California they seized the opportunity, bought a motorhome and hit the road. Megan shares the struggles and joys of their nomadic lifestyle and use of the Internet from the road. Over five years later they continue to live this nomadic lifestyle. Available at book stores and *http://www.amazon.com.* Autographed copies are available at *http://www.roadtripamerica.com/book/order.htm.*

Survival of The RV Snowbirds by Joe and Kay Peterson. Covers boondocking, how to do it safely, finding places to park and the equipment necessary. Order from RoVer's Publications, 100 Rainbow Drive, Livingston, TX 77351, (888) 757-2582, *http://www.escapees.com/website/knowledge/books.htm,* *books@mail.escapees.com*

Resources

The RVer's Friend: North American Diesel/Parking Directory from The Trucker's Friend lists valuable information, including the location of truck stops, KMart, Wal-Mart, state and national parks, and dump stations. It also tells what facilities and services truck stops offer, including roadside service and repair. Available at truck stops or PO Box 476, Clearwater, FL 33757, (800) 443-4921. *http://www.truckstops.com*

RV Buying

The RVer's Bible: Everything You Need to Know About Choosing, Using & Enjoying Your RV by Kim Baker & Sunny Baker.

Solar

RVer's Guide to Solar & Inverters by Noel and Barbara Kirkby. Available at alternative energy dealers nationwide, or by contacting RV Solar Electric, 14415 North 73rd Street, Scottsdale, AZ 85260, (800) 999-8520. *http://www.rvsolarelectric.com*

Taxes

Selecting An RV Home Base: State Tax & Registration Information published by Trailer Life Books and currently packaged with ***Complete Guide to Full-time RVing*** by Bill and Jan Moeller. To order call (800) 234-3450.

Bus Conversions

Clubs

Bus Nuts. This is a chapter of FMCA (Family Motor Coach Association) and you must be a member of FMCA to join. Contact FMCA at (800) 543-3622.

Magazines

Bus Conversions, MAK Publishing, 3431 Cherry Ave., Long Beach CA 90807. *http://www.busconversions.com/bcindex.html*, (562) 492-9394

The National Bus Trader, *http://www.busmag.com*, (815) 946-2341.

The Private Coach, 46481 246th St., Colton, SD 57018, (605) 446-3791, *http://www.privatecoachmagazine.com/*.

Camping

Membership Organizations

Adventure Outdoor Resorts (AOR), 1125 US Hwy 98 South, Suite 200, Lakeland, FL 33801, (800) 934-3443, *http://www.membershipcamping.com*

Camper Clubs of America, 2800 South Rural Road, PO Box 25286, Tempe, Arizona 85285-5286, (800) 369-2267 or (602) 966-3085, *http://www.camperclubs.com/*

Coast to Coast, 64 Inverness Drive East, Englewood, CO 80112, (800) 368-5721, *http://www.coastresorts.com*

Passport America, 18315A Landon Road, Gulfport MS 39503, (800) 681-6810, *http://www.join2save.com/*

Resort Parks International (RPI), PO Box 7738, Long Beach, California 90807-0738, (800) 635-8498, (562) 490-0669 (in Long Beach area). *http://www.resortparks.com*

Thousand Trails/NACO, *http://www.thousandtrails.com*

Public Camping

BLM (Bureau of Land Management), Office of Public Affairs, 1849 C Street, Room 406-LS, Washington, DC 20240. Request information about camping on BLM land at *http://www.blm.gov/nhp/index.htm.*
National Forest Service, PO Box 96090, Washington, DC 20090-6090, *http://www.fs.fed.us/.* Campground reservations (800) 280-2267, *http://www.reservausa.com/.*
National Park Service, reservations (800) 365-2267, *http://www.nps.gov/.*
National Wildlife Refuges, write to US Fish & Wildlife Service, 1849 C St., NW, MIB 3012, Washington, DC 20240, (202) 208-4717.
US Army Corps of Engineers, Reservations (877) 444-6777 or (800) 280-2267.

Camping Web Sites

Federal Recreational Opportunities, *http://www.recreation.gov*
Florida Camping Information, *http://www.floridacamping.com*
Pet friendly Campgrounds, *http://www.petswelcome.com*

Communication Tools

Free ISP's, *http://nzlist.org/user/freeisp/index.htm*
Free Faxes via e-mail, *http://www.efax.com/*
PocketMail, (800) 762-5386, *http://www.pocketmail.com/*

Nation Wide Cellular

AT&T, *http://www.attws.com*
Bell South Mobility, *http://www.bellsouth.com*
GTE, *http://www.gte.com*
Nextel, *http://nextel.com*
Primeco, *http://www.primeco.com*
Sprint, *http://www.sprint.com*
Verizon Wireless, *http://www.verizonwireless.com*

Educational Programs

Escapade Twice a year thousands of serious RVers and those interested in the lifestyle gather to attend RV lifestyle seminars, check out the latest in RV products, socialize and meet others with the same interests. For more information contact Escapees at 100 Rainbow Drive, Livingston, TX 77351, (888) 757-2582 or (936) 327-8873, *http://www.escapees.com.*

Life on Wheels Join hundreds of RVers at Life on Wheels. Whether you are experienced, a novice, or just want to join the RV lifestyle, you will find classes to fit your needs. Life on Wheels is an exciting and unique program taught by RV Lifestyle experts. For information on the Idaho program contact:

➢ Enrichment Program, University of Idaho, PO Box 443224, Moscow, ID 83844-3224, (208) 885-6486, *http://www.lifeonwheels.com*

Information on the extension programs in Texas, Kentucky and Pennsylvania can be obtained from:

➢ Office of Continuing Educ. Aquarena Center, Southwest Texas State University, 601 University Drive, San Marcos, TX 78666, (512) 245-2507
➢ Western Kentucky University, Institute for Economic Development, 2355 Nashville Road, Bowling Green, KY 42101-4144, (270) 745-1900
➢ PRVCA Life on Wheels, 4000 Trindle Road, Camp Hill, PA 17011, (888) 303-2887

Escapees

Escapees RV Club, 100 Rainbow Drive, Livingston, TX 77351, (888) 757-2582, (936) 327-8873. Information Packet Requests: *info.packet@escapees.com, http://www.escapees.com*

BOF (Birds of a Feather) Groups

You must be a member of Escapees to join these groups:

Aerial Recreation Vehicles
Alternative Medicine
Amateur Radio
Amateur Photography
Barbershop Quartet Singing
Bible Study While You Travel
Biking/hiking
Birders
Books on Wheels
Boomers
Boondockers
Buff
Bus Nuts
Canoeists/Kayakers
Christian Fellowship
Computers on the Road
Escapee Elks
Food Allergies
Friends of Bill W
Genealogy
Yehudim al Galgalim
Law Enforcement/firefighters

Marriage Encounter
Medium-duty Truck
Metaphysical
Model Railroaders
No Limits
Nu-Wa Owners
Penwheels
Pet Lovers
Prospecting and Metal detecting
Quiltlovers
Racketeers (tennis)
Rockhounds/Lapidary
R(o)Ving Rods (fishing)
RVing with Kids
SOLOs
Speakers
Square Dancing
Traveling Threads
Vegetarians
Woodcarvers
Workers

Financial Planning

Dave Loring, PMB 465, 146 Rainbow Drive, Livingston, TX
77399-1046, (800) 260-1615 or (936) 327-1237. Investments,
financial planning, estate planning.

Homeschooling and Kids

Associations and Organizations

Home Education and Family Services, PO Box 1056, Gray, ME
04039, (207) 657-2800, *http://www.HomeEducator.com/HEFS/*
National Homeschool Association, PO Box 327, Webster, NY
14580-0327, voice mail (513) 772-9580, *http://www.n-h-a.org/.*
Publishes a travel directory in which permanent homeschooling

families are willing to host traveling families as a way of providing social contact for the children, as well as the adults.

Books

Home Education Resource Guide by Cheryl Gorder. A comprehensive resource guide for the parent-educator.

Homeschooling for Excellence by David Colfax and Micki Colfax. While this book was published in 1988 it still sells well at Amazon.com and has received excellent reviews from Amazon readers.

Home Schooling from Scratch: Simple Living—Super Learning by Mary Potter Kenyon, 1996. Looks at home schooling on a budget.

Home-schooling Resource Guide and Directory of Organizations by Mary Hood. Order through Ambleside Education Press, PO Box 2524, Cartersville, GA 30120.

Strengths of Their Own—Home Schoolers Across America: Academic Achievement, Family Characteristics, and Longitudinal Traits by Dr. Brian Ray. This book shares the results of a home-schooling study commissioned by the Home School Legal Defense Association (HSLDA).

The Home School Manual: Plans, Pointers, Reasons and Resources by Theodore E. Wade Jr. and others, 7th edition, April 1998

The Simplicity of Homeschooling: Discover the Freedom of Learning Through Living by Vicki Goodchild and Jack Goodchild, June 1997

Several books: Blue Bird Publishing, 1713 East Broadway #306, Tempe, AZ 85282, (888) 672-2275, *http://www.bluebird1.com/home.html*

Conferences

Listing of Conferences by State:
http://www.sound.net/~ejcol/confer.html

Groups

RVing with Kids BOF You must be a member of Escapees to join this group. Contact Escapees RV Club, 100 Rainbow Drive, Livingston, TX 77351, (888) 757-2582, (936) 327-8873, *http://www.rvnetwork.com/members/kids/, http://www.escapees.com*

Homeschoolers Web Sites

Blondins' Travels, *http://www.ncmc.cc.mi.us/Blondin*
Graham Family, *http://www.usatrip.org*
Heather's Home Page, *http://www.madrone.com/home-ed.htm*
Moxon Homeschool, *http://www.moxon.com/journey98*

Internet Addresses

Answers to Objections about Homeschooling,
http://www.hsu.edu/faculty/worthf/argue.html
Growing without Schooling, *http://www.holtgws.com*
Homeschooling, *http://homeschooling.miningco.com/*
Homeschooling Information and Resource Page,
http://www.home-ed-press.com/
Kaleidoscapes, *http://www.kaleidoscapes.com/*
Part-time Homeschooling,
http://ww2.whidbey.net/webplay/teach.html
The Gathering Place,
http://www.thegatheringplace.com/homeschool.htm

Legal Information

Home School Legal Defense Association, Box 3000, Purcellville, VA 20134, 540-338-5600, *http://www.hslda.org* and *http://www.hslda.com/hslda/*
Home School Legal Defense Association of Canada, 2-3295 Dunmore Road SE, Medicine Hat, AB T1B 3R2, (403) 528-2704, *http://www.hslda.com/hslda/canada.html*

Magazines

Growing Without Schooling, (617) 864-3100,
http://www.holtgws.com/
Home Educations, (800) 236-3278, *http://www.home-ed-press.com/*
Practical Homeschooling, *http://www.home-school.com/*
The Teaching Home, (503) 253-9633, *http://www.teachinghome.com/*

Materials

There are many places to obtain materials, new and used. These are just a few:

Curriculum Swap, *http://www.theswap.com/*
Homeschooling and Homelearning Resources Catalog, Christian Book Distributors, PO Box 7000, Peabody, MA 01961-7000, (508) 977-5000, *http://www.bridgestonemultimedia.com/cbd.htm*
Used curriculum and resources,
http://www.homeschoolclassifieds.com

Newsletters

Families on the Road, Editor Shelley Zoellick, PMB #191, 2601 S. Minnesota Ave., Suite 105-191, Sioux Falls, SD 57105, *http://www.familiesontheroad.com*

Schools

There are many homeschooling curriculums. Here are just a few used by full-timers.

Calvert School, 105 Tuscany Rd., Baltimore, MD 21210-3098, (410) 243-6030, *http://www.calvertschool.org*
Christian Liberty Academy, 502 W. Euclid Ave., Arlington Heights, IL 60004-5495, (800) 348-0899, *http://www.homeschools.org/*
Keystone National High School, School House Station, 420 W. 5th Street, Bloomsburg, PA 17815-1564, (800) 255-4937, *http://www.keystonehighschool.com*

Insurance

Licensed Insurance Agents

Miller Insurance Agency, Inc., 5805 SW Willow Lane, Lake Oswego, OR 97035-5342, (800) 622-6347. Specializes in RV insurance, umbrella policies and Mexican insurance. *http://www.MillerRVInsurance.com*

Roger E. Thomas Insurance/ Insurance Concepts:
- ➤ For Life and Health Insurance issues and quotes: 221 Country Wood, Livingston, Texas 77351, (800) 497-8798 or (936) 327-2133
- ➤ For RV Insurance: 301 Loop 59 South, Suite B, Livingston, TX 77351, (800) 736-5622 or (936) 327-5626

Medical Insurance

Prescription Purchase Savings with femScript® and aVidaRx™, 8536 Crow Drive, Suite 105, Macedonia, OH 44056, (800) 511-1314. Wal-Mart pharmacies sometimes carry brochures on the program. Check to see if your prescriptions qualify for the program before joining. Small enrollment fee, which is waived in some cases.

RV and Vehicle Insurance

Foremost Insurance Group, PO Box 3357, Grand Rapids, MI 49501, (800) 262-0170, *http://www.foremost.com*
National General Insurance or Good Sam's VIP insurance. May require membership in Good Sam or Coast to Coast. 800-847-2886, *http://www.ngic.com/*
Progressive Insurance, Attn: National RV Product Manager, 760 Beta Drive, Mayfield Village, OH 44143, (800) 309-7878, *http://rv.progressive.com/about.htm* or quotes at *http://www.rv.progressive.com/homepage.htm*
RV Alliance America, 11100 NE th Street, Suite 900, Bellevue, WA 98004-4441, (800) 521-2942, *http://www.rvaa.com*

Internet Sites

Camping

Camping in America,
http://www.suite101.com/welcome.cfm/camping
Federal Recreation Areas, *http://www.recreation.com*

Equipment

RV Solar Electric, *http://www.rvsolarelectric.com*

Full-timing

Full-timing America RV Lifestyle, *http://www.fulltiming-america.com*

Movin' On, *http://www.movinon.net/*

My Prime Years, *http://www.myprimeyears.com/rv*

RV Full-time, *http://www.concentric.net/~Lmchaney*

Full-timers Web Sites

American Dreamin, *http://www.americandreamin.com*

RoadTrip America, *http://www.roadtripamerica.com*

RV Living on the Road Full-time Lifestyles for Baby Boomers, *http://www.webworker.com/index/fr.rv.html*

General Information

Falcor's Findings, *http://www.angelfire.com/nm/debshome/rvers.html*

Gentle Adventures, *http://hometown.aol.com/winfield3/*

Happy Camper, *http://www.happy-camper.com*

Hi-Teck Camping Site, *http://www.boondocker.com*

Lists camping, clubs & dealers, *http://www.campnetamerica.com*

Post Cards America, *http://www.postcardsfrom.com/971013.html*

Quest-4, *http://www.quest-4.com*

Roadnews, *http://www.roadnews.com*

Roads to Adventure, *http://www.roadstoadventure.com*

RV Advice from a Service Manager, *http://www.rvadvice.com*

RV America, *http://www.rvamerica.com*

RV Camping, *http://www.rvcamping.com*

RV Club, *http://www.rvclub.com*

RV.com, *http://www.rv.com*

RV Design, *http://www.worldwideclassified.net/rvdesign/*

RV.Net, *http://www.rv.net/*

RV Net Linx, *http://www.rvnetlinx.com*

RV Network, *http://www.rvnetwork.com*

RV USA, *http://www.rvusa.com*

RV Search On-line, *http://www.rvsearch.com*

RVers Online, *http://www.rversonline.org/*

The RV Site, *http://www.rvsite.com/*

Trader on Line, *http://www.traderonline.com*

Woodalls, *http://www.woodalls.com*

Organizations

American Recreation Coalition, *http://www.funoutdoors.com/*
Escapees RV Club, *http://www.escapees.com*
Go RVing, *http://www.gorving.com*
National Assoc. of RV Parks and Campgrounds',
http://www.gocampingamerica.com
RVIA, *http://www.rvia.org*

Pets

PetPatio, *http://www.petpatio.com*

Recreational Sites

Great Outdoors, *http://www.gorp.com/gorp/activity/rv.htm*

RV Buying Information

NADA RV Pricing, *http://www.nadaguides.com/valueshome.html.*
Also offers a lemon check by VIN number.
RV Buyers Guide, *http://www.rvbg.com*

RV Manufacturers

See RV Manufacturers Section

RV Services

A 'Weigh We Go, *http://www.aweighwego.org*

RV Rentals

Cruise America, *http://www.cruiseamerica.com*
RV Rental Referral, *http://www.rvrent.com*

Women's Full-timing Sites

Women's RV Forum, *http://www.womensrvforum.com*

Jobs

Books

Camperforce Directory Lists more than 2,000 resorts, lodges, parks and campgrounds nationwide that are interested in offering free or reduced cost campsites in exchange for labor by campers willing to assist in chores. Order from Camperforce, PO Box 1212, Cocoa, FL 32923, (407) 633-1091.

Finding Your Perfect Work: The New Career Guide to Making a Living, Creating a Life by Paul and Sarah Edwards, the Self-Employment Experts. This career guide provides advice on how you can bring your personal goals and dreams together with a prosperous and meaningful livelihood.

Road Work: The Ultimate RVing Adventure by ArleneChandler. This book covers different jobs available on the road and shares experiences of many individuals. Emphasis is placed on jobs obtained through ***Workamper News.*** Available in book stores and at Workampers bookstore, (800) 446-5627, *http://www.workamper.com.*

Travel While You Work: Earning Money as you RV by Kay and Joe Peterson. A look at some of the different job options and what someone working on the road must consider in seeking a job or working for themselves. Order from RoVer's Publications, 100 Rainbow Drive, Livingston, TX 77351, **(888) 757-2582,** *http://www.escapees.com/website/knowledge/books.htm, books@mail.escapees.com.*

Groups

Workers BOF You must be a member of Escapees to join. Contact Escapees RV Club, 100 Rainbow Drive, Livingston, TX 77351, **(888) 757-2582, (936) 327-8873,** *http://www.escapees.com*

Employers that hire RVers

Camping World Job Hot Line, (877) 612-5627
Disney World Casting, (407) 828-1000, *http://www.disney.go.com/disneycareers/*
Hamilton Stores, *http://www.hamiltonstores.com,* *jobs@hamiltonstores.com*

Newsletters

The Caretaker Gazette, This newsletter lists property and personal caretaking positions worldwide. To order: PO Box 5887, Carefree, AZ 85377-5887, (480) 488-1970, *http://www.caretaker.org, caretaker@uswest.net.*

Workamper News, Lists jobs by state and has a bookstore which handles books on the RVing lifestyle. To order: 201 Hiram Road, Heber Springs, AR 72543-8747, (501) 362-2637, *http://www.workamper.com, info@workamper.com.*

Workers On Wheels, At press time Workers On Wheels was expanding their services for working RVers. Please see the web site for the latest details. Contact: 3213 West Main—306, Rapid City, South Dakota 57702, *http://www.workersonwheels.com, wow@workersonwheels.com.*

Internet Sites

The following sites either list jobs; link to sites that list jobs or have forums for RVers who work. Some of the sites listed in the Internet Sites section may also have job listings.

Amsoil, *http://www.amsoil.com/opps.html*
Baehre Real Estate, *http://www.rvparksforsale.com/*
Bik's Cyber RV,
http://www.geocities.com/Yosemite/Trails/5280/
Campgrounds for Sale, *http://www.rvpark.org/cg4sale.htm*
Career Mosaic, *http://www.careermosaic.com*
Career Path, *http://www.careerpath.com*
Contract Employment Weekly, *http://www.ceweekly.com*
Coolworks, *http://www.coolworks.com*
Fulltiming America,
http://www.fulltiming-america.com/workcamp.html
Government Jobs, *http://www.usajobs.opm.gov*
> This site is a little hard to figure out. To find out about jobs in the National Parks select "Current Job Openings," then select "Agency Job Search," enter keyword "interior," and finally submit "National Park Service."

Hospitality And Tourism Jobs,
http://omni.cc.purdue.edu/~alltson/career.htm

Hot Jobs, *http://www.hotjobs.com/*
Info Space, *http://www.infospace.com*
Monster Board, *http://www.monster.com*
Morgan Drive Away, *http://www.morgrp.com*
Nation Job, *http://www.nationjob.com* ·
Road Rat, *http://www.roadrat.com/*
RV Living, *http://www.webworker.com/index/fr.rv.html*
Seasonal Employment,
http://www.seasonalemployment.com/index.htm
Telecommuting Jobs, *http://www.tjobs.com/*
Travel for Pay Secret, *http://www.roadrat.com*

Another way to search for jobs is to check the Chamber of Commerce, city web sites and newspaper web sites for the communities you are interested in.

Training Opportunities

Camping World RV Institute, (800) 356-0311, ext. 1903. Camping World offers training courses to teach individuals how to diagnose and repair RV problems.

Magazines/Newspapers

Coast to Coast, for members of Coast to Coast, 64 Inverness Drive East, Englewood, CO 80112, (800) 368-5721, *http://www.coastresorts.com*
Escapees, for members of Escapees RV Club, 100 Rainbow Drive, Livingston, TX 77351, (888) 757-2582, (936) 327-8873, *http://www.escapees.com*
Family Motor Coaching, for members of FMCA, 8291 Clough Pike, Cincinnati, OH 45244, (800) 543-3622, (513) 474-3622, *http://www.fmca.com*
Gypsy Journal, 1400 Colorado St., #C-16, Boulder City, NV 89005, *GypsyJrnl@aol.com.* Publishers Nick and Terry Russell travel full-time gathering stories for their newspaper along the way.
Highways, for members of Good Sam Club, PO Box 6888, Englewood, CO 80155-6888, (800) 234-3450, *http://www.goodsamclub.com/highways/*

MotorHome, P.O. Box 54461, Boulder, CO 80322, (800) 678-1201
(U.S.) *http://www.motorhomemagazine.com*
Out West, 9792 Edmonds Way #265-A, Edmonds, WA 98020,
(800) 274-9378, *http://www.outwestnewspaper.com*
RV Companion, PO Box 174, Loveland, CO 80539, (888) 763-3295,
http://www.rvcompanion.com
Trailer Life, 2775 Vista Del Mar, Ventura, CA 93001,
(805) 667-4100, *http://www.trailerlife.com*

Mail Services

Escapees RV Club (for Escapee members), 100 Rainbow
Drive, Livingston, TX 77351, (888) 757-2582, (936) 327-8873,
http://www.escapees.com
FMCA, (for members of FMCA), 8291 Clough Pike, Cincinnati, OH
45244, (800) 543-3622, (513) 474-3622, *http://www.fmca.com*

To obtain General Delivery Addresses, US Postal Service,
(800) 275-8777

Message Services

Escapees RV Club (for Escapee members), 100 Rainbow
Drive, Livingston, TX 77351, (888) 757-2582, (936) 327-8873,
http://www.escapees.com
FMCA, (for members of FMCA), 8291 Clough Pike, Cincinnati, OH
45244, (800) 543-3622, (513) 474-3622, *http://www.fmca.com*
Remote Link, contact Cliff Parrish, (800) 362-9446
Freedomstar Communications, (888) 324-8686,
http://www.freedomstart.com/
Worldlink, (800) 432-6169, *http://www.premtec.com*

Newsletters

Two-Lane Roads, PO Box 23518, Fort Lauderdale, FL 33307-
3518, (888) 896-5263, *http://www.two-lane.com*
The Road Princess Gazette, Janet Wilder, Editor, PMB 198, 102
Rainbow Drive, Livingston, TX 77351-1002, *Prinjrw@aol.com*.
Sample copy for 50¢ and legal SASE.
http://www.concentric.net/~Lmchaney/author/road_princess.htm

Organizations

National Association of RV Parks and Campgrounds (NARVC), 113 Park Avenue, Falls Church, VA 22046, (703) 241-8801, *http://www.gocampingamerica.com*
RVIA (Recreational Vehicle Industry Association) 1896 Preston White Dr., PO Box 2999, Reston, VA 20195-0999, *http://www.rvia.org*
Recreational Vehicle Dealers Association, 3930 University Dr., Fairfax, VA 22030-2515, (703) 591-7130, *http://www.rvda.org*

Physically Challenged

Automobile Mobility Programs
Buick Motor Division, (800) 521-7300
Cadillac Motor Division, (800) 458-8006
Chevrolet Motor Division, (800) 222-1020, opt 3
Chrysler Auto Mobility Program, (800) 255-9877
Ford Mobility Motoring Program, (800) 952-2248
GMC Division, (800) 462-8782
Oldsmobile Division, (800) 442-6537
Pontiac Division, (800) 762-2737
Saturn Assistance Center, (800) 553-6000, TTY (800) 833-6000

Books
Great American Vacations for Travelers with Disabilities by Donna Cornacchio and Auto Howard.

Groups
HTC (Handicapped Travel Club), Merle Young, 12555 Lantern Road, Fishers, IN 46038, phone (317) 849-8019, *Mry@netdirect.net, http://www.sohoconnection.com/htc/*
No Limits BOF, (you must be a member of Escapees to join). Contact Escapees RV Club, 100 Rainbow Drive, Livingston, TX 77351, (888) 757-2582, (936) 327-8873, *http://www.escapees.com*
Society for the Advancement of Travel for the Handicapped (SATH), 347 Fifth Avenue, Suite 610, New York, NY 10016, (212) 447-0027, *http://www.sath.org/*

Paralysis Society of America, 801 Eighteenth Street, NW Washington, DC 20006-3517, (888) 772-1711, (202) 973-8422 (TTY), *http://www.psa.org/*

Internet Sites

Access-Able Travel Source, http://www.access-able.com
Dis-abilities, http://www.dis-ablities.com/
Handicapped Access to the Net,
http://www.vr-usa.com/vr-ct/Handicap.htm
RV Accessibility for the Disabled, http://www.theautochannel. com/content/vehicles/mhrv/guide/disabled.html

Magazines and Newsletters

Diabetic Traveler Quarterly, PO Box 8223 RW, Stamford CT 06905, (203) 327-5832, *http://www.tds.net/rhodes/links.htm.*
Disabled Outdoors, Box 395, Grand Marais, MN 55604, (218) 387-9100
Paraplegia News, 2111 East Highland Avenue, Suite 180, Phoenix, AZ 85016-4702, (602) 224-0500

Resources

ABLEDATA, 8401 Colesville Road, Suite 200, Silver Spring, MD 20910, (800) 227-0216, *http://www.abledata.com.* A national database of information on assistive technology and rehabilitation equipment available from domestic and international sources. The database also contains information on noncommercial prototypes, customized and one-of-a-kind products, and do-it-yourself designs
Mobility International USA, PO Box 10767, Eugene, OR 97440, (514) 343-1284 (voice/TTY), *http://www.miusa.org/*
Moss Rehabilitation Hospital—Travel Information Service, 12th Street and Tabor Road, Philadelphia, PA 19141, (215) 456-9900, *http://www.einstein.edu/aehn/moss_rehab.html*
National Rehabilitation Information Center (NARIC), 1010 Wayne Ave., Suite 800, Silver Spring, MD 20910, (800) 346-2742, (301) 562-2400, (301) 495-5626 (TT), *http://www.naric.com/*
Travelin' Talk Network, PO Box 1796, Wheat Ridge, CO 80034, (303) 232-2979, *http://www.travelintalk.net.* Travelin' Talk is a global network of persons with disabilities who have joined together and formed a unique family of friends around the

world. They share knowledge about their hometowns, or extend a hand to other members when visiting or passing through.

RV Clubs

Escapees RV Club, 100 Rainbow Drive, Livingston, TX 77351, (888) 757-2582, (936) 327-8873, *http://www.escapees.com*
Family Motor Coach (FMCA), 8291 Clough Pike, Cincinnati, OH 45244, (800) 543-3622, (513) 474-3622, *http://www.fmca.com*
Good Sam Club, PO Box 6888, Englewood, CO 80155-6888, (800) 905-9911, *http://www.goodsamclub.com* Good Sam Chapter Hotline: call (800) 314-3510 and provide a zip or postal code and you will be given information on the local chapters, including any memberships specifics (families, singles, women etc.). You are then given the opportunity to leave a message for the state or provincial director who will call you with more details.
The RV Club, *http://www.rvclub.com/*

RV Consumer Groups

RV Consumer Group, Box 520, Quilcene, WA 98376, 360-765-3846, order desk 800-405-3325, *http://www.rv.org*
RV Group Wise, 41 South grant Ave., Columbus, OH 43215, (877) 525-5477, *http://www.rvgroupwise.com*

RV Manufacturers

Airstream, *http://www.airstream-rv.com*
Allegro, *http://www.allegromotorhomes.com*
Alpenlite, *http://www.wrv.com*
Auto-Mate Recreation Products Inc., 150 W. G Street, Los Banos, CA 93635, (209) 826-1521
Beaver, *http://www.smccorporation.com*
Bigfoot, *http://www.bigfootrvs.com*
Blue Bird, *http://www.wanderlodge.com*
Born Free, *http://www.dodgen-bornfree.com*
Chinook, *http://www.chinookrv.com*
Coach House, *http://www.coachhouserv.com*
Coachmen, *http://www.fleetwood.com*

Country Coach, *http://www.countrycoach.com*
Damon, *http://www.damonrv.com*
Dynamax, *http://www.dynamaxcorp.com*
Excel, *http://www.petersonind.com*
Firan Motor Coach Inc., Box 482, Elkhart, IN 46515, (219) 293-6581.
Fleetwood, *http://www.fleetwood.com*
Foretravel, *http://www.foretravel.com*
Georgie Boy, *http://www.georgieboy.com*
Gulf Stream, *http://www.gulfstreamcoach.com*
Harney Coach Works, *http://www.smccorporation.com/*
Holiday Rambler, *http://www.monaco-online.com*
Home & Park, *http://www.roadtrek.com*
Horizon, *http://ww.horizonsrv.com*
Jayco, *http://www.jayco.com*
King of the Road, *http://www.chiefind.com/rv.htm*
Kit, *http://www.kitmfg.com*
Lance Camper, *http://www.lancecamper.com*
Lazy Daze, *http://www.lazydaze.com*
McKenzie, *http://www.monaco-online.com*
Monaco, *http://www.monaco-online.com*
National RV, *http://www.nrvh.com*
Newmar, *http://www.newmarcorp.com*
Nu-Wa, *http://www.nuwa.com*
Play-Mor Trailers, Inc., PO Box 128, Hwy. 63 South, Westphalia, MO 65085, (573) 455-2387.
Pleasure-Way, *http://www.pleasureway.com*
Rexhall, *http://www.rexhall.com*
Roadtrek, *http://www.roadtrek.com*
Royale Coach, *http://www.monaco-online.com*
Safari, *http://www.smccorporation.com*
Shasta, *http://www.shastaind.com*
Space Craft Manufacturing Inc., *http://www.spacecraftmfg.com*
Sportsmobile, *http://www.sportsmobile.com*
Starcraft, *http://www.starcraftrv.com*
Star Ship Custom Vehicles, 103-C Village Green Lane, Carmel, IN 46032, (317) 844-8143.
SunnyBrook, *http://www.sunnybrookrv.com*

Teton, *http://www.tetonhomes.com*
TrailManor, *http://www.trailmanor.com*
Travel Supreme, *http://www.travelsupreme.com*
Travel Units, *http://www.travelunits.com*
Triple E, *http://www.tripleerv.com*
Winnebago, *http://www.winnebagoind.com*
Xplorer, *http://www.xplorermotorhome.com*

RV Accessiblity for the Disabled lists RV manufacturers who work with disabled RVers.
http://www.theautochannel.com/vehicles/mhrv/guide/disabled.html

RV Services

A 'Weigh We Go, 211 Mae McKee Road, Chuckey, TN 37641, (423) 257-7985, *http://www.aweighwego.org, awwg@rvamerica.com.* John takes pride in responding to every letter and e-mail they receive. However, a SASE (self addressed stamped envelope) would be greatly appreciated with letters.

Singles

Clubs

Loners of America, PO Box 3314-TB, Napa CA 94558-0331, (888) 805-4562, *http://www.napanet.net/~mbost/*
Loners on Wheels (LoW), P.O. Box 1355, Poplar Bluff, MO 63902, *http://www.lonersonwheels.com/*
RVing Women Inc., P.O. Box 1940, Apache Junction, AZ 85217, (888) 557-8464, (480) 983-4678, *http://www.rvingwomen.com/*
Wandering Individuals' Network, Inc., P.O. Box 2010, Sparks, NV 89432-2010

Internet Sites
Mark's Full-time RV Adventure,
http://bart.ccis.com/home/mnemeth/

Solar

RV Solar Electric, 14415 North 73rd Street, Scottsdale, AZ 85260, (602) 443-8520, *http://www.rvsolarelectric.com*

Tourism Web Sites

Alabama, *http://www.state.al.us*
Alaska, *http://www.state.ak.us*
Alberta, *http://www.atp.ab.ca*
Arizona, *http://www.arizonaguide.com*
Arkansas, *http://www.arkansas.com*
British Columbia, *http://www.gov.bc.ca*
California, *http://www.gocalif.com*
Colorado, *http://www.colorado.com*
Connecticut, *http://www.state.ct.us*
Delaware, *http://www.state.de.us*
Florida, *http://www.flausa.com*
Georgia, *http://www.georgia.org*
Hawaii, *http://www.gohawaii.com*
Idaho, *http://www.visitid.org*
Illinois, *http://www.enjoyillinois.com*
Indiana, *http://www.state.in.us/tourism*
Iowa, *http://www.traveliowa.com*
Kansas, *http://www.kansascommerce.com*
Kentucky, *http://www.state.ky.us*
Louisiana, *http://www.louisianatravel.com*
Maine, *http://www.visitmaine.com*
Manitoba, *http://www.travelmanitoba.com*
Maryland, *http://www.mdisfun.org*
Massachusetts, *http://www.massvacation.com*
Mexico, *http://www.mexico-travel.com*
Michigan, *http://www.michigan.org*
Minnesota, *http://www.exploreminnesota.com*
Mississippi, *http://www.mississippi.org*
Missouri, *http://www.missouritourism.com*
Montana, *http://www.visitmt.com*
Nebraska, *http://www.visitnebraska.org*

Nevada, *http://www.travelnevada.com*
New Brunswick, *http://www.tourismenbcanada.com/web/*
Newfoundland and Labrador, *http://www.newfoundland.com*
New Hampshire, *http://www.visitnh.gov*
New Jersey, *http://www.state.nj.us*
New Mexico, *http://www.newmexico.org*
New York, *http://www.iloveny.state.ny.us*
North Carolina, *http://www.visitnc.com*
North Dakota, *http://www.ndtourism.com*
Northwest Territories, *http://www.nwttravel.nt.ca*
Nova Scotia, *http://www.explore.gov.ns.ca*
Ohio, *http://www.ohiotourism.com*
Oklahoma, *http://www.travelok.com*
Ontario, *http://www.travelinx.com*
Oregon, *http://www.traveloregon.com*
Pennsylvania, *http://www.state.pa.us*
Prince Edward Island, *http://www.gov.pe.ca*
Quebec, *http://www.gouv.qc.ca*
Rhode Island, *http://www.visitrhodeisland.com*
Saskatchewan, *http://www.sasktourism.com*
South Carolina, *http://www.travelsc.com*
South Dakota, *http://www.state.sd.us/tourism*
Tennessee, *http://www.state.tn.us/tourdev*
Texas, *http://www.traveltex.com*
Utah, *http://www.utah.com*
Vermont, *http://www.vtlife.intervis.com/travelvt/*
Virginia, *http://www.virginia.org*
Washington, *http://www.tourism.wa.gov*
Washington, DC, *http://www.washington.org*
West Virginia, *http://www.state.wv.us/tourism*
Wisconsin, *http://www.tourism.state.wi.us*
Wyoming, *http://www.wyomingtourism.org*
Yukon, *http://www.touryukon.com*

Volunteerism

Habitat for Humanity Care-A-Vanner, 121 Habitat Street, Americus, GA 31709, (800) 422-4828, ext. 2446, *http://www.habitat.org/gv/rv.html*
Laborers for Christ, 1333 South Kirkwood Road, St. Louis, MO 63122-7295, (800) 433-3954, *http://mission.lcms.org/laborers/*
Campers on Mission, Special Ministries Department, 4200 North Point Parkway, Alpharetta, Georgia 30202-4174, (770) 410-6000, *http://www.freeyellow.com/members4/com-va/*
US Fish and Wildlife Service, *http://refuges.fws.gov/NWRSFiles/general/volunteers.html*

Index

Notes

Notes

Notes

Order Form

Copy the form below and send with a check or money order made out to Stephanie Bernhagen to:

Stephanie Bernhagen
164 Rainbow Drive, PMB 6431
Livingston, TX 77399-1064

or e-mail *stephanie@escapees.com* for updated and foreign ordering information. Please allow 6-8 weeks for delivery.

Order Form
Please send _____ copies of
Take Back Your Life! Travel Full-Time in an RV at $19.95 (U.S. funds) per copy to
Name:
Street Address:
City:
State and Zip Code:
Number of Books: @ $19.95 U.S.   = $
Book Rate Shipping and Handling $3.00   = $
Priority Shipping and Handling $4.00   = $
Shipping and Handling Add. Books $2.00 each = $
South Dakota residents add sales tax   = $
Total Enclosed   = $